CROCODILE JULIETTE

JACK LAWRENCE

Published by Crocodile Juliette™ Projects
             P.O. Box 319, Landsborough, Qld. 4550 Australia

Telephone   61 7 5439 9033
Fax   61 7 5439 9044
Website   www.crocodile-juliette.com
Email   jackcroc@mail.cth.com.au

Final editing by Catherine Gale.
Cover design and illustrations by Dennis Hill.
Internal layout and design by Lindsay Parry.

Printing by Queensland Complete Printing Services,
28 Price Street, Nambour, Qld. 4560 Australia - Phone 61 7 5441 7775

National Library of Australia cataloguing-in-publication data:
Lawrence, Jack,
Crocodile Juliette - ISBN No: 0 9577913 0 5

<u>Dedication</u>

For Bryce Courtenay and Juliette.

They made me write this book.

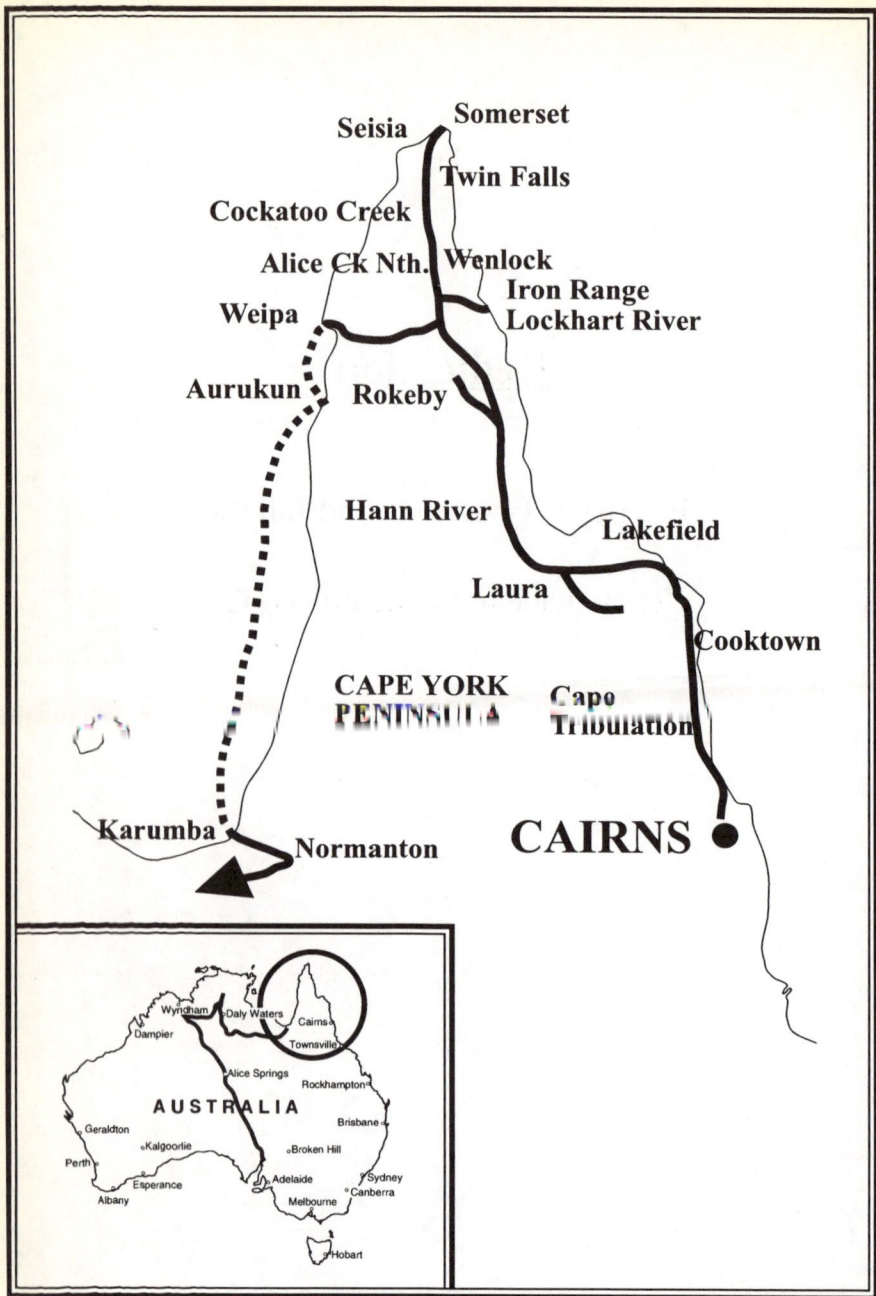

Seisia · Somerset

Twin Falls

Cockatoo Creek

Alice Ck Nth. · Wenlock

Weipa · Iron Range
Lockhart River

Aurukun · Rokeby

Hann River · Lakefield

Laura

Cooktown

CAPE YORK
PENINSULA · Cape Tribulation

Karumba · Normanton · CAIRNS

Wyndham · Daly Waters · Cairns
Dampier · Townsville
Alice Springs · Rockhampton
AUSTRALIA
Geraldton · Brisbane
Perth · Kalgoorlie · Broken Hill
Esperance · Adelaide · Sydney
Albany · Melbourne · Canberra
Hobart

That Cape York Jaunt

4

Introduction

The writing of this book is the most insane thing I have ever done.

I was driven to write it by something totally and completely beyond my control. The experience has been one of profound enlightenment, terrifying in the extreme for fear of losing my sanity, and indeed, at times, in fear of my continued existence. It has given me, at times, a better insight into the workings of the female mind, and I have discovered that it is terrifying terrain for the uninitiated. At other times I believe that I am probably far more confused than I am enlightened.

Despite the aforesaid, and the multitude of other insurmountable obstacles and threats that continually presented themselves, including the only person to believe that this book would ever be completed, it is now done and forevermore will remain so.

This is a completely factual account of the adventures, escapades, trials and tribulations of Juliette, physiotherapist, accomplished violist, pianist, mezzo-soprano, sailor and ornithologist extraordinaire who was courageous enough to accompany me on an expedition to Cape York and then into the Great Outback in the Dry Season. Neither she nor I knew who we really were at the time. We took off totally unbeknown to each other who we, each other and ourselves, really were at the time - and still don't know.

The story covers in detail the joint emotional crisis we had and the subsequent development of our friendship. It briefly deals with the vital importance this friendship, and the writing of this book, held for us both a year later as we dealt with our independent catastrophic circumstances from opposing ends of the planet, and later, together.

The people described in this book existed with the exception of Ding and Dong Battle-Bickering, who did exist, but whose identity must of necessity be protected. All the events experienced by Juliette on the Jaunt and described herein are true in every respect. There has never been any intent to do anyone any harm whatsoever. The intent has, in fact, always been quite the contrary.

Included are some partially biographical campfire yarns I told Juliette which perhaps contain some sensible but unidentifiable nonsense. I blame the latter on some of the best African campfire storytellers and bush philosophers who told me very many stories when I was growing up. It is a way that is used in Africa to tell stories about one's self without being inhibited or obliged to tell the full truth. It allows one to exercise some literary license by pretending to once have known someone very well. Indirectly, they shared with me life's highly complex philosophies that I am still trying to understand, but fully know that I never will.

I readily succumb to the impassioned plea of my young fifteen year old country born and bred Tasmanian friend James Carins' request to pass on a message to teenagers to please refrain from taking drugs. No matter how innocent and adventurous the softest of drugs might appear to be, they will kill you in the end.

Please don't go *tripping* in many more ways than one for there are many more adventurous and rewarding trips in life. Try the harmless, natural trips like this one instead. You will live longer, and you will also experience a far more meaningful, richer and happier life.

A strong word of warning to travelling youth. Never go anywhere with strangers without taking the precautions Juliette did, and was made to take, to ensure her safety. It was I who made the mistake of not taking proper precautions to find out who Juliette really was. I consider myself incredibly lucky to still be alive to tell this tale. I have lived dangerously all my life. I now continually, but with complete futility, try my very best never to do so again.

I am unsure at this juncture whether or not the sage-provided idiom of *The path makes us stronger* is valid or not - perhaps it does at a later stage. I just don't know at the moment because I still occasionally find myself emerging from the wrong end of a meat grinder.

One specific comment which was raised more often than I would like to have heard from readers and others who perused the manuscript, in particular those who know Juliette very well, was *'The more successful you are, (writing as Juliette) the more confusing you are.'*

I am quite unable to determine exactly where the reader's confusion lies, as I am the author, and not the reader. Some found parts of it quite jarring at times, and continually had to remind themselves that it was written by a man - me. This aspect has caused me the greatest difficulty from the time I first started writing and it still does. Don't even think about asking me why for the moment. When you have finished reading this book you will find that you won't need to ask me why.

I have decided not to modify the text, but to just let it be Juliette's story, for that is exactly what it is. This confused logic is perhaps quite inexplicable so be forewarned. Feel free to be confused, and I cheerfully welcome you to the club.

You are about to share our story of joy, happiness, laughter, tears, trials and tribulations, and finally triumphing over our tragedies. I hope that that you enjoy it all. Not for one instant did we whinge or complain when the gods had not smiled benignly upon us - we just kept going relentlessly forward.

The joint decision to share our friendship, and this precious time in our lives with you, was not made without great difficulty. The decision was made over a very long period of time, and sometimes quite loudly, very loudly - even now. We entrust you not to abuse this privilege, and we can only hope that this trust will never be misplaced.

Acknowledgments

This is primarily a tribute to the Rangers of the National Parks and Wildlife Service of the Cape York Peninsula and all the National Parks of Australia. Their task of preserving these unique wildernesses is, more often than not thankless, lonely and largely unappreciated. The part they played in our enjoyment and appreciation of the Cape York Peninsula and the Outback was enormous to say the least.

We also wish to pay tribute to the Aborigines and Islander people who we so infrequently managed to talk to, and regretfully barely got to know, for affording us their hospitality and the opportunity to visit their missions and communities.

The Royal Flying Doctor Service must get due acknowledgment for providing us with medical care in our times of need, and we extend our grateful thanks to them for their timely assistance.

We also wish to thank all the other people who played a part in our Cape York and Outback adventure. It is without doubt the ultimate Australian odyssey.

The Department of Environment and Heritage in Brisbane is thanked for their kind permission to use information from their pamphlets. Kerryn Lyon of Cairns kindly drew some cartoons for the book, and Juliette drew some of the sketches. Jon and Adrian, both close friends of Juliette's father, reviewed and extensively commented on the first draft and provided valuable encouragement, and for that I sincerely thank them both.

Little Helen Corr and her tribe of teddy bears were just there when I started writing. Her moral support, surprise teddy bear attacks, and warm, innocent friendship were invaluable during my very darkest times.

Gavin Rawlins' inquiring, six year old, mischievous, trick-playing mind kept mine going when it most needed stimulation while I was writing the first draft. He was, at one time, my one and only friend, and the only person with whom I could sensibly converse.

Mike and Irene Christie and their four children Anthony, Bryce, Richard and Chiomi, Louise Welch, Max West and Sharon Daniels, all of Cairns, must share responsibility for the parts they played in the completion of this book. They kept me intact and prevented me from going completely insane during that critical time. They are all top quality people from the very top shelf. The world needs many, many more of them.

Bryce Courtenay was the only person in the world to evoke an appropriate response to my desperate and silent screams for help in the moment of my greatest despair. He did so a few days after his youngest son Damon had died, and while his wife was in hospital for a triple by-pass heart operation. He once saved a valuable life - mine, and I don't forget things like that.

'Writ with the quill from an angel's wing' was how Bryce wanted this book to be written. I hope I have fully justified his valuable mentorship and his confidence in my ability to write.

Kate, my late baby daughter, tells me that if he continues to poach those feathers from Up There we all know what is going to happen to him, and where he will finally end up!

Margaret Gee of Sydney and Dr. Cath Filmer-Davies of the University of Queensland both did independent, objective evaluations of the first self-produced, unedited book. Cath was instructed to totally ignore the fact that I had an ego, and did. I was justifiably literally caned by these two good ladies into doing what they told me to do and finally producing what you now have in your hand.

Then there was Madiba, alias Nelson Mandela, whose spirit accompanied me every one of the painful, weary, final miles of this - the excruciatingly long, incredible and most profound journey of my life. This is what he said one day:

'Our deepest fear is not that we are inadequate.
Our deepest fear is that we are powerful beyond measure.
It is our Light, Not our Darkness, that most frightens us.
We ask ourselves, who am I to be brilliant, gorgeous, talented,
fabulous?
Actually, who are you NOT to be?
You are a child of God. Your playing small does not serve the World.'

Prelude

He ever so casually, in his uniquely inimitable way, wandered into my wide-eyed, innocent, peaceful, idyllic, blissfully happy and carefree life, touched it where it hurts most, and in so doing, indelibly left his mark. To this day I still am unable to determine whether or not he was saint, sinner, angel or bastard. He rattled my unshakeable cage completely. There is absolutely no telling what can happen to a woman travelling on her own in foreign climes. This is what happened to me:

I had some ten months previously migrated from Chichester, England to New Zealand, where I had been working as a physiotherapist in Whakatane, a small seaside town on the sweeping Bay of Plenty on the North Island. The approaching English winter prior to that time posed a serious threat to my health. It had the potential to lay me low for a few years due to a dormant, but imminently awaited medical condition. It was due to strike, which I could do nothing about, but do my best to stay warm and dry.

My going to New Zealand put me in a position to possibly delay, and even avoid a catastrophe. This, together with the subjective, conformist, controlled, confined, staid and manipulative circumstances which I strongly felt that I was living under, and which were inhibiting my spontaneity and sense of adventure, made me very unhappy. You know what it is like when you no longer feel free to do the things you want to do, and you have to make a big break and run to save your life, when no-one else is about to do so for you.

Thoroughly disillusioned with life overall at the time saw me dejectedly turn up at the New Zealand High Commission in London. New Zealand was on the opposite end of the planet, and as far away from England as I could possibly go. They spoke English there, and the Antipodes had summers lasting for eight months of the year, and mild winters. I filled in the migration application forms, had my medical examination, attended the interview, and then let matters take their natural course.

I had then come to Cairns, Far North Queensland and Australia at the insistence of my dear twin brother Pete, who had been working for the previous year in Sydney with Greenpeace, the environment protection people. Pete was on his way back to England and had decided to visit Cairns to complete his sojourn to Australia.

I had more than happily agreed to his idea as my locum contract terminated at that fortuitous time and my next job in New Zealand was due to start in mid-September. I had three months to fill in, no fixed itinerary, and enough money to allow me to spend this time travelling in Australia. Getting away from the New Zealand winter, and into the warm Australian tropics for this time, further allowed me respite from the impending catastrophe that I was dreading.

Flashes of lightning continually, and dramatically, illuminated the midnight sky as the Qantas Boeing 767 finally, and thankfully, touched down in tropical Cairns. As I disembarked the oppressive heat and humidity was still to be felt despite the time of night, and the time of year. When I had left New Zealand it had been cold, wet, grey and depressingly miserable. The sudden change of climatic conditions needed quite some adjusting to. I continually had to remind myself that late May was close to mid-winter in Cairns.

There were no courtesy buses from the various hostelries waiting for me as I had expected. Lugging my heavy backpack around, I finally found my way to the taxi rank long after the last passengers had disappeared. I asked the lone taxi-driver to take me to the Esplanade where I understood reasonable economy accommodation was available. There was only one place still open at that time of night to receive late arrivals. It reminded me a lot of the rather basic Thai hotels I had spent some time in during my travels in South East Asia.

Lying wearily in my bed at three o'clock in the morning, with an overhead fan lazily circulating the musty, humid air, I could smell the damp from the walls, a common problem in the tropics. Weary from the day's travelling, I was soon asleep.

Very early that morning, and much to my great annoyance, my earplugs fell out. There was an over-abundance of early morning noise coming from the Esplanade below and I couldn't get back to sleep again.

After a quick breakfast I was on my way in search of a more comfortable, and more pleasant, place to stay. I finally found what I was looking for further along the Esplanade. There was a swimming pool surrounded by palm trees, and a nice open area in front of the dormitory. The rather disgusting and badly equipped kitchen had to be overlooked when balanced against the other more pleasant aspects.

It is a sad reflection of us travellers when toasters and kettles have to be chained to the walls and cutlery goes walkabout I thought. I had already started to think like an Australian.

I was most pleasantly surprised when Katie, whom I had met with her sister Taura in Fiji the previous year, greeted me at the front desk. The world continued to get smaller and smaller. We had a quick chat about the things we had done, and places we had been to since, before they had to dash off on some excursion or other. I spent the rest of the day all alone walking around the shops and taking in the sights, smells and delights of tropical Cairns.

There were numerous cheap eateries about. The health food section of a large supermarket was disappointing and rather small, but I did manage to find a superb vegetarian take-away shop on the Esplanade. A large market called Rusty's Market, a few streets from the Esplanade that opened on Saturday and Sunday mornings, sold organic vegetables and exotic fruit that were grown in the nearby moist Atherton Tableland.

The Esplanade, with its solid, orderly date palms overlooking the tidal mud flats, and the unusual marine bird life such as pelicans, storks, spoonbills and the like frequenting the area, created a superb vista. I thought that the bird life was a lot more attractive than the mobs of semi-clothed people lazing about getting sunburnt.

I saw Australian Aborigines for the very first time sitting in noisy groups under the trees on the Esplanade. Some of them were snoozing on the pavement in the heat of the day. Cairns was abuzz with four-wheel-drive vehicles, and an equal number of cool dudes wearing Akubra hats, to match. All in all, it was a good day to acclimatise, and to orientate myself to the Far North Queensland culture. Life was far from intense.

Pete and I should have some good fun I thought to myself, eagerly anticipating his arrival. There seemed to be no end of adventurous and fun things to do. Cairns was just my kind of town!

Sipping a delightful cup of tea in a cafe over the road from the bus station at sunset, whilst waiting for Pete to arrive, I started to get quite excited. Having not seen him for eighteen months, I was really looking forward to seeing him again. It was going to be good to have some company after a whole day on my own.

It was all very pleasant looking out over the harbour with the rainforest-covered foothills in the background, and the great variety of seafaring boats and little dinghies bobbing about on Trinity Bay. The larger cruise ships reminded me that the Great Barrier Reef was not very far away. The multitude of marlin and game-fishing boats made a silent statement,

'This is a man's world!' they proclaimed.

'Ha! Girls can do anything!' I reassured myself.

Pete's bus finally arrived on time, much to my great delight. As he alighted we hugged each other and, bubbling with happiness at being together once more, we danced a little jig on the sidewalk. Twins are like that. It was so good to see dear old Pete again!

We collected his baggage and then walked to the hostel on the Esplanade where I was staying where we speedily got him comfortably installed. That done, we immediately went straight out to have dinner. Pete was absolutely exhausted after the three day, 2,800 kilometre long bus journey from Sydney, and he very reluctantly decided to retire rather early. Had he not done so he would surely have fallen fast asleep on the restaurant floor for the night.

The next day we had a very early 5:30 am start. Twenty of us were picked up in Cairns for the three hour coach trip to Cape Tribulation. We wound our way through the most spectacular bushland, rainforests, fords and slips. I was glad I wasn't driving, for it was a very winding road to the Daintree River ferry, and a ghastly, muddy dirt road from there to Cape Tribulation.

Included in the trip was a cruise for an hour down the Daintree River in a boat hugging the bushline all the way in search of crocodiles. We did see one, but he wasn't exactly very visible, nor did he move much.

I thought perhaps he is stuffed, and is a set-up for us tourists.

The guide was equipped with binoculars, and he assured us that the crocodile was very real. He profusely apologised for the dreadful weather, and I didn't think he was relishing the prolonged wet season either. The rain kept pouring into the boat as we sped along the river.

Rain, rain and more rain. Cape Tribulation must surely have been the wettest place on earth then! For most of the time it absolutely hosed by the bucket load as the unseasonable monsoon downpour continued unabated. It was far worse than the English weather. The temperature was also quite cool, resulting in me having to report to reception where I borrowed a woolly jumper to keep me warm.

As a result of the poor weather the trip to the Great Barrier Reef which we had booked was cancelled. We did plenty of talking, eating, drinking and socialising over the next two days instead. There was nothing else to do except to sleep, get wet and shiver from the unexpected cold. There were a lot of people frantically rushing around trying to keep warm and dry, but without much success.

When the rain temporarily ceased one day, we took a northerly walk along the beach to the Cape Tribulation headland to see what we could find. The transition from rainforest to beach was instant, and the thought of the possibility of a saltwater crocodile attack was a great novelty, and an adventure in itself.

There was an abundance of organised activities available, weather permitting, which it didn't do for most of the time. We chose to do an organised bush walk with Jim, a True Blue Aussie, through some very dense rainforest.

With wit and skill he enlightened us on epiphytes, (natural baskets of plants hanging from the branches of trees), the cassowary, (a rather large bird), wait-a-while, (a very thorny shrub which made me wait a for a good few whiles), the dreaded stinger tree, (don't go anywhere near them!), the fan fern, the pixie cup, the ant tree, which bears tiny yellow fruit on the bark, and so much, much, more. Nearby, he told us, were ancient, one hundred million year old pockets of forest. It was a botanist's dreams come true.

The violent cassowary female appealed to my sometimes-wayward sense of humour. She beats her husband up before and after sex, and then lets him get on with the job of rearing the chicks after they hatch. Way to go!

Jim pointed out to us many fresh pig-rooting holes. Unfortunately feral pigs, which are not an indigenous species, were left to run wild a long time ago, eat the cassowary eggs and the young rainforest shoots. This in turn endangers the longer-term existence of the indigenous cassowary and prevents the rainforest from regenerating. There are an ever-increasing number of feral pigs, and they have inadvertently acquired the status of protected species by default.

The dingo, the only predator of the pig, is vigorously being killed off with DF 118, a poison. The pigs also eat turtle eggs, thereby threatening the continued existence of the sea turtle. These pigs are, without doubt, a monumental environmental tragedy as they are diseased, and therefore, serving no commercial purpose, are left alone to multiply uncontrolled, locked into the rainforests, and protected from hunters.

On our last night at Cape Tribulation we danced in the disco and had a right merry time. Pete in particular, enjoyed himself immensely as he had recovered from his long journey by then, and he was back to his normal self.

The tour returned to Cairns via Mossman Gorge on the last day of the tour. Due to time constraints, we weren't allowed to be there for more than half an hour. We also sped past Port Douglas as if it didn't exist, but we fortunately did stop at the golden, sandy Ellis Beach for a quick leg-stretch and breather.

That evening, on our arrival back in Cairns, Jo, Pete and I hired a swish new car and drove to Mrs Miller's Youth Hostel in Kuranda, high up on the plateau above Cairns. We arrived there hot and tired to find that the hot water was going to be turned off at 9:00 pm. When we discovered that Frog's Restaurant took last orders at 8:30 pm, we really got our skates on. We had 10 minutes to have a shower and to get our meals ordered.

After the frantic rush we managed to sit down and enjoy crocodile fillets wrapped in bacon with a sweet and sour sauce for starters, accompanied by a delicate Australian white wine. This was followed by salmon fettuccine, and then passionfruit cheesecake which was washed down with Brandy Alexander. It was a superb meal in a pleasant, alternative atmosphere.

Very early the following morning we started the day by hiring canoes for a paddle along the Barron River. The foliage was dense, there were a lot of strange noises from elusive animal life and pink, orange and blue flowers, fluorescent kingfishers and other abundant bird-life were to be seen. Mist enshrouded the rainforest. It was a puffingly steep ascent to the top of the Barron Falls, and a hot and sweaty return. The sun appeared briefly, thankfully, and for long enough, to dry out the clothes we were wearing.

It was market day at Kuranda, so we ambled over after the canoeing to investigate. All sorts of things were for sale, from tee shirts, fresh sugar-cane juice extracted on the spot to holidays in Papua New Guinea. The food on sale was quite expensive generally, and a bit beyond our budgets. The market was set in a lively and pleasant atmosphere in the rainforest. The scones and honey, which were delicious, were hungrily devoured while we waited for yet another rainstorm to clear. Rain again!

The butterfly house in Kuranda, which we had heard so much about, was indeed fabulous. We had an enthusiastic and knowledgeable guide who told us so much, very clearly, and with great perseverance and patience to our many questions. The magnificently bright electric blue Ulysses butterflies, for which Far North Queensland is renowned, were spectacular.

We learnt that a butterfly lives from three weeks to fourteen months depending on its colours. Reds and yellows distract and deter birds that prey on butterflies, and blues attract them. The blue Ulysses flutters around furiously, literally batting itself to death in order to perform all its duties in case a bird devours it prematurely. The main aim in the life of a butterfly is to mate, which I thought was quite sensible enough.

The female mates once only, but she won't tell the male if she has been mated or not, and makes him flutter around her forever and a day. There were a lot of frustrated male butterflies around. During the prolonged process of mating, the larger female is attached to the comatose smaller male for many hours. Each type of butterfly has its own specific plants on which it lays its eggs, the leaves of which sustain the caterpillars after hatching.

The butterflies attracted to reds, pinks and whites, which they apparently see as fluorescent, fluttered around our brightly coloured clothing. The butterfly display was indeed wonderful, and must surely rank in world class.

Also on display were very large moths with wingspans of up to thirty centimetres. We further learnt that the female vibrates her antennae at ninety times per second to attract the male. Bats, being the main predators, are also attracted to her vibrations but, when the bat's radar locks on to the target, she changes her frequency, and the bat's radar goes haywire and it gets diverted. A rather nifty trick I thought.

We watched Sir John Geilgud on television at the hostel that night. It was so pleasant to feel totally relaxed, and quite at home, in a home so far away from home.

After a rather hectic start to the next day, when chaos seemed to reign supreme with everyone either getting lost, misplaced or misinformed, the three of us, together with John and Amy, whom Pete had met in Tasmania, merrily bombed around the Atherton Tableland in our hire car for a wonderful scenic day.

The Atherton Tableland, with gently undulating hills and pockets of rainforest, and being elevated on a plateau, was quite cooling compared to Cairns. We visited Lake Tinaroo, Crater Lake, Lake Eacham and Millaa-Millaa Falls. The falls were full due to the late wet season, and the surrounding rainforest lush, glistening, and resounding with birdsong.

After a scrumptious Devonshire tea at Malanda, we had to make a dash for Cairns, firstly to get Pete to the bus station in time to catch his bus back to Sydney, and also to return the hired car. We got Pete there in the nick of time, only to find that his bus was going to be forty minutes late in departing.

I was extremely sad to say goodbye to Pete at the bus station. Leaving him before his bus departed didn't seem quite right to me, but we really had to return the hire car before we incurred an extra day's charge. Having returned the car, we then clumsily ran in thongs all the way back to the bus station, only to find Pete's bus had already departed.

I shall miss Pete a great deal, but I'm glad he made me come out here I thought sadly, between heaves and gasps as my lungs shrieked for oxygen.

Alone once again, I stopped on the Esplanade for a while to further catch my breath. The tide was high, supporting the pelicans gently floating away. It was a calm, warm, barmy evening, and a full moon was rising. I could have killed for a Foster's Lager, but I couldn't afford it at $2.40 a can.

I finally gathered all my belongings, wearily walked across town to the Youth Hostel in Macleod Street, and checked in there for the night. It seemed to me to be a lot quieter, and more peaceful, than the backpackers' establishments on the Esplanade, and nowhere near as busy.

I had booked, and prepaid, for a scuba diving course on the Great Barrier Reef due to start the following morning, which I was so eagerly looking forward to as it was to be the highlight of my visit to Cairns. I had come to see the Great Barrier Reef, and how better to see it than *a la* Jacques Cousteau - underwater. I had grave doubts about passing the strict medical examination before the course even started because I had caught a cold. Colds cause blocked sinuses, ruling out diving entirely, or so I was told.

Who wants to see the Great Barrier Reef peering like the average tourist through a glass-bottomed boat? Not me, I thought to myself.

This is going to be the real, dinkum thing, or nothing at all!

The most extraordinary thing happened as I was checking in at the Youth Hostel. I had asked Judy, the girl at the desk, where I could find some guy named George who was reportedly going to Cape York and, whom, according to rumours I had heard, had a spare seat available.

She didn't know the George I was inquiring about. However, there was this short, skinny, stern-eyed, anaemic-looking, chicken-chested, bespectacled, nondescript sort of chap at the reception desk at the time who had overheard my inquiry.

South of England, convent educated, well spoken, probably hockey sticks. Good looking, intelligent and a strong pair of walking stalks. Blonde, but does she have any brains? Tennis anyone? he assessed as I was to discover later. He managed to get the hockey sticks wrong by a country mile. I couldn't play hockey for toffee, and was unfortunate enough to be the only girl at convent with that dubious distinction. I handled a hockey stick with the most dangerous and injurious dexterity.

'My name is not George, but I am going to Cape York, and I do happen to have an empty seat available,' he volunteered.

He is so scrawny! I thought to myself. If I needed an X-ray of his chest, I wouldn't send him to radiography. I would just hold him up against the window and lift his vest, was my first impression of him. He much later mentioned to me that I should have seen him before he took up bodybuilding!

He invited me over to his room to discuss matters once I had settled down in my dormitory.

Chapter One

'Not George' was quite open in telling me that he was still grieving the death of his only child, a baby daughter Kate, twelve months previously. She had died as a result of Trisomy Thirteen Syndrome, a chromosome disorder, when she was nineteen days old. It was the most devastating event in his life.

He had then been fired from his job as a mining engineer in Indonesia and Borneo, due to not being able to perform as a result of acute grief following Kate's death. He said that he had known some of the most delightfully pleasant, mongrel bastards imaginable in his life.

He had left his home and wife four weeks earlier following advice from his two doctors to do so. He was told that he and his wife were both dying from grief, and that if he did not run away from home to find some solitude, and to get some rational order back into his life, he would die. The prognosis was that he had three months to live if he did nothing. He was strongly urged to run for his life.

He had a new Toyota Landcruiser GXL four-wheel-drive station wagon which was very well equipped for all emergencies in the bush. He seemed a likeable and genuine sort, but he was a very sad and tired man.

He told me that he was not taking a calendar along, because he did not know how long it would take. Perhaps three to four weeks was his estimate at the time, and he needed maximum flexibility. He had no desire to break an arm and a leg to get back anywhere, for anything, or for anyone. Having deadlines and due dates were no longer his style. He had endured them for far too long, and was trying to give them up.

He had booked the Toyota on a landing barge from Weipa to Karumba, a two-day voyage sailing down the Gulf of Carpentaria. This was done in order to avoid doubling back on his tracks back to Cairns, and more specifically, in preparation for him possibly going to the Northern Territory, and then on to the Kimberley in the far north of Western Australia.

'I've got ten weeks left to do whatever has to be done in Australia. I have no particular plans in mind at this stage,' I said. That seemed to please him.

'I have had all sorts of people wanting to go with me,' he said. 'You would be amazed at some of the people I have spoken to about the trip.

I once had two guys come up to me saying that they had three spare days available, and asked if they could come to Cape York with me!' he continued shaking his head with a faint smile on his face.

He told me that his name was Jack. He was born and raised near Sabie in the Eastern Transvaal, South Africa, a picturesque village surrounded by waterfalls and trout streams, and nestled in a valley on the Drakensberg escarpment, not very far from the Kruger National Park. It was 'Jock of the Bushveld' country he said. After a long, contemplative silence, he said that God lived there. He had migrated to Australia and had gone to live in Wollstonecraft, a suburb of Sydney.

'Not because of the political problems in my native land, but despite them,' he explained. I couldn't understand what that meant then, and I still, to this day, don't understand what it meant. He said the strangest things at times.

I phoned my mum and dad in England that night, and told them that I was thinking of going bush with him. Their reaction to my unexpected plan was, understandably, one of great concern. I told them what he had told me about himself, and this appeared to immediately have created a vast amount of apprehension and anxiety. I had to admit that an Englishwoman going into the Australian Outback with an emotionally disturbed South African man would, at first appearances, be sheer folly.

He was somewhat older than I was, colonial, non-Catholic, and had even worked as a coal shoveller in an underground coal mine at one time. He was a white ex-South African, and my parents were vehemently anti-Apartheid. I knew it was very difficult for them to judge character from twelve thousand miles away.

'Could we not take a third person with us? I really would feel safer if this were possible,' I asked him the following morning. My dad had told me to insist on a third person going with.

'There will be no room for a third person as things now stand,' he replied. 'If a third person were to come the rear seat which has been laid down, would have to be raised to accommodate that person, thereby displacing vital vehicle recovery gear. A heavy-duty roof-rack would then have to be purchased and fitted at a cost of six hundred and fifty dollars. This is an unnecessary expense that I have no desire to incur - especially as it would be to my detriment. The roof-rack and the extra load would alter the centre of gravity of the vehicle adversely, and make the vehicle unstable to an unacceptable degree.'

'In addition, taking a third person along would, all in all, result in overloading the Toyota by an additional two hundred and fifty kilograms in body weight, baggage and supplies,' he continued. 'Buying a trailer is equally out of the question for financial reasons. Besides that, the trailer would be torn apart before we were halfway up the track. I have already considered all the options' he concluded with authority and finality. I had not the faintest idea of what he was talking about!

'What will you do if no one wants to go with you?' I asked him.

'I will simply go alone with Ted as originally planned,' was his firm reply. There was clearly no way that he was going to be convinced to take a third person with him. It was definitely, and beyond any shadow of doubt, totally out of the question.

'What on earth do you mean by going alone with Ted?' I asked. He didn't reply, he just avoided the question.

Why would he want anyone else to go with him on this trip at all? I pondered for not too long. I later discovered that Ted was his late baby daughter Kate's teddy bear.

First of all, I have this Great Barrier Reef scuba diving course to attend to over the next few days, and I shall thoroughly think this Cape York trip through while I am at sea, I reasoned to myself.

What a great time we had on the diving course! I somehow managed to pass the medical examination, even though my cold was particularly green and unpleasant. The weight of the eighty cubic foot air tank on my shoulders, and extra paraphernalia dangling all over, definitely did not contribute to my comfort and well being. It took some time to become accustomed to it.

We were on board the *Tropic Breeze* bobbing around furiously in the strong winds. The weather was fine for a change, the red sunsets looked optimistic, and the forecast was for finer weather. However, my bunged up nose and sinuses didn't help me much. My ears equalised to the pressure at depth generally, but it was quite surprising how easy it was some times, and not at others.

We learnt mask clearing, buddy breathing, and many other scuba diving skills. Surprisingly no one freaked out and all the students completed the full course. My dive buddy, Amber, had some ear problems initially, but managed quite well overall.

The freedom of our first independent dive was fantastic as we writhed, twisted and dived down with the fish. We took an underwater camera down with us and took some photographs that came out surprisingly well. There was a great shot of me with my eyes nearly falling out of my head, and me panting at what, I believed, could have been a shark! Thankfully, we had a thirty-six exposure film and could snap away at everything to our heart's delight.

We anchored off Saxon Reef for a dive in a shallow six metres of water. It was quite the best dive of all. The sergeant major fish, small striped fellows, were particularly hungry, and frenzied at the bread we offered them. The Saxon Reef coral garden was a magnificent experience, never to be forgotten.

I AM A CERTIFIED OPENWATER SCUBA DIVER! I said to myself triumphantly, and with a great sense of achievement, and finding it hard to believe that all this was happening to me. If my medical practitioners had seen me, they would have totally disowned me for daring to defy their advice. I had also totally disregarded my own professional counsel for that matter, but I got away with it.

As we sailed back through Trinity Inlet to Cairns harbour late that evening, leaving the Great Barrier Reef behind us, I hoped that I could one day return. It had been an absolutely fabulous experience, and one far beyond my wildest expectations.

I again checked in at the Macleod Street hostel late that evening. I settled down in my dormitory and then went in search of Jack. I found him at the swimming pool talking to some of the other residents. I went on, and on, about the brilliant time I had on the dive trip.

'You really should try scuba diving,' I said to him. He took out his wallet and passed his Rescue Diver's card over to me. The least he could have done was to tell me about it first. He had even dived a live underwater volcano in Indonesia once. He was crazy about volcanoes. He even had a pet active volcano on the French island of Reunion in the Indian Ocean.

I then went straight to bed. Utterly exhausted I was quickly lulled into a blissful sleep, and dreams of the Great Barrier Reef.

I awoke completely refreshed at 10:30 am the next morning which, to me, was pure, decadent luxury. Jack cornered me to discuss more about the trip as I was about to go to town to do some shopping. He told me of all the things he had been doing, many of which I did not understand at the time. We had a really good talk exchanging all sorts of personal information that he said was vital if, for any reason, we found ourselves in difficulty. He told me that he was very tired, in reasonably good shape physically, and did not anticipate any health problems to arise.

I reciprocated by telling him that I had Ankylosing Spondylitis, an arthritic condition that is a disease of the spine and joints, that it was in remission, but could flare up at any time. I explained that I was extremely concerned at the prospect of an occurrence in the wilderness, and the lack of medical facilities north of Cairns.

'The Royal Flying Doctor Service is exceptionally competent and efficient. What is the prognosis?' he asked.

'The long term prognosis is extremely unpleasant,' I answered. 'The final result, due to start at any time now, is the slow fusion of the spine, and possible fusion of the spine to the hips. I will become a hunch-backed old hag. I also, at times, cannot walk without crutches,' I informed him.

I was suddenly terrified that this information would make him change his mind. Perhaps he didn't want to be saddled with a cumbersome lame duck on his hands in the middle of nowhere. My previous experiences had been that, when it seemed that I was building up a lasting relationship with a man, the ardour had cooled and died soon thereafter when this fact became known. I was wrong this time. It had entirely the opposite effect on him.

'Mmmm!' was his response followed by a long, pensive silence.

'What specific objectives do you have for the trip?' he suddenly continued with his inquisition.

'I want to learn bush survival skills,' I said.

We then spent some time discussing what skills there were to learn out there. Apparently, there was an awful lot that I didn't know about. I couldn't understand why pigs could be dangerous. Crocodiles were understandable threats, but not pig attacks.

'What specific interests do you have; hobbies, activities, special interests, and so forth?' he continued probing.

'I do have a long-standing passion for bird watching,' I replied.

'We will get a lot of that out there, and a great variety of it. What particular problems do you have in life generally, and what are your greatest fears?' he probed persistently.

'The single, most vexing problem I have, is with one-to-one relationships.' What a revelation to make to a virtual stranger!

'Don't we all. Why do you think that is the case?' he asked.

'Because I have been spoilt rotten all my life. I wrap everyone around my little finger, and I get whatever I want all the time. If I don't get what I want, then I throw non-stop, rampant tantrums until I do. I want to stop doing that,' I confessed.

'We will fix that problem for you in a hurry. What the bush doesn't fix, I will. That is a firm promise,' he assured me. 'Be prepared for the adventure of your life. When it is over, don't expect your life ever to be the same again. It won't be!'

Little did I know at the time what all that really meant. He was a man of very few words, and not exactly what one could describe as being big on diplomacy. There was still a lot of Borneo jungle left in him it seemed.

I then had a few hours on my own in town buying up toothbrushes and basic commodities, including a long-sleeve, anti-mosquito shirt from Woolworth's. Because of my medical background, I had been put in charge of first aid and medical supplies, and I had to buy a vast prescription for what amounted to almost a Royal Flying Doctor medical chest. It was quite fun, and I thoroughly enjoyed doing all the shopping. I had a huge lunch at The Pier overlooking Trinity Wharf and the dive boats. I so longed to go diving again.

I went to see the doctor for a pre-trip checkup as Jack had told me to do. She also supplied me with a prescription for medicines and a list of useful items for the first aid kit. That afternoon, we went to the dentist for a checkup and he patched up a troublesome, broken tooth of mine. He checked Jack's teeth and found that no dental repair work was necessary.

The dentist had been to Cape York the previous dry season, and he kept us in his surgery for another half an hour chatting away and telling us all the things we had been asking other people about.

He was the only person we spoke to who actually knew a lot, and was willing to impart his experience, which was greatly appreciated by us. No one seemed to really know what was going on, or were not prepared to tell us. The information we had been given before, was a morass of speculative guesses, and an overabundance of very obvious bum steers.

That night was our night at Magnum's nightspot to celebrate becoming Certified Openwater Divers. I was so exhausted from the shopping, medical visits and pre-trip run-around, that I could hardly drag myself away from my dozy, early-evening horizontal position to get there. I was glad that I did, as everyone from our group turned up, and they were such good company.

There was Hendrick the Dane, Ebba the Swede, Kathlin the Dutch girl, Leo from the UK, Amber my dive buddy from the UK, Roan, Debbie, Andrea and Paul; all from Canada, Greg, the dinkum Aussie who thought I was old - the cheeky little rotter, as well as Sara and Danny from the UK. The obligatory snorkel and fin treatment was hilariously funny as we were initiated into the scuba diving fraternity in the most appropriate style.

The next two days were spent preparing and packing for the Cape York trip. I had decided to definitely go to Cape York with Jack despite the protestations from my parents. My dad was especially concerned about *being attacked in the bush!*' He had said that, after three weeks of isolation in the bush, strange things happened to people - especially to men. He knew, for he was a man, had been an officer in the British Army, and therefore knew men well.

A lovely English lass Helen, another of Jack's friends, allayed most of my fears of going into the wild blue yonder with him. Jack seemed to be quite popular with the residents at the hostel.

I could well understand my parent's fears, concerns and apprehension, so I decided to talk to them again and to tell them that I was definitely going bush with Jack despite all their advice to the contrary which I, under normal circumstances, always respected.

My father had previously given me some good advice when assessing men. He had told me to check for personal hygiene, which, he said, was a good first impression. Jack managed to pass that critical inspection. His clothes were always clean and ironed, he was clean-shaven, he showered every day, he had a good set of teeth, and his room was neat, clean and tidy. He also possessed the social graces, and treated a lady like a lady - a most welcome change.

He was well-spoken and had a reasonable good taste in music. I did notice a few rough, bushy edges about him that needed a bit of polishing. He offered me his Australian passport and his driver's licence to examine together with photocopies thereof.

'Just in case you need to know who I really am, and for you to let your next of kin know. You never go anywhere with someone you don't know from a bar of soap,' he said. He ensured I did the latter by insisting on being present when I posted the letter with the appropriate photocopies of the information on him to my parents. Somehow, deep down, my instincts and intuition told me that I was right about this man.

He then drove me to the Cairns Police Station. With his documents in my hand, and the Senior Constable standing in front of me, he told me to tell the policeman that I intended going bush with him, and to please have a check done on him. Jack was as clean as a whistle - not even a driving offence was on record.

'If only other people like you would make similar inquiries, our job as policemen would be a great deal easier. Innocent travellers do disappear, and they do get killed, by going off with total strangers. Have a look at the Missing Persons board to see what I mean. Enjoy your adventure,' the policeman concluded. I felt completely comfortable about going to the police then, and much more at ease about going bush with Jack.

We had a look at the board on our way out. There was over a dozen photographs of international travelling youth pasted on the board. For all Jack knew about me, I could have been an axe murderess. I wasn't of course. Jack then took me back to the Youth Hostel.

'I was holding my breath in the cop shop for a while,' Jack cheerfully told me on the way to the hostel. 'I once was arrested near Venice, and I spent the night in a real dungeon after I crashed a brakeless motorcycle through a plate glass window, and straight into a pharmacy.'

'A few weeks later, I was again arrested, and spent a night in jail in Istanbul after Dudley, the Aussie farmer, Lex, the Kiwi seaman and I, legally borrowed a boat. We rowed it across the Bosphorus and back again one night, dodging the Soviet Navy passing through at the time and leaving them in total disarray. It happened when I was raising wholesale colonial hell in Europe. Those events are not on record, so they don't count as far as I'm concerned.'

'I did the crimes, I paid the fines, and I did the times. It cost me a fortune for that pharmacy and the motorcycle, and we had to get out of town in a hell of a hurry both times. The Soviet Navy we left to sort themselves out. Bloody outrageously good four months the three of us had though. I have been clean ever since,' he added.

Colonial boys will be the boys they were in Europe, I thought, so I couldn't hold that against him. Besides, Europe was used by the colonials as a big playground as much as the colonies were used by the Europeans as playgrounds. I was where I was with serious intent to play up big-time, and I had no idea what impact I was going to have on Australia. Quid pro quo

I guess. I would have loved to have been a fly on the wall in the Kremlin at the time though!

Jack then went to see his friends Mike and Irene Christie and their children to say goodbye to them. Mike was the manager of the Red Dome Gold Mine near Chillagoe, some three hours drive west of Cairns. He told me that he and Mike had been on a few adventurous capers together, including running Jack's brand new ocean-going sloop *Tokolosh* aground on the first night of her maiden voyage during a storm.

Jack was a qualified Yachtmaster who ran a dry ship, and Mike was a very experienced yachtsman then. The reason that Jack offered for running a dry ship was that 90% of drowned yachtsmen whose bodies were recovered had their flies open, their willies hanging out, and a high blood alcohol level. It had nothing to do with their seamanship, nor the storm, but everything to do with their coastal navigation skills poorly applied. I was also a yachtie, so I could tell what the two fools had done that night, but I didn't say so.

My parents DID phone the next day! I was in bed for the first call, in the shower for the second, and in tears of relief for the third!

Jack and I were very well prepared for this critical telephone call. I felt a little guilty about it, for it was almost like plotting against my parents, but I knew in my heart of hearts that what I was doing, was right. It was not as if they were wrong, but they could not judge a strange man's character from twelve thousand miles away. It similarly was not as if I could, but all my instincts told me that it was all right. They had to rely on my ability to judge character for just this once.

'Well?' asked my father, 'What have you decided to do?'

With Jack by my side I told my father all of what I knew about him, what precautions I had taken, and had been forced to take, and then, in the most definite and careful manner, I told my father that I had made a firm decision, and that we were departing for Cape York the next day.

My father was somewhat taken aback when I told him that Jack was standing by my side, and was prepared to talk to him. I handed the phone over to Jack without waiting for a reply. I somehow forgot to tell my father about a highly irate, arm-waving Italian pharmacist and a very confused Soviet Navy.

They started off by getting the time of day wrong. Jack said 'Good morning,' and my father said 'Good evening.' They finally agreed to settle on 'Gidday.'

Jack explained to my father that he had an appreciation of the tyranny of distance in determining a man's character, and the fact that he was a competent bushman. He further explained that he had been experiencing emotional problems for some time which he had no reason to hide, because he had nothing to be ashamed of. He empathised with Dad with regard to me being his youngest daughter, and his justifiable concern over my safety. Jack told my father that I was about to embark on the adventure of my life.

The two of them then discussed regular communication to assure my parents of my continued well-being. Jack arranged with my father that we would telephone collect on a weekly basis, if we could. Telephones in the Cape York Peninsula were very few and far between, and we would also be camping out in some of the remotest places for indefinite periods of time. Cape York was a wilderness after all.

My father asked Jack if he was fully aware of my health problems, in particular the Ankylosing Spondylitis that could flare up at any time, and possibly terminate the trip prematurely. My father was concerned that, should this happen in a remote place, I would not be able to get medical attention without great delay.

Jack explained that we had two-way radio communication, and that the Royal Flying Doctor Service was more than capable of handling any emergency in the bush. Jack further explained that we had discussed, in some detail, all aspects of our health with each other, and had recovery plans in place should anything serious eventuate to either, or both, of us.

I was positive that I had made the right decision to go with Jack. My father seemed happy enough, and my mother was pleased to hear that my main fears were the rivers and crocodiles, and not Jack. All four of us were very relieved, and a heavy weight had been lifted from my shoulders. I had their blessings to go. Yahoo!

It was an emotional start that I really hadn't anticipated. Speaking to my parents, made me wonder whether Jack really did want to take advantage of me, but I continually kept telling myself that it was nonsense. We continued to prepare for our epic journey unhindered.

Jack had spent the previous two weeks in Cairns preparing for the trip. He had been living at the hostel in a single room, sharing it with detailed topographic maps, distance and fuel supply and demand calculations, and an assortment of other bits and pieces. He had been informed that the road to Cape York was still closed at the time, and no traffic was being let through.

The northern Australian tropical Wet Season was exceptionally prolonged that year. For the benefit of tourism, and for political correctness, it had been renamed the Green Season. Normally, from about mid-December, when the summer rains start falling, until mid-May, the road to Cape York is totally impassable. It was mid-June at the time, and the road was still closed to traffic north of Laura on the day we left. Laura was some five hours driving north of Cairns.

The Queensland Police determine when the road is trafficable. They generally keep it closed until they are reasonably certain that they will not be called upon to rescue some unfortunate victim from the evils of 'The Track', as it is colloquially known. It exacts a heavy toll on the less experienced, and ill-equipped, adventurers.

Even if the road is not completely dry, and a vehicle can get through, the police still keep the road closed, as in a semi-wet state, deep ruts are left behind which, when they dry up, make it very dangerous for traffic thereafter.

Jack had collected all sorts of paraphernalia for the Toyota. He had bought a complete second spare wheel, a puncture repair kit, a high-lift jack to change tyres in mud and sand, a heavy duty Tirfor hand-winch including snatch-blocks and shackles for winching the vehicle out of mud bogs and sand, a Snatchum strap which stretches until taught, then snatches the towed vehicle out of difficulty, fifty metres of strong marine rope, a heavy-duty spade for digging the Toyota out of mud bogs and heavy sand and for human waste disposal, two twenty litre jerry cans for spare fuel and a twenty litre can for fresh water.

A full set of tow-bars and tow hooks had been fitted in Cairns. A ten thousand kilometre, and *Cape York Special Service*, had been done to the Toyota in Cairns. On board were a complete set of radiator hoses, a complete set of belts for the fan, power steering, air conditioning and water pump, as well as a change of spark plugs, points, condenser, jumper leads and half a dozen cans of water dispersing WD40 to protect the electrical system at deep river crossings.

Jody and Mike, two hardened and experienced bushmen residing at the hostel at the time, kindly, and ceremoniously presented to us a contraption called a *snake catcher* for precisely that purpose. We had, by then, accumulated two large first aid boxes that would have been adequate for a general hospital casualty ward. Goodness knows what could happen in the Outback! It all seemed a bit exaggerated and melodramatic to me to have all this equipment on board.

Whatever will become of us if we have to use any of it I wondered. 'Wouldn't a horse and a pack mule be a much less complicated way of doing things?' I asked Jack.

'It is all something similar to a Colt .45. You don't always need it, but when you do, you need it awfully badly,' he smiled back.

It was only then that I understood why Jack said that there would be no room for a third person. There was just so much gear and supplies to take with us that, if we had taken any more, we most certainly would have required a roof rack. As it was, the packing was done with absolute geometric precision inside the Toyota. The only thing to be strapped to the outside of the vehicle was the canvas water bag on the bullbar.

We started the pre-departure day getting our supplies together which, in the main, constituted $280.00 of food from the local supermarket. It was great fun choosing all the luxuries like smoked oysters and mussels, cashew nuts, and all sorts of other delectable goodies that were to supplement and enrich our rather simple diet.

We selected a Jackaroo three-man dome tent that ultimately proved to be a very wise choice. Jack had intended buying a swag and sleeping under the Toyota if it rained had he gone off by himself. I bought myself an Akubra hat at Jack's insistence, as I don't normally wear a hat.

'It will probably save your life up north. It is a vital and essential piece of bush survival gear. I also don't want to deal with an hysterical, troppo female going bananas in the sun while we are bogged up to our eyeballs in mud,' he said.

At times that day I could understand only half of the things he said as he gave me half answers, and seemed to speak in unintelligible riddles. I knew full well that he had his mind fully occupied with all sort of things to get, and to provide for every possible eventuality.

He did appeared to be a rather bossy sort. It seemed to me at times that he had lost the ability to say 'Please' and 'Thank you'. It was 'Do this!' and 'Do that!' most of the time.

I will teach him that he is not commanding his troops on his mining projects in Borneo racing them around the jungle, but that he was dealing with a refined gentlewoman with breeding, I decided. Deep down I really did hope that I had made the right decision. We would both have to learn to tolerate each other's shortcomings over the next few weeks it seemed.

When we got back after our shopping expedition, Peter, Lori and the rest of the crowd at the hostel teased us, and said we would want a Jacuzzi bath next. Peter was a nice fellow we had met the previous night. He was quite charming.

What a shame I couldn't be going with him, I thought to myself. Going with Jack instead is going to be jolly hard work. Jack by comparison was a pain-in-the-neck perfectionist, and a pragmatic, dogmatic non-Romeo.

On our last evening in Cairns I felt a little insecure and apprehensive not knowing quite what the next four weeks were to bring. All I knew was that we were to leave the next day, and we most certainly weren't going to starve.

Soon, I was to be losing contact with time, dates and the other problems that beset the real world when Jack and I started on our great adventure to Cape York, the northernmost tip of Australia, and one of the last remaining wildernesses on earth. We had agreed that we were not taking a calendar with us, and our general plan was to stop over at any one place for as long as we liked it there.

On the Saturday the 'Big Day' had eventually arrived. We set about in the early morning packing all the vehicle recovery gear into the Toyota. We had previously packed all our supplies into containers, and the containers were then packed into the vehicle. It took a lot of organisation and patience.

Jack went to the camping store around the corner to get some last bits and pieces from his friend John including a rifle and ammunition.

A rifle? I asked myself with some alarm. I am going to have to watch this man!

We next went to pick up some dry ice for the Esky cooler to keep our perishables frozen and edible. The idea was good, but it didn't work for as long as we would have liked it to have. We also bought some block-ice for the second Esky cooler to keep the cans of Foster's Lager cold. It meant fresh food and cold beer for perhaps a week.

We simply couldn't wait to get on the road out of Cairns. It seemed as if the last bits and pieces and finishing touches were hampering our departure, and would never let us go, but at last the time had come.

There was a mob of about twelve people who had turned up at the hostel to see us off. All the buying, packing and preparation had been so laborious, but the fun was about to begin. It was midday exactly when we took off.

Jack was such a fastidious and meticulous 'everything has got to be just so and so' that I deeply hoped that I would be able to cope with it all in the bush. Four weeks of this was going to be a very long, long time.

As we drove out of the driveway I turned around to wave goodbye to the mob. I was wondering if I ever was going to see Peter again, or my home and family for that matter.

LOUGHRIGG TARN

Chapter Two

Jack drove to the northern outskirts of Cairns on the Captain Cook Highway to Cape Tribulation. We made a last stop at the Smithfield shopping centre to stock up on Foster's Lager and some wine. If my father had been there to see what we had bought, and packed into the Toyota, he would have had a frightful fit. There was enough there to float HMS Hermes in!

We soon discovered that it didn't last very long, given a few beers at lunch time and a good few more in the evening. The last of the shopping completed, Jack headed for the passenger side of the Toyota.

'You can drive for a while. I am too tired,' he said. I hadn't expected him to relinquish the driving to me so soon.

If I as much as make one mistake, he will probably want to kill me, I thought in near-panic, as all women do when they drive a man's vehicle. It was the first time I had driven a four-wheel-drive vehicle, and I had never driven anything that large before.

Jack read my thoughts accurately enough, and ensured that I handled the Toyota well enough by offering more than adequate advice from the passenger seat. However, he soon felt comfortable about my driving ability, and he nodded off to sleep. Poor Jack - he was absolutely exhausted.

The Toyota was equipped with power steering and was quite easy to handle. She went like a Roller, and later went into, and got out of, places no Roller could possibly have survived. We arrived at the Daintree River ferry crossing at about four o'clock that afternoon, just in time to catch the next ferry across. I was furiously looking out for crocodiles, but again, in vain. Jack and I took photographs of each other on the ferry. We both looked pale, tired and very tense.

I continued driving on the dirt road through some quite spectacular rainforest until we reached The Village at Cape Tribulation. It was the same road I had been on two weeks previously, except that this time, it wasn't raining, the road was drier, and I could better appreciate the rainforest. It was supposed to be 'a good road', but there were ruts and potholes in the road which called for very skillful driving. It was impossible to maintain the road in the wet season and, more likely than not, untrafficable most of the time then.

We stopped at the little cafe across the road from The Village for a cup of tea. The kind lady there told us that there was a camping ground on the beach about a kilometre north of Cape Tribulation called Pilgrim's Place.

How many cafes like this one are we going to encounter en route to Cape York? I wondered to myself. I found it rather strange seeing the backpackers at The Village where I had stayed earlier. I half wanted to be with them, and have a party, but Jack wouldn't let me drive the Toyota on my own.

'There are two things a man does not lend out. They are his vehicle, and his rifle,' he said.

'What about the women in your life?' I asked him.

'The feminist extremists tell me that they are perfectly capable of looking after themselves,' he responded flatly and without a trace of emotion in his voice.

'Don't misinterpret what I have just said, because I like women a lot - perhaps too much for my own good. I believe that they have every right to get out into the real world to realise their full potential.'

What on earth have I let myself in for? I asked myself. I wasn't a feminist - not by a long shot.

'We are on a totally different sort of adventure. Discos on this trip are Oh, Tee, Ee - out!' Jack reminded me. It must have been some really bushy grammar school that he went to!

We most certainly found the most delightful campsite at Pilgrim's Place. We were told by the owners that that particular spot was the only one vacant, was very wet, that it wasn't very good, and we could refuse it if we wished without offending. It turned out to be the perfect spot in the rainforest for our spacious dome tent which we erected for the first time. It popped up in no time at all, and we had our very first real camp. All in all it was very comfortable.

We were surrounded by cane toads, possums, wallabies, goannas and a canopy of fan palms. The nocturnal animals were abundant, curious and noisy. This included a bunch of middle-aged New Zealanders on a group tour camping further down near the beach. They were merrily singing away one night and were having a wonderful time.

Cape Tribulation National Park, which was 16,959 hectares is size, had, as its boundaries, the Bloomfield River to the north, the McDowell Range to the west, the Daintree River to the south, and the Coral Sea to the west. It was listed as a World Heritage Wet Tropics area in 1988.

We had agreed to a fundamentally essential operational rule in camp. If one of us noticed anything that needed doing, we did it immediately. We did not consider any particular job was either his or mine. There was no job demarcation at all - one just did whatever it was that needed doing without looking to the other to do it, unless help was needed for a particularly difficult task.

We had the most delicious barbecue, thanks to Jack with his excellent bush skills carefully making a campfire with totally saturated wet wood. He slowly, and painstakingly, kept whittling away at the firewood with the hand-axe until he had a more than respectable pile of kindling in front of him. Once a flame was established, the kindling dried out under its own heat and it took flame.

We were the only party to have a campfire amongst the twelve others at Pilgrim's Place. Passers-by looked on with envy as our fire cheerfully blazed away. They all complained bitterly that their wood wouldn't burn. It was gas burners to the fore, and baked beans and bully beef from a can for those without cookers. We had copious amounts of Foster's Lager and CC chips before dinner to celebrate our first camp, and campfire, in the Cape Tribulation rainforest.

After dinner, I left Jack to hold the fort, while I went for a long, leggy walk on the beach alone. It was pitch dark, and the moon was yet to rise. The stars twinkled brightly in a cloudless sky, and the gentle surf quietly kept rolling in. I followed a hermit crab scurrying along the beach, all the while shining my torch on him until he dug himself deeply into the sand. Magic!

That night we went to sleep in our tent lulled by the sounds of rainforest night life, and the occasional thud of a seed-pod falling from the nearby tree-tops to the ground below.

Very early the next morning, Jack and I went for an amazing walk on the beach. The sun had arrived, illuminating the dense rainforest behind us which was positively alive with sunbirds and butterflies. Jack was enthralled at how satisfying it was to collect shells on the beach. He was bum-up and head-down crawling along the sand digging here, there, and everywhere, making all sorts of happy sounds and grunts whenever he found a patch of good shells. They were different shades of brown, with dots and zigzags - there were heaps of them. Shelly beaches are common to find in name on maps, but extremely rare to find in reality. We didn't know then that we weren't allowed to collect shells. Sorry.

Jack had entrusted me with the loan of his Nikon binoculars to spot birds and butterflies. The binoculars, and my bird book, were never to leave my side for the rest of the trip, ever-ready for a new exiting discovery. The most unusual birds would always appear on a toilet stop when one was least prepared, it seemed.

'Isn't it strange how one can be totally absorbed in the environment, and be made to feel incredibly content and lazy,' I had remarked to Jack over lunch one day. 'I find it strange not having any high or low moods - just a steady, tranquil and happy equilibrium.'

'That, is what this jaunt is all about,' explained Jack. 'All we have to do from here on, is to be totally relaxed and to enjoy ourselves,' he added.

Jack spent that afternoon going over the Toyota with a fine tooth comb. Every electrical connection was liberally sprayed with WD40 water dispersant. Jack then called me over to the Toyota and started my bush survival skills orientation.

'If you don't look after your vehicle, it is not going to look after you,' he told me. He had me crawling under the Toyota examining suspension and steering systems, while he explained the various components, and their functions, while he looked for oil and fuel leaks. The Toyota was in good shape.

That afternoon however, after a long, hot stroll along the beach, I felt tired and a little restless. On my return, I vented my discontent on Jack by criticising him, and pointing out his shortcomings. He listened intently, stared me straight between the eyes, but offered no reply. Not even a raised eyebrow did he proffer.

She has been in the sun for too long, probably has been walking far too fast, too far, and has gone bananas, Jack thought to himself. I will talk to her later when she is more receptive he sensibly reasoned. He went over to the Toyota, spooned some Staminade into a mug, filled it with ice water from the Esky cooler, and handed it to me.

'Drink this! It contains glucose and electrolytic salts and minerals,' was all he said as he handed the mug to me.

After I had a refreshing hot shower later in the day, I felt fine and rearing to get the campfire going. I apologised to Jack for my outburst and went off to collect firewood.

'Always keep your hat on in the sun. That is precisely what it is there for. You must also ensure that you drink enough water, so as not to get dehydrated. From now on, midday naps are also in order,' he said to me later that evening.

Does he think I am some infant in kindergarten? I asked myself. No doubt the rest of the trip was going to have its turbulent moments.

I must be out of my mind being here. Turn back at Cooktown! It's my last chance to escape part of me was saying, but my adventurous spirit demanded the experience, whatever it was to be. We had hardly started on our trip, and I was full of anticipation.

I really couldn't make head or tail of this strange man. I tried very hard to find out more about him by probing into his background. All I got back were unintelligible monosyllables. After some consistent, gentle persistence, he finally relented, and said that he would tell me about someone he said was Lighty's father. You are on your way to some African high adventure......

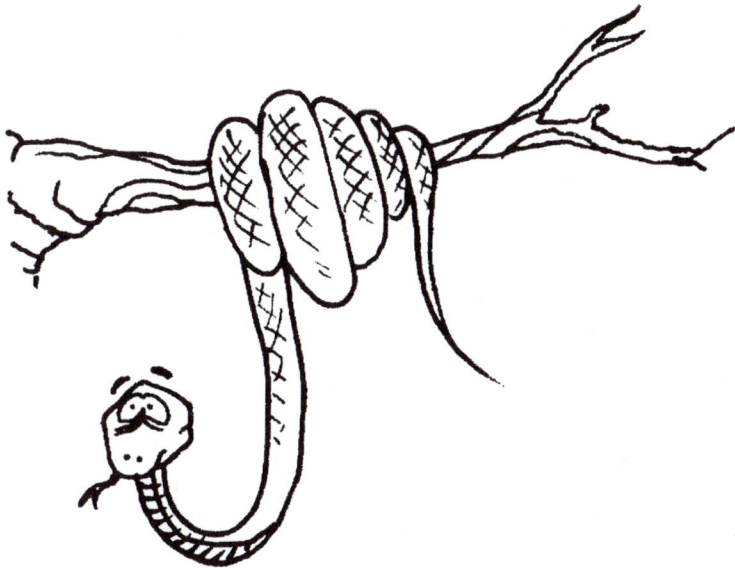

Chapter Three

Lighty's father had a rather unusual childhood. He had been born near Ladysmith, Natal, a British colony in those days. Lighty's paternal grandfather was from England, and his paternal grandmother was French.

Lighty's grandfather had left his non-English speaking French wife and three infant sons on their farm near Ladysmith in Natal, and had joined the British forces to fight against the Boers of the Transvaal and Orange Free State Republics during the Anglo Boer War at the turn of the century. Ladysmith had a rather mixed English and Boer population at the time and, as part of Natal, was under British rule.

Being very close to the Transvaal and Orange Free State borders, Lighty's father and uncles had learned to speak Zulu well by that time, some French, some Afrikaans, but no English.

During the war the British Forces were rounding up the Boer women and children and sending them to concentration camps in the Transvaal. Arriving at the farm, the British soldiers found three Afrikaans speaking boys, and a mother who could not speak English, so off they went on a train to a concentration camp in the Transvaal.

Lighty's grandmother and one uncle died in one of the infamous epidemics there. His grandfather returned to the farm at the end of the war only to find it razed to the ground by the British, all the livestock dead, and reports that his family had been taken away to an unknown concentration camp.

His grandfather took off on horseback searching the human remnants in the concentration camps he encountered. His reception by the victorious British forces left a lot to be desired he found. He also found that the Boer grapevine was far more reliable, and helpful, even to an Englishman and old foe who spoke Afrikaans fluently, and dressed, shot, rode, and even looked like a Boer. His love for King, Country and British Empire died forever when he arrived at the Balmoral concentration camp, some eighty miles east of Pretoria in the Transvaal, to find only two sons left; Lighty's father aged four, and his father's younger brother, aged two.

He took them back to the farm near Ladysmith, where he left them in the care of the Gumede tribe there. Once he had ensured that they had been safely ensconced in a Zulu family, he departed for Mozambique to hunt elephant to sell the ivory and to get some money to start farming again.

Mother Africa took him to her bosom; she was like that. The drums, the vital heartbeat of Africa, long since silenced by the post, the telegraph, the wireless, the telephone and the newspaper, spoke.

They brought a message that he had been killed; gored and trampled to death under the horns and hooves of an enraged African buffalo bull he had the misfortune to wound, and then had to go out alone and get. Such were the hunting laws amongst gentlemen hunters in Africa then, for the wounded African buffalo is the most formidable, and unpredictable, of all animals. The chances of returning alive were less than fifty percent, so one had to go out man alone.

His grandfather was never heard of again, half-crazed with fear and terror as he died, his last remains in the form of hyena, jackal and vulture turds indiscriminately dispersed across the vast expanses of the African veldt. Left then to bleach bone dry and white in the harsh unforgiving African sun, and to meld back into nature, back into the parched, dry, red earth as the next summer rains came and went, leaving no trace of his ever having even existed.

Lighty's father grew up as a Zulu in the Gumede kraal on the farm near Ladysmith for a while because there was no one else to look after him and his younger brother then. Lighty's father's Zulu name was Nyanyan, the Little One. His brother became known as Chirrichir, The Cricket. Nyanyan's Zulu friend was Ndlovo, The Elephant, because he was big for his age, and used to walk like an elephant.

The Gumede family eventually feared that they were living too close to Ladysmith. They feared that the white people might take Nyanyan and Chirrichir away from them, and teach them the ways of the white man. They retreated to the remotest part of Natal that they could find, which found them at the steep foothills of the Drakensberg in a place where the white man would not want to farm, or settle, and an infinity away from them.

Some white men did later try to settle there, but their livestock never seemed to want to stay at home. The Zulu's arranged matters such that it was impossible for any white man to want to come anywhere near the place. It became known as Manzi Mhlopi, The Place of White Water, because of the cold mountain streams cascading through the valley.

The sangoma was called from Inginginghluvu, and she bewitched the area with tagate for the white man, and it was made known as such far and wide.

It was also made known that Tokolosh was there. The tagate was the black magic of misfortune for the white man, and the Tokolosh was the little mythical man, no bigger than knee high, who was held responsible for all inexplicable events leading to the pregnant status of young, un-married maidens.

Nyanyan and Ndlovo would play to their hearts content in the African veldt doing the happy things African boys did in those days. Their major preoccupation was sculpturing pretend cattle from clay which they found near the perennial spring which fed the creek near to the kraal, and from which the women drew water for the kraal in clay pots and calabashes.

Cattle were of major concern then, for the number of cattle a man owned, was living testimony of his wealth. The number of wives he had, was additional testimony of that wealth, as cattle were used as dowry for a new wife. A man having more that one wife was not unusual, as inter-tribal warfare took a great toll on the warriors, and there were many widows, for there were many wars - mostly because of stray livestock.

Cattle and goats in those parts of Africa were very undisciplined, for they used to deliberately wander in the path of someone for miles on end, and quite often to the wanderer's kraal. Of course, they had to be watered and fed there, and the owner eagerly and sincerely sought to restore rightful property. That was the honourable code of proper conduct in face-saving African custom, but it always seemed to occur in a direction opposite to which the livestock had come from.

Taking care of stray livestock was a decent enough thing to do, and the least that could be done for a distant neighbour. Getting caught with errant livestock wandering in front of the wanderer, was a big problem, for it was insisted on by the owner that they always walked faster than the owner knew they could walk, and always further, and faster, than the owner wanted them to walk.

So the boys grew up in harmony with nature at Manzi Mhlopi, and they knew the beauty of being as one with nature, playing in the veldt endlessly with little, if any, restraint on their curiosity and sense of adventure. They played kleilat with sticks and blobs of clay stuck to the ends. The older boys used to make shields, and assegais, and knobkerries for them to play the invincible Zulu warrior, and to have stick fights with.

They caught frogs and tadpoles. They chased rock rabbits and duiker. They had meerkats and bush babies for pets and always looked after them very well, because animal husbandry was a precursor to their later way of life, which was always centred on animals.

And they knew of the delicate balances of nature. That between leopard and baboon was the most important, and central, to their being. The leopard ate the baboons, and if there were insufficient baboons, then the leopard ate the livestock. When there was no livestock left, the leopard ate the people.

If the baboons had insufficient crops to feed off, then there would be too few baboons for the leopard to eat, so crops had to be planted by the people to feed themselves and the baboons. There was room aplenty in the mountains for everyone to live in harmony.

They had been living in the hills, mountains, and streams for seven happy, carefree years, with many mothers and fathers, and brothers and sisters, when the first missionaries penetrated as far as Manzi Mhlopi. They had disregarded the advice that it was bewitched for the white man, and foolishly feared not. They set up a tent camp not far from Manzi Mhlopi, and started their work.

Much to their consternation, they found Nyanyan and Chirrichir, and immediately took them into their care, believing that white children belonged with white people, and should be raised as such rather than as non-believing savages.

The missionaries later took Nyanyan and Chirrichir to their Ladysmith mission where they were locked up in a classroom for many hours every day. They tried to teach them strange things, and foreign ways, and they tried to tame them. They tried very hard to make them wear strange clothes, and to eat strange food, but not with their fingers.

They also spoke a language that both Nyanyan and Chirrichir could understand, but could not speak. It was a language they feared a great deal, and had good reason to do so for their memories were young and fresh.

They were told by the missionaries, in a breastless and brotherly manner, that they were loved, but it did not feel like the love that they knew, and it was not the warm bosom of their mothers, and the love of their fathers, and of the brothers and sisters they knew, and loved, and understood so well.

There were no mothers there, and no fathers, and no sisters, and no brothers. They had no one to play with, and the things that they used to play with, they no longer had.

At night they would have to wash themselves with a strange slippery stone, and were made to sleep on a soft thing called a bed. There were no sleeping mats there, and they had to sleep alone in a room by themselves, which frightened them.

They were never allowed by the missionaries to go outside of the mission for fear that they might be lost, or perhaps run away. They looked through the windows and saw white people like themselves riding on horses, and in horse-drawn carts, and on ox wagons.

And they saw Zulus like themselves, mothers, and fathers, and brothers, and sisters, and they could not talk to them, or play with them. It was very bewildering to them to see the hustle and bustle around the mission which they could not be part of.

Nyanyan also did not like the way the missionaries tried to make him talk in English, and do sums, and to say God and Gentle Jesus, and Mother Mary, and please, and thank you. The missionaries used to get very alarmed when they spoke Zulu to each other. Chirrichir used to cry a lot every day, and Nyanyan would have to comfort him.

Nyanyan and Chirrichir were very unhappy there, so they decided to run away one very dark night when there was no moon. They planned, and they plotted, and they schemed, and conjured up ideas on how to escape the strange and dislikeable ways that had so changed their happy lives.

They knew that they could run far and fast, because that was the way they had been taught to do as warriors when they were chasing the enemy, or were being chased by a leopard, but they did not know who they could trust any more. There were no Zulus at the mission, so they could not talk to anyone, and no one could understand what they were saying. They silently screamed for the freedom they knew of, but no one listened, no one cared, and no one did anything about it.

One day Nyanyan looked out of the window onto the street and he saw Ndlovo standing in the street looking back at the window. It was in a manner that said that he was not looking there, but elsewhere. Nyanyan rushed to the window and put his face against it. Ndlovo's eyes lit up, and then quickly looked away again. Nyanyan shouted at Ndlovo, again and again, but he just walked slowly away.

That night, a fire broke out in the mission stable. All the missionaries went there to save the horses and to fight the fire. Nyanyan and Chirrichir heard the commotion and ran to investigate. They ran to the front of the mission. The missionaries had, in their haste, left the front door of the mission open.

Nyanyan and Chirrichir ran like the duiker, they ran like the cheetah, they ran outside to where the missionaries had told them the devil was to be found. They ran straight into hell, and they disappeared like the mystical wind.

They ran and they ran. And the moon was full, and directly above them. And they ran west, for that is what their hearts told them to do. And they ran to where the moon went down. They ran towards their home in the mountains. They ran toward Manzi Mhlopi.

They ran all night until the skies behind them turned to grey, then to purple, then to red. Their bare feet feared not the stone and the thorn, for their feet were thick with callous, and impenetrable.

When the sun sky was orange, they stopped to find a stream, for they were thirsty and tired. They found one and drank until their bellies were full, and they rested. And they drank again. And again, and again, and again, until the water they drank no longer would stay in their stomachs.

They knew that they had run faster than the horse that night, and faster and further than any man could run. They knew they were safe, but they had to find a safe place to hide in until the moon sky came again. Then they could continue their flight to safety in the dark of night. They knew that they could run for many miles, and for many days without food, but they could not run too far away from a stream of life-giving water.

They walked along the creek until they found a place where there was a shady tree with thick bushes beneath it. There, they lay down to sleep for the rest of the day. They took turns to sleep, while the other kept a close guard, just like the baboons did when the baboons raided the crops. They did as the baboons wisely did. They saw no one, heard no one, and so could speak to no one.

As the sun sky turned to orange, and then to red, they drank their last bellyful of water from the creek, and ran away from the creek, for they knew that was where the white men would look for them. And they ran to the sunset, and away from the moon, leaving the creek to the right of them. When the moon was difficult to run away from because there was too much cloud in the sky to see it, they stopped running.

They could see the high mountains of Manzi Mhlopi in front of them, and they knew the mountains were still two moons away, and their bellies were talking to them, and they were hungry and thirsty. They turned to the right to find the stream again, and found it after a very long time.

In front of them, they saw a kraal with Zulu beehive huts, built in a circle on a kopje not far from the stream. There was a larger than normal fire burning in the centre of the kraal. And the indunas, the elders, were sitting around the fire drinking millet beer from calabash gourds. Together with them were the war chiefs of the Zulu, mighty and fearless men all.

Nyanyan and Chirrichir carefully stalked the kraal, mindful that sentries were likely to have been posted, and to safeguard the cattle. As they got closer, they saw many, many warriors, Zulu impi, in full war dress, and all were carrying shields, knobkerries, sticks and assegais. They were sitting around fires, and groups of them took turns to leap up, and to do a fierce Zulu war dance.

They danced the dance of the warrior, stabbing the imaginary enemy lying on the ground with the assegai, and they trampled his mere mortal remains into the ground, for they knew not the meaning of mercy in times of war.

The women constantly kept bringing food and full calabashes of beer to the indunas and war chiefs, who did much talking and debating. They were having a royal indaba, discussing matters of great national importance.

The indunas were passive, and thoughtful, and calm, while the war chiefs and the warriors were restless, and troubled, and thirsting for the blood of battle.

Nyanyan and Chirrichir had not seen such a great gathering of chiefs before, but they knew that, when the warriors were dressed for battle, and the indunas were doing much serious talking at an indaba with the war chiefs late in the night, then a mighty battle would surely ensue.

At the head of the indaba sat the Paramount Chief of the Zulus. He was dressed in the royal dress of leopard skin. He had come all the way from Ulundi, the Royal Kraal, and some five suns away.

He was talking slowly, but very deeply, about the children that the Singise abalungu had stolen from him. The English white strangers had stolen his children. And the warriors danced, and ululated the glory of great warriors, and of great battles past, and of Chaka Zulu, the mightiest warrior of them all.

The bellies of Nyanyan and Chirrichir were sore from thirst and hunger, but their hearts were happy to hear the language that they could talk and understand. And they knew that they were the children of which the Chief spoke of with much sadness and anger. And their heads told them that that was good.

They came out from hiding and approached the kraal, shouting warrior cries, and stamping their feet in defiance of the white man's prison that they had been in, and with great joy. An impi sentry heard their shrill cries, and was alarmed to find little children in the veldt so late at night when there was great danger in store for them and at a time when the nation was in foment about the children.

'Abantwana bakona! Abantwana bakona!' Nyanyan cried out to him. We are the children!

The warrior took them immediately to the kraal to present them in front of him at the entrance to the kraal. He shouted for all to hear that the children were there, and that they were safe. He kept on shouting as he ran, and then stopped at the entrance to the kraal, and waited to be acknowledged. The message was passed to an induna who rejoined the indaba, and who then waited his turn to be acknowledged by the Paramount Chief before relaying his message.

The women came and took Nyanyan and Chirrichir away to the women's fire, where they were given water to drink from a calabash gourd, and they were fed until their bellies were swollen, and until the fleas in their stomachs told them that they could eat, and drink, no more. One of the women took them into a hut and lay them gently to sleep on a sleeping mat. She sang lullabies to them, while the indunas spoke softly to the war chiefs, and the war chiefs spoke loudly of war.

'My children must go to Pongola where they will be safe!' the Paramount Chief commanded. 'Ten impi of the very best must take them to our Swazi brothers in the Lebombo Mountains, for the Singisi will not look for them there. They must fly by night, and rest by day. They must go now!' he commanded.

Nyanyan and Chirrichir had barely fallen asleep when the impis came to get them for the long and dangerous journey. Chirrichir started crying, but Nyanyan told him that the time had come for him to be hard like a warrior, for there was still much hardship to follow that night and for many days thereafter.

They ran again that night, and when they got tired they were carried in the arms of the impi who each took turns to carry them. Then they ran again for miles on endless miles. Across ditches and dongas, across veldt and vlei, across rivers and streams, through the mud and the rain, and across hills and valleys. And they ran.

The drums spoke loudly across the whole of Zululand that night. They spoke the following day into Swaziland, and to Egoli, the gold mines in Johannesburg, and to the diamond mines in Kimberley, and to the Shangaan of Mozambique, and to the Ndebele and Matabele in the north, and deep into the heart of Africa.

The drums said that the children were safe, and were going to Swaziland. And they said that there was to be no war if the children stayed safe. The drums told the people to look after the children and the Zulu impi.

The impis heads were hardened, for their assegais had not yet been red with the blood of the Singisi. The Zulu warriors had not done bloody battle with the white man for many years, but their hearts were soft for the children.

By night they ran, and by day they ate, and drank, and slept while the sun shone hot. And they lay hidden in wait for the darkness of the night. The first night they ran north, away from Ladysmith, and away from the Singisi.

They ran for another thirty miles that night, for sixty miles the following night, and for another sixty miles the next night where they reached the place of Blood River - where the river ran red from the blood of the Zulu when the Voortrekkers, the Sibunu, (Boers) had defeated the mightiest nation on earth. All along the way the Zulu people kept fires going all night for the impi to see them, and they were always well fed and looked after. When they were fed, the drums spoke again to the north, and to the east, to let them know that the children were coming.

They slept at Isandlwana, where the earth was red with the blood of the Singisi, where the Zulu had defeated the might of the British Empire who had come to tame them. Then they ran another sixty miles the next night until they reached Hlobane, the cliff of the cowards, where the cowards who ran away from battle were forced by Chaka Zulu to jump to their inglorious deaths.

They slept near the Kongalana River that day, and again that night, for they were too tired, and they knew that it was only two more nights of running to reach Pongola. And the boys were very tired and weary. And so were the warriors. And none cried, for they were all too tired to cry.

They spent the next day in the shade under the trees on the banks of the Kongalana River, and they rested. That night they went on their way again, over the Hlobane Mountain, and they followed the Pivane River downstream to Golele where they slept the day.

The next morning they were near to Pongola. There were sentries awaiting their arrival all along the way, and they were fed and sped on their perilous journey to the Dlamini kraal on the Swaziland border, which they finally reached at sunrise.

The Swazi women took the boys away to feed them, and to let them rest and sleep endlessly, for they were very tired. And the boys had the hard look and demeanour of manhood about them, far in advance of their brothers.

The impi were fed great gourds of millet beer, and there was much festivity. A young ox was slaughtered for their reception, which was a great honour bestowed on the impi. The roasting meat, and many fires, could be smelt for many miles down the wind. The neighbours came from far and near to celebrate, to welcome the impi of great honour, and to ululate of great deeds of courage and endurance - for the sake of their children.

The drums again spoke across Africa, and they said that the children were safe at last from the Singisi. The impi slept the sleep of the weary warrior wherever they came to rest in the dry, African dust.

The impi were much admired by the Swazi maidens as they slept. The maidens took great care of them as they slept, and basted their cracked and bleeding feet with the fat from the slaughter, and the sangoma nursed their wounds with her magic herbal ointments.

And the mothers clucked and brooded over the two little white-skinned warriors lying sleeping at their feet, whose skin was nearly black from the sun, and whose straight hair had turned white from the sun. The Dlamenis took the two little warriors as their own, and the mothers took them to their bosoms as they slept. The mothers of Africa wept with great joy.

Nyanyan and Chirrichir ate not with the little mfanyanes, nor with the initiated mfanes who tended the cattle, nor with the married Swazi amadoda, but with the Zulu impi, for they were true warriors of proven endurance by then, and accepted as such.

After three more suns the impi were rested and healed, and they slowly prepared to return to their kraals all over Zululand, for each was the mightiest warrior of their sub-tribe, and each had his own kraal and people to go back to.

The time had come for the Swazi to farewell the Zulu impi, and there was much reluctance for them to leave, for they did not want to leave, and the

Swazi maidens helped them a lot to not want to leave. There were many sore hearts, and many promises of soon return.

Nyanyan and Ndlovo were initiated into Zulu manhood in their thirteenth winter. They later underwent their warrior training, and had been accepted as warriors in their sixteenth year. They decided then, that herding cattle was much too tame for them. They decided to venture forth to seek their fortune.

There was talk that there were cattle aplenty in a place where the Bechuana lived further to the north, and west, across the Limpopo River. There was also talk that there were many lions, leopard, buffalo, crocodile and elephant to the north of the place called the Okavango. Those places were called Moremi, Savuti, and Chobi. It was a place known to be very dangerous for a man.

It was the paradise of Africa, as it had a never-ending supply of much water, and not many great white hunters had ventured that far afield to plunder the wildlife with the thunder of the smoke-stick, and to try to subdue an untameable Africa.

To the north of the Okavango in Matabeleland, was the much feared Matabele tribe which had deserted Chaka Zulu, and they had gone further north in search of a better life. They took their warrior skills with them, for they were needed to fend off Chaka's warriors in the rear and in hot pursuit, and to subdue the tribes in front of them as they fled.

The Voortrekkers, the great white tribe from the Eastern Cape Colony, were tired of endlessly fighting the Fingo, the Pondo and the Xhosa, and to eke out a threadbare subsistence on the land. They despised the British-ruled Cape Colony, and the Afrikaner tribe was born, the White Tribe of Africa, and they too, headed north to the hinterland. The Great Trek had started.

The paths of the Voortrekkers and the Matabele crossed in the trans-Orange River territory where a bloody and decisive battle was fought at Vegkop, the battle hill, which the Voortrekkers won, and they then took possession of, and created, the Orange Free State. The Matabele took flight after the battle, and headed further north for the Witwatersrand, the ridge of white water.

Some of the Voortrekkers headed even further north over the Vaal River, and again they encountered the Matabele to the north of the Witwatersrand. Another mighty battle ensued. The Matabele headed clear across the Limpopo River, and toward Victoria Falls, the Cloud That Thunders. Once across the Limpopo, the Matabele subdued the local tribes, killing all the able men, and the old and fragile, and they incorporated the fertile women, and the children, into the Matabele tribe. They dispersed the Mashona tribe yet even further to the north, and to the east.

The Matabele started to spread themselves out there and continued to be a very fierce force to be contended with. These were the places Nyanyan and Ndlovo went to.

In their first winter there, Nyanyan and Ndlovo managed to find some 200 stray cattle, and they drove them south through Matabeleland all the way across the Limpopo River into the Transvaal where they sold them to the white farmers there who desperately needed new stock. They were paid in gold coins, and they hid the gold in a safe place.

For three winters did they do this, until they found that the chase was far too close for comfort. What firmly made their minds up, was that they discovered that the British South Africa Police had put out wanted posters for the two of them. They then found their way to the Pilgrim's Rest alluvial goldfields where they mined for more gold, and they hid that.

After another three years, they dug up all their gold and returned to Manzi Mhlopi. There, they found that a white farmer had settled there, and he had taken over legal title to Manzi Mhlopi.

Nyanyan, also being white, and who already knew about white man's titles, and the way in which they were come by, took half of the gold and very easily bought the whole of Manzi Mhlopi for himself. Then, according to the white man's rules, legally converted it into perpetual, and indelible, tribal trust land for the tribe forevermore. They used the rest of the gold to buy many cattle, and the tribe prospers to this day'

Jack went on to tell me that The Okavango, Moremi, Savuti, Chobe, Caprivi, trans-Kalahari safari to Namibia, the Namib Desert and northern Namibia was his favourite stamping grounds. He said that nature's predators such as crocodile, lion and leopard were allowed to eat people there, and get away with it.

He said that the Okavango was a paradise for the variety of birds there - unparalleled anywhere in the world. He told me about the sight of some 30,000 African buffalo on the plains in the late afternoon; black it was, as far as the eye could see. Awesome!

He told me about coming to within six feet of being killed by a lioness in Moremi while she was guarding her cubs. He was stalking a waterhole to take some photographs of game early one morning when he saw her crouched, ready for the kill, some ten feet in front of him, her enraged body aquiver as he was unwittingly stalking through the long, dry grass, straight toward her and her cubs.

He also told me about the time when he woke up one afternoon in Chobe, to stare straight into the right front foot of a bull elephant. The elephant's foot was a foot away from his head. His beer-dazed gaze slowly made eye contact with the elephant staring down at him. He was lying flat on his back then, and as vulnerable as the day he was born. He silently pleaded with the elephant not to do him any harm. He then rolled over, and put his face to the ground, and waited for the elephant's foot to crush him to death, or for the trunk to grasp him and smash him against a tree, or onto the ground before trampling him to death.

He told me about the time that he accidentally stumbled into six full-grown leopards in northern Namibia - unarmed. He told me that many of the things that Wilbur Smith wrote about, he had lived in their harshest, bloodiest, raw reality.

He confessed to me that Nyanyan was his father. He said that Nyanyan had told him that story many, many times over as a child, and every time it was exactly the same story, and it never ever varied. Jack said that what he had told me, was the short version of the story, and that he was, one day, going to write the long one.

He told me about the time when he was about four years old, on a fishing trip to the Mariti River. He, his Zulu friend John, and his dog Tony, had gone for a walk into the trees on the river's edge, and had walked straight into about twenty deadly green mamba snakes, basking in the sun on a sandy spot.

He had gone on a hunting expedition with Nyanyan and Ndlovo when he was five years old. A rogue elephant bull had charged them. He held onto his father's trouser leg, and waited. His father took aim, and waited, and waited, and waited. The rifle roared. His father grabbed him by the shirt, flung him up in the air, and then bolted himself. The elephant stumbled, and then crashed down on the very spot that they had been standing on seconds before. Jack had peed in his pants.

And many other things did he tell me. He said that he never told anybody about these events in Australia, because no one would ever believe him.

'If I had died, everybody would believe me,' he said. Not even his very best friends did he tell - never ever. I believed him then, and I still do. Perhaps he will take me to that savage, unforgiving paradise one day. Hopes and dreams.

54

Chapter Four

The next morning we had a luxuriously slow rise, with a hot mug of tea, which we drank while lying in our sleeping bags. Jack had contrived the most decadently ingenious trick where all the tea-making things were at the immediately ready outside the tent. All that was required, was to light the single-burner gas cooker to boil the billy can, and then to brew our mugs of tea. All this was done from the very horizontal position of course. This early morning ritual continued for the entire ten weeks of our jaunt.

That day, it was followed by a hot birdwatch along the beach. The birds were a rainbow of colour - honeyeaters, pheasant, coels, sunbirds, spectacled and shining monarchs.

After lunch, we went for a walk along the road in a northerly direction. Every now and then, we got glimpses of the azure blue sea below us through the dense rainforest. It was hot in the sun again, and the rainforest prevented the cool sea breeze from reaching us. My Akubra hat certainly saved the day for me then.

We went in to see the *Bloomfield Blockade*, where the greenies had set up camp to blockade heavy earthmoving equipment, which had been used to build the controversial Bloomfield Development Road from Cape Tribulation to Cooktown. The frightful mess they left behind, with discarded hardware, and their garbage still strewn all over the countryside, was an absolute disgrace.

They had also left a long-drop dunny nakedly open into which unwitting animals had, no doubt, fallen, and which was potentially fatal to humans had they fallen into this ghastly trap. Falling into a well-used bush toilet was not a pleasant prospect. The environmental legacy they left behind certainly left a lot to be desired. We had reason to debate their real intent, and general purpose, in life, as it did not appeared to be that they had any respect for their immediate environment at the time.

'Their type should be denied the very air that they breathe. I have had more than my fair share of dealing with the dole-bludging, pot-smoking, no-hoper feral variety of greenie who calculate that, on pay day, if there was enough money for a box of beer, a bottle of bourbon and a bong, who cared what the children had to eat or wear,' Jack mentioned to me as he was looking down the dunny. The things he could say!

Further along the road, we walked up the most delightful, bubbling creek with cascades, deep pools, fan palms, and butterflies galore as far as we went. The canopy was dense, and permitted the occasional sunbeam to pierce through, and find its way to the rainforest floor. It was very pleasant there, so we decided to have a nap lying on a sun-warmed, flat rock in the middle of the creek, with the brook bubbling away over the rocks beside us.

I awoke with a mighty start when Jack touched my knee to wake me up when it was time to go.

'Crocodile!' was my first thought, as I scrambled around hastily flailing my limbs, and going nowhere in particular; my eyes wild with panic, and as big as soup plates.

At night around the campfire, Jack continued my education on bush survival skills. Over the next few nights, he kept asking me how I would deal with hypothetical situations like snake bites, scorpion stings, eye piercings, extensive burns, bush pig savagings, crocodile attacks, stonefish stings, and even the Toyota falling on top of him.

I knew sweet blow-all about anything. I soon learnt, and very quickly too, as he made absolutely sure that I responded. It helped him no end, when he suddenly started to ask me what I would expect of him in the event of similar accidents, and mishaps, happening to me. That made me sit up and take note!

We spent five nights in the Cape Tribulation rainforest. Our days were taken up by beachcombing, birdwatching, sunbathing, and doing very little in particular. Each day, the big plan was not to make any big plans at all.

We had a reasonably early start breaking camp and then taking a quick shower. On our way out of the campsite, a vehicle with New South Wales number plates blocked our path. It was parked dead in the middle of the single-lane road, with no room to pass on either side. There was more than adequate space to park no more than ten metres away. It was somewhat inconsiderate we thought.

'They are, in all probability, Sydneysiders. Country people don't do this sort of thing,' Jack said, and went off to find the driver of the vehicle.

'Can you wait another twenty minutes? I want to have a shower,' was the response to Jack's silent inquiry, with his thumb pointed over his shoulder. Stone the crows! The very nerve of some people!

'You will move your truck! Right now!' demanded Jack, his pleasant disposition having temporarily deserted him. I thought, for a moment that Jack was going to, well, sort of, you know, gently help him along a little. He

Crocodile Juliette

1. *SCUBA*
2. *Daintree River Ferry*
3. *Helen, Jack, Juliette, Prince Charming*

didn't need much provocation to race someone up a gum tree! I made a mental note to be careful not to offend him unnecessarily.

Less than a minute later, we were merrily heading north along the Bloomfield Development Road to Wujal-Wujal, on the banks of the Bloomfield River, and then on to Cooktown. It was not a road to take for the regular Sunday afternoon drive in the family sedan. It was strictly four-wheel-drive terrain, and adequate ground clearance was a pre-determined necessity.

We drove through rainforest, with a multitude of creek crossings. There were no bridges or culverts, just plain creek. The scenery was superb, with the sea to our right, and the green foothills to our left. Every so often, we would stop to admire the landscape, and to take photographs when we found some scene that commanded our attention. It was an exceptionally pleasant drive. At one of our stops the offensive vehicle, which had blocked our path at the camp, went whizzing passed us without as much as a wave. They, unsmilingly, appeared to be much cleaner.

'When does the real action start?' I asked Jack as we were going along. I had not seen much to warrant the recovery gear we had on board.

'As soon as we get to some decent water,' he assured me.

It started right on our arrival at the Bloomfield River. Lo and behold! The jokers in the blue vehicle had come to a stop in the middle of the river, because they had flooded the electrics' of their engine. The engine bonnet was up. The two men had their heads embedded in the engine compartment, while the two women were frantically on crocodile watch. They apparently hadn't heard of water dispersant to protect the electrical system of their vehicle.

Jack climbed out of the Toyota and, none too silently, said a few unkind and derogatory things about them. He had been there ten days before, and he knew what the situation was. He had not crossed at the time, as it was late afternoon, and the tide was rising then.

The Bloomfield River had always been a rather difficult river to cross at the best of times. It had no bridge, was tidal, and therefore best crossed at low tide when the water level was at its lowest. It was also infested with salt-water crocodiles, the man-eating variety. We had arrived half an hour before low tide, the optimal time, which allowed for possible mishaps midstream, and time to recover before the tide turned. Jack assessed the situation.

'To the left of them is a deep pool. Very deep, too deep to even think of taking it at the moment. To the right is insufficient room and it falls off into a deep lagoon. If we go that way, we will roll over into the lagoon, and that will be the end of us - crocodile fodder. To wait for these jokers to get their act together, and to get out of the way, could take any amount of time. The tide will also be going against us in thirty minutes. The next low tide is at midnight tonight, and there is no future there. The headlights will be under water, and, with a new moon offering no light to see by, visibility will be zero. It will also be spring tide, an impossible situation. Our next best option is to camp here for the night, and to cross tomorrow at midday; if these clowns are out of the way by then,' Jack reasoned. He was not at all very happy.

He took another walk around, again reassessed the situation, whistled to attract their attention, waved his arms at them, and got back into the Toyota.

'We are going in. We'll go to the left of them, through the deep pool. Hold onto your socks, false teeth and bubble gum!' he advised me.

'I don't have any of those!' I protested.

'Try the panic bar in front of you then,' he offered.

We engaged low four-wheel-drive and plunged into the river, hoping the WD40 water dispersant would do its job. The headlights immediately went under water, and a wall of water came crashing over the bonnet, and up against the windscreen.

So this is how one floods a vehicle, I thought, firmly and grimly grasping the panic bar right in front of me, and the panic handle above me to my left. White-knuckled we splashed on. The two men and two women in distress slowly waded their way to the right hand side of their vehicle.

As we approached them, Jack snap-judged that there would be sufficient space to pass on their right hand side, but with nothing left to spare. He altered course and headed straight for the mob.

The frantic clambering onto their vehicle grabbing windscreen wipers, and anything else grabbable, and thrashing around in more than a metre of water to get out of the way, was a sight to behold. The gap was frighteningly narrow, and got narrower the closer we got to them. I was sure then that Jack had made a mistake.

As we passed them, with our right hand side wheels halfway on the rocky edge, and the other half hanging over the deep lagoon, we were left with no choice but to smash their wing mirror off. It was either that, or for us to go swimming with the crocodiles.

Once past them, the water gradually got shallower. We continued until we got to where the water was about seventy centimetres deep. Jack stopped the

Toyota, got out, and asked them if they wanted a tow out by clenching his fists, and drawing them toward his stomach.

'No thanks!' came the reply from our intrepid heroes, crocodiles watching them intently from the river bank all the while.

'So much for that lot. They probably think that I was indicating to them that I wanted to box,' Jack remarked with a laugh as he climbed back into the driver's seat. I fully agreed, although I wasn't quite sure whom it was I was agreeing with.

We continued further until we reached terra firma again, and parked up on the north bank where we joined the Aborigines from Wujal-Wujal, who had gathered there to witness some of the more spectacular crossings. It was a wonderful past-time for them, for there were a lot of hapless victims. It was something they did every day.

There was an hydraulic excavator working away on the riverbed, digging a trench for some culvert piping that was to be laid and covered. The water was to be diverted through the culvert, and so reduce the water level to safer proportions, but, despite the piping, crossings would still be confined to low tide. Another adventure was disappearing, as was the daily entertainment of the people of Wujal-Wujal.

By this time some eight vehicles had pulled up on both sides of the river, anxiously watching the tide rise, and their hopes of crossing for the day, rapidly fading. They expressed more than mild surprise at the refusal of the stranded party to be towed out. They were downright angry, and were vocally quite derogatory in their comments.

The fearless adventurers eventually got their engine started, and drove out of the river. They just kept on going, without stopping, not even as much as a flippant wave, still not smiling. We were not surprised that they did not stop. The rest of the vehicles then crossed, having been shown the safe way to do so. We watched the frolics for a while and then set off again.

Chapter Five

We took the road that branched off to the left on the north bank of the Bloomfield, and drove for five kilometres up the river. As the road stopped very abruptly against a gum tree, we concluded that we had very obviously taken the wrong turning, and had managed to get ourselves lost. We decided to boil the billy and have some lunch there, before going back and to go on the right road.

As we got out of the Toyota, we heard the roar of a waterfall nearby and decided to investigate it after lunch. We looked for, but could not find any indication of, a waterfall on any of the maps we had.

Suitably fortified internally, we headed along a footpath in the general direction of the watery noise. About two hundred metres upstream, we fell upon a thundering waterfall. What a pleasant surprise it was! After the recent heavy rains, it was flowing very strongly. The bottom of the falls was still some one hundred metres away, and I decided to be a bit adventurous. I clambered over the rocks to get closer.

'Tootle-doo,' said Jack as he sat down under a shady tree. 'Keep a sharp lookout for snakes and crocodiles will you?' he warned.

Fifty metres further I froze in fear of my life. I saw my first snake. It had a greeny-yellow tummy and was about a metre long. It slithered away into a crack in some nearby rocks, and I crashed headlong back to where I had come from, barking the skin off my shins on the rocks in the process and scurrying back to safer ground. I figured that, because he had got there first, he was jolly well entitled to his territory.

I joined Jack again, and we had a refreshing, and exhilarating, swim in a protected pool alongside the rapids below the falls, after we had carefully scouted around for crocodiles, and had found none. The general safety rule was, apparently, that crocodiles were not normally to be found where there were rapids in the rivers, as they didn't like fast flowing water. We plunged into the pool, thoroughly enjoying the cool, crystal clear water.

On our way back to the Toyota, we came upon the friendliest group of Aborigines who were camped on the banks of the river catching fish, rock painting, and generally passing the time of day. We had seen them on our way to the waterfall, but they were some distance away then. They told us that the snake was a *Bag-ae*, a harmless water snake. Jack seemed to get along very well with the Aborigines. I was of the understanding that, in those parts of the world, they and the white people were not on the friendliest of terms.

The ten or so of them invited us to partake in a large mug of sweet, billy tea which was on the boil, and for a short smoke break. We sat around the campfire with them gassing away at ninety to the dozen. There were no barriers between us at all. It was such a delightful experience for me, and one I had been relishing for a very long time. With great reluctance we took our leave from these warm, friendly people and headed for Cooktown, this time on the right road fortunately.

We most certainly had an experience in Cooktown. On our arrival at the campsite, we were compressed into a camp spot about the size of my toenail. The camping ground was filled to overflowing with Cape York expeditioners, with screaming children and out-of-control dogs, all named Blue, being reddish in colour, careering all over the countryside. We also seemed to have mislaid fifty dollars somewhere along the way. A frantic search failed to deliver the desired result, unfortunately.

That evening we drove up to the Cooktown lighthouse to see the sunset. There was a chilly southeasterly wind blowing strongly which called for warm jumpers and windcheaters. We drank a few cans of Foster's while we leisurely took in the marvelous three hundred and sixty degree panorama of the sea to the east, Cooktown below us, and the sunset reflecting off the vast expanse of the Endeavour River and mangrove swamps to the West, until all light had faded.

We then proceeded to an up-market restaurant where we drowned our misfortune of the fifty dollars, and the dismal campsite, with a bottle of superb Australian Chardonnay. We had barramundi and chips, followed by black forest gateau. Barramundi was certainly the best fish I had ever tasted, and it is said to be the best eating fish Australia has to offer. It occurs only in the northern, warmer parts of Australia, and is a lively game fish to catch. Barramundi fishing was the consuming passion of northern Australians.

Jack was unshaven, and very scruffy-looking after having lost his razor in the Cape Tribulation rainforest. He never, ever replaced it. I was wearing a pair of filthy denim shorts. When we got up to leave, I was halfway across the restaurant when Jack noticed how filthy my trouser bottoms were, and started laughing out aloud.

'What is so funny?' I asked him.

'You want to see your dirty bum!' he replied, continuing to have a good laugh.

I have no idea what the other restaurant patrons must have thought about this strange dialogue. It was only then that I noticed how smartly the other diners were dressed, as they all stared at me. It seemed that, when one has been in the bush for a while, peculiar things are said and done - and our journey had only just started. I had time to write a few last post cards that night, so that I could post them the next day. We had no idea when we would see a post office, or post box, again.

I phoned my mum the next morning. She was quite pleased to hear from me, and to hear that I was still alive, and had not been taken by a crocodile yet.

We topped up our food and beer supplies, filled the water containers, refueled the Toyota, filled the jerry cans with spare fuel, and then went to visit the Cook Museum. It really was a good museum for a tiny settlement such as Cooktown, and full credit to the town's folk for their efforts. They had managed to preserve not only a vital part of early Australian history, but also the entire history of Cooktown, the northern goldfields, and the Entire Cape York Peninsula.

It was near Cooktown where James Cook, the famous British explorer, ran the barque *Endeavour* aground on the Barnes Reef not far off Cape Tribulation, and had holed her during a violent storm. It happened during his epic voyage up the eastern Australian seaboard in 1770 to chart the coast for the first time. The *Endeavour* was then sailed into the Endeavour River and careened. It took them over a year to effect repairs and to put to sea again.

The first motor vehicle to travel up to Cape York was a 1928 Baby Austin - in 1928 as it so happened. At many of the river crossings the car had to be stripped down, carried across piece by piece, and then reassembled on the other side. Makeshift rafts were used to float the parts across the deeper, and wider, rivers. It took the adventurers a month to complete the expedition.

Cooktown in its hey-day was a lively place when the goldrush of the Palmer River alluvial gold diggings was at its peak. It also served as the port to ship cattle from the vast cattle stations on the peninsula. Cooktown certainly was steeped in history, all of which had been well documented and preserved. At the time of our visit, the population was contracting as the recession was biting deeper, and people were leaving to go south to greener pastures. It had not lost any of its charm despite the circumstances.

We departed Cooktown late that morning bound for Lakefield National Park, keen to get a move on to the real Outback. We took the Battlecamp Road up to Lake Emma. I had been driving along sand and gravel roads, which I found quite tiring, and I was glad to hand over the driving to Jack. It was long, straight, dusty, red roads amongst the gum trees. I also drove through my first river, which was about a metre deep.

'Go! Don't stop!' Jack yelled at me. 'If you bog the vehicle, you dig it out! I'll watch from under a shady tree on the bank of the river!' he told me in the middle of it all, when the Toyota started going sideways.

'He really means what he says!' I fully realised. 'If he expects perfection, I'll demonstrate that to him!' I didn't have to dig her out, but only just, only just.

That ought to get her adrenalin pumping and her reflexes sharpened thought Jack with a benevolently wicked look on his face.

Sometime after that, when we were in a totally safe place, Jack told me to stop the Toyota. He then took out the rifle and ammunition.

'Now you are going to learn how to fit the bolt to the rifle, load it with ammunition, aim it properly, and fire it so that you hit the target,' he told me. I had never in my life handled a rifle, let alone fired one.

'First put the *safety* catch on *safety*.' he told me, then showed me how, and then made me do it.

He then showed me how to fit the bolt into the rifle. He then made me do it myself. Then he showed me how to load the ammunition into the rifle; again making me do it myself.

He then showed me how to hold the rifle ready to take aim at a Foster's Lager can some thirty metres away. I wrapped the leather sling around my left arm, gripping the barrel of the rifle with my left hand. I lined the beer can up with the sights.

'You can't fire it unless you switch the *safety* to *fire*,' he said, and then showed me how to do that.

'Now to cock the rifle,' he told me, and showed me how to do that.

'Now take aim, and squeeze the trigger. Don't pull or jerk it! Squeeze it!' he said.

I lined the beer can up in the sights, squeezed the trigger, and the beer can jumped into the air! The recoil on my shoulder hurt me a bit.

'Put it back on 'safety' he said, which I did.

'Next time, make sure that the butt of the rifle is pulled firmly into your shoulder before firing' Jack told me.

'Back onto *fire*, recock, aim and fire!' he instructed. I did, and the beer can again jumped into the air! I was getting good!

'Keep shooting until the magazine is empty,' he instructed. I missed a few times, but hit the can any amount of times.

'Safety!' he said. I did. 'Bolt undone!' I took it out to a rest position as shown.

'Reload!' he said. I did.

'Fire as before!' he said. I did.

When the magazine was empty again, I put it on 'safety', removed the bolt, and put the lot back into the rifle-bag.

'Take it all out again. You have to clean it first,' Jack said. He made me do it - piece by piece before I could put it back into the rifle bag.

'Now you can handle a firearm when you need to,' Jack said. I was glad that he had shown me the workings, and the basics, about shooting. The cleaning bit he could keep for himself, I thought.

Shortly afterward we entered Lakefield National Park and stopped at Lake Emma. It was singularly the best day of birdwatching of my whole, entire life. It was a paradise of bee-eaters, northern kingfishers, egrets, black throated finches, honey-eaters, brolgas and much, much more. Without doubt, a Johnson crocodile was somewhere to be found.

We boiled the billy and had cucumber sandwiches, and a large mug of tea for lunch on the shady banks of the lake. How civilised cucumber sandwiches and tea were in the bush. My birdwatching stroll after lunch was so incredible that I really didn't see any reason to leave Lake Emma, but Jack gently urged me on.

'We can't stay at the first place we get to forever. We still have many other places to see,' he told me.

We stopped for a while at the Old Laura cattle station at the road junction from Laura to the New Laura Ranger Station in Lakefield. The Laura homestead had been restored, and preserved, as it had been a century before.

We wandered around for a while, stretching our legs and marvelling at the relatively primitive technology of the times. Life was so much simpler in those days. We did not loose sight of the extreme hardships, and isolation, those hardy pioneers had to endure.

The Ranger at New Laura Ranger Station, a lovely lady Clare Blackman, assigned us a very special spot on the banks of Caulder's Lake, which was a twenty kilometre drive through some very rugged roadless country. We had told her that our interests were birds, fauna, flora, peace, quiet and solitude. We were not in the least bit concerned about hot showers, sewered toilets or tap water. Clare shared, and appreciated, our interests, and was quite surprised to have visitors who didn't want to go barramundi fishing.

The site Clare directed us to, was her favourite place, and she very rarely allowed anyone else to go there. She made sure that we were totally self-sufficient, bush-wise, competent and capable before she pointed us in that direction. She did not want to effect a rescue.

'Be very careful, because there are some very big bushpigs out there!' she warned us. Stern-faced she was too, so we took her words of caution very much to heart.

That evening at sunset, we were singing *You'll Come A-waltzing Matilda With Me* beside a tinder-dry campfire on the banks of Caulder's Lake, with the twitter of nestling birds all around us. It was difficult to describe the incredible stroke of good fortune that had come our way. We were miles away from the nearest human beings, camped all alone by a billabong with kangaroos, crocodiles and bushpigs. We saw a pig across the billabong, which had come for a drink of water. It looked to me to be as big as a Jersey cow. Those bushpigs were really scary.

Jack and I agreed that we were getting the very best first. It was magical at Caulder's Lake. As the orange light deepened to red, and then to purple at sunset, the hysterical laughter of the blue-winged kookaburra pierced the air followed by the cacophonic chorus of millions of frogs croaking.

'We could be in Africa,' Jack said. He seemed to be very comfortable, and was totally in his element. Living in the Outback came as second nature to him.

'I don't for the life of me know how I managed to survive the past fifteen years in cities, nine of them in Sydney, and still work in the bush and jungle,' he added.

Our peace was rudely interrupted on a few occasions by my nightmares. I would find myself, or rather Jack did, racing around the tent in my sleep trying to find a way out. Jack seemed to understand, and he would calm me down when it happened. He would then tuck me in to sleep again. He seemed to have the patience of a saint.

'We can't have too much of this somnambulant kerfuffle! There could be a very nasty accident at some time or other!' Jack thought to himself as he lay back in wide-eyed anticipation of my next trick. I had a big bag full of tricks and surprises with me. It was to take me quite a while to get used to being crammed together in a tent at night.

On the longest and hottest day in the Northern Hemisphere, and supposedly the shortest and coldest in Australia, we were desperate for shade in the midday heat. The gum trees had sparse foliage and therefor, did not provide us with much shade.

We erected the tarpaulin that we had bought to provide shade for such an occasion, but it seemed as if it were hotter under the tarpaulin than it was elsewhere. The dry heat was unbearably stifling and energy draining. There was simply no place to hide, whichever way we turned. It was going to get hotter as time went by, with summer approaching, and with us going further north.

Clare had told us that we wouldn't be disturbed, and she was true to her word. No other people came anywhere near us, nor did we hear any other vehicles. The odd mail plane flying high overhead between Cairns and Weipa, were the only signs of civilisation we were aware of.

One morning, we found evidence of pigs, which had been rooting for food close to our tent in the night. From then onward, we made doubly sure that we did not leave any food, or food scraps, lying around, but fed them to the crabs in the lake instead.

As promised, the following morning, Jack made the coffee, and I didn't move a finger. I slept much better that night and waking to the dawn chorus of birds was fabulous. I could view all the activity on the lake with binoculars from the comfort of my sleeping bag, using my backpack as a backrest.

After a scanty five-point *bush-wash* to conserve our precious water, we set off on a wander west along the lake's edge. Egrets, sacred ibis, sea-eagle, blue-winged kingfisher and heron were some of the sightings that day. Thankfully, pigs did not accost us, although we did see some at a distance, and there was abundant, very recent, evidence of their presence. The lake, which was covered in bright green lily pads, occasional patches of reeds on the banks, and gum trees growing in the lake with their roots firmly under the water, was exceptionally photogenic.

Tired and hot, we returned from our excursion for a brunch of eggs, bacon, steak and toast. It was all cooked over a campfire of course. It turned out to be not such a very clever idea; cooking a hot meal over a campfire in the midday heat. Jack went troppo a short time afterward, and crashed down in the tent to sleep it off. The tent was unbearably hot, but it offered the best protection there was.

We were both suffering from severe heat exhaustion then. The tent, tarpaulin, and Toyota offered very little relief from the heat and sun. Exposing skin to get some cooling effect from an almost non-existent, searingly hot breeze, only served to attract flies which sucked up the salt and moisture of our perspiration, and resulted in sunburn.

There was just no way of winning the battle, and it was to take some time for us to acclimatise to the heat. We had to bite the proverbial bullet between ten o'clock in the morning until four o'clock in the afternoon when a modicum of relief was to be had.

We played a game of Canasta one night, which ended up in a terrible row. Jack was winning and he started to gloat. I promptly had another temper tantrum and threw in my hand. We decided not to play Canasta again or any other competitive game thereafter.

Jack taught me to simply stare into the campfire at night, which, after the initial frustration, was a far more pleasant, and peaceful, way to pass the time of night. It was amazing what that campfire could make me see, think, and feel, as I experienced the primeval sense of well-being and safety, as I silently stared into the flickering flames at night.

I asked Jack one night, while looking into the campfire, and at the stars, to tell me more about himself, as I still really knew very little about him. He chose instead, to tell me a little bit more about this little character named Lighty, who, he said, he once knew very well.

Chapter Six

Lighty was a lightweight. He was always smaller than the rest of the boys, and he never ever seemed to be big enough. It all started when he started playing with the other boys that he discovered this sad fact of life.

However, he first started answering to his African native nick-name of Mzenze, The Flea. Perhaps it was because he was always racing around like a holy terror, bouncing around, popping up all over the place, and generally getting into all sorts of strife and mischief, that he was called Mzenze. Zit-zit!

Perhaps it was because that the mischief he got up to very often was subtle enough to go unnoticed. It was only so, until the consequences of his actions suddenly bit deeply and painfully on some poor, unsuspecting victim - when he was nowhere to be found. Zit-zit! That was when he would really cop it - that is, after they had found him, and had then managed to corner him. Zit!

He was smart enough to know that, even if it was blatantly apparent that he was the cause of the belatedly discovered, and lamentable, discomfort, but no definite evidence was forthcoming, he could get away with it - but only just. He couldn't get away from a well-earned reputation though - ever. He soon learned that a native name, once given to one, is a painfully fair reflection of one's characteristics.

Perhaps the name Mzenze had something to do with the size, and shape, of his willy, but no-one ever told him so. He had been circumcised earlier. Having been virtually all foreskin before, he was, by then, half-sized. And it even looked like a flea.

He cried a lot that day they did the circumcision, loudly too. When he woke up from the chloroform anaesthetic, he found himself alone in a cot in the hospital, with a big bandage around his willy. There were only white bars around him, and his very dusty, one-eyed teddy bear had fallen out, and was lying on the floor.

It happened one day, not long after he had learnt to walk, that Mzenze disappeared. Gone he was, and no-one knew where to. His mother went looking for him so that she could take him to tennis with her, and she couldn't find him anywhere.

Mass hysteria broke out, and a massive man-hunt was under way everywhere. Katie, his Swazi wet-nurse and nanny heard the uproar as she was walking toward the house and then asked everyone what the fuss was all about.

'Mzenze e'balekile le!' everyone shouted in Zulu panic. Mzenze has run away to a very far place!

'Xha! Nango!' Katie said, and calmly pointed her thumb over her shoulder. No! Here he is! She was carrying her twin son and daughter John and Nondwe, where they were firmly, and warmly, ensconced in a gaily coloured blanket which was secured around her breasts to keep it up, and also around her stomach to keep John and Nondwe from falling out.

No-one worried too much about his whereabouts after that, they knew where to find him. He no longer had to be dressed up like a ponce, and had to behave, every Saturday afternoon, when he wasn't taken along to that bing-bong, bing-bong, bing-bong, paff, 'deuce' senseless tennis any more.

Although John and Nondwe could walk, it was expedient for Katie to carry them in a blanket on her back over longer distances. Perambulators didn't exist for the black people in those days, and he couldn't remember his younger sister, or his younger brother, to have had one either. Perambulators didn't last very long before they became a wheel-less statue in the back yard, and a brand new soap-box cart with shiny wheels was launched at frightening speed down the hill.

Sometimes Mzenze and John were lucky enough to be in the soap-box cart with one of the big boys when it went down the hill, and when it actually got to the bottom of the hill. At other times, they were very unlucky indeed to be in it when it didn't get to the bottom of the hill. That was when the wheels fell off, and when it crashed, or capsized, and those things happened very often.

From the time he started toddling, and could move about a bit, being adventurous, and getting into all sorts of scrapes, mischief and trouble, his first independent steps led him instinctively to the far corner of the yard. There the African servant's warm, smoky, wood fireplace was, and where they congregated to have their meals, and to socialise under the corrugated iron shelter constructed for that purpose.

He and the other piccaninnies liked to stand around the warm fire in the wintertime, where the flames from the fire warmed their bare bums. It was also probably his instincts which told him that he was less likely to get a clip on the earhole there, than he would in the house.

The African way to discipline children was on the extended family principle. If a child misbehaved in the presence of any adult of the extended family, they copped it sweet right there and then. No questions were ever asked by the natural parents, for there was never any need to.

It was difficult to get away with anything, and he collected his fair share of discipline, as it never seemed to be in short supply. Besides that, the spontaneous fun the servants had, seemed to be more sensible than inside the house, even if it was light-heartedly at his expense at times, and more often than not about his prematurely circumcised, and under-sized, willy.

His mum, his brother, or one of his older sisters, would put a pair of baggy, home-made, khaki short trousers, equipped with built-in braces, on him in the morning, and he would discard them as soon as he got out of the house. They were frightfully awkward, far too big for him, and it was a devil of a job getting his near-non-existent willy out in time and clear for a pee. They invariably ended up being peed in, only to then get discarded thereafter anyway.

Even when he did manage to get everything right, and had done his pee, he would put his willy back only to have the last few drops drizzle down his leg. Besides that, the black piccaninnies that he played with never wore trousers anyway, so why should he have to have been any different?

Having to go for a poo while wearing over-sized khaki shorts was quite catastrophic, and got him entangled in his braces so that, if he did manage to get them off down to his knees, he would poo on his braces, and still pee on his pants anyway. This happened often in the springtime when the apricots and guavas started getting ripe. He would eat them when they were half-ripe, while sitting in the fork of a fruit tree.

The consequent acute diarrhoea resulted in him developing exceptionally strong legs for the rest of his life, so it was not all such a bad thing after all. He really couldn't see any purpose in wearing trousers at first. Off they came first thing every morning, and he avoided peeing and poohing in his pants, and avoided the resultant wallop, which would inevitably follow.

It wasn't very long before some maidens made a modesty apron for him as worn by all the other African boys to cover their willies. He didn't think that the maidens liked to see his willy because they always seemed to be scared of it. Bums didn't seem to matter to them. The modesty apron was a real beauty made of exceptionally colourful beads woven into the brightest of patterns, and fringed all around with tanned leopard skin. There was always fierce competition amongst the boys as to who had the brightest bead modesty apron.

The fact that he used to wander back to the house at sunset absolutely filthy, and wearing his modesty apron, and with his clean trousers in his hand, didn't seem to perturb his mum at all.

He used to have his breakfast, and lunch, with the servants and their children in the back yard under the shed by the fireplace. After, he and the other piccaninnies, would go about satisfying their curiosity and sense of adventure in the bush, initially close to home, but continually venturing further, and further, afield, to horizons new, and adventures more bold.

At sunset, he would make his way to the cowshed next to the garage where his father kept the family sedan, a 1928 Chevrolet. The family had five cows, each one assigned to one of the children. His cow was named Coffee. One would think it was because that was her colour, but she was a black and white Friesland. He never was able to determine the nexus.

When the cows had been milked, he would collect his trousers and saunter into the kitchen, where they would again be jammed onto him, and the course khaki drill would painfully chafe his willy raw again, as well as run the risk of being drizzled in. This was done to be 'decently attired for dinner'. Dinner was the main meal of the day and, for some unknown reason, very important.

It happened one cold winter's morning, when the icy chilly wind from the northwest was blowing down from the snow-capped Mount Anderson, straight down through the Sabie Valley in the Drakensberg. He, and his older sister Margaret, had walked the half a mile or so down the footpath with his older brother Derick and his older sister Marie, to the school bus-stop. When Derick and Marie had climbed into the dicky seat of the grey 1936 Ford, and had gone off to school in a cloud of red dust, they walked back home, and he had stubbed his big toe on a rock in the footpath.

Ripping the skin off from under one's big toe, from end to end, so that it peeled back to the base of the toe, was not very funny. It was very painful indeed. It was far worse than toothache, or earache or any other kind of ache, including headache, and even heartache too. It was even worse than being hungry, or cold, or either together, or maybe all of them put together for all he knew.

When he reached the house, he had gone hobbling on the ball of the heel of his sore foot to his mother, all the while bleeding blood on the floor. His mum first saw the blood dripping onto everything, removed his three-week-old little sister Verity, whom she had just started feeding from her breast, and gave him a wallop on the earhole for dripping blood all over the place. Damn it!

His mum went to the sewing cupboard, ripped off a strip of linen from an old flour sack, which had been boiled to partly remove the printing dye from it, and wrapped it around his toe to stem the bleeding. It hurt like all hell as it was being wrapped around, especially when she got to the end, which was then split, and the two ends firmly tied around his big toe to secure it.

His yelling at the pain, his mum yelling at him, his sister Verity bellowing for her interrupted feed, and his sister Margaret shrilly joining the choral melee for no particular reason, completed the scene. The place was a madhouse!

The old flour sacks were used to make bloomers for his sisters and shirts for his brother and he, on his mum's treadle-powered Singer sewing machine.

'Premier Milling Company Ltd.' his little shirt told the world where he came from. He wasn't wearing any trousers.

It wasn't his mum's fault for belting the bejesus out of him. It was the second time that day that he had collected a clobbering. The first was his regulation whacking he got every morning for peeing in the three-quarter bed that he shared with his brother and two older sisters.

They didn't seem to mind him getting whacked by his mum, because he didn't think that they found being peed on every night was very funny either. Peeing in the bed was social suicide for little children, they were scums then. Getting whacked didn't fix the problem either, it only made it worse.

His poor mum had given birth to five children in the space of seven years. From the time he started toddling, his mum told everyone who was prepared to listen to her, that her nervous breakdown was imminent. She was utterly exhausted and drained, by the time Verity arrived, she really couldn't cope with his shortcomings, trials, tribulations and catastrophic accidents any longer, because Verity had, by then, been demanding her almost full attention. His mum was totally worn out, burned up, and used up, by then.

After the makeshift bandage was secured to his toe, he got another light clip on the ear hole from his mum, and told to go and play outside, and not to get into any more trouble. He hobbled off in a big hurry. His life as a truly independent and self-sufficient human being had begun. In the African bush, one was actively encouraged to grow up fast for one's own good. He had just turned two years old.

He limped out to the front verandah, where he had left his only other toy, which was his pride and joy, a real motor car made from eight- and sixteen gauge wire. He was really lucky to have that wire car, it was a beautiful work of art. It had Nugget shoe polish tins for wheels, and an ingeniously designed, and brilliantly constructed, independent, coil-spring front suspension.

It also had a magnificently built steering system, with a length of eight gauge wire protruding from the top of the car, with a real steering wheel on the end of it, which reached up to his chest. It really steered, and it went wherever he dictated. There was a special place in it where he could put his one-eyed, dusty teddy bear.

The three teenage Shangaan herd boys, who tended and milked their five cows every day, had built it especially for him. He would grab the steering wheel, and go racing around the countryside, fiercely so, driving his own real car, with his dusty teddy in it. What a magnificent piece of engineering it was! It never got a flat tyre, and it never ran out of petrol. What more could a two year old boy ask for?

His only problem then, was that stubbed toe. Unbeknown to everyone, including himself, was the fact that a small bone in his big toe had also fractured. It was the most painfully prolonged stubbed toe in all of history, and he couldn't play with his wire car any more. Damn it again!

Katie found him there that day, sitting on the verandah steps crying his little heart out, his big toe sticking out like the true proverbial. She was carrying little John, and his twin sister Nondwe, on her back as usual.

'We come into this world alone, and we depart this world alone. It sometimes takes us a lifetime to discover that, while we are in this world, we really are alone,' said Katie in a gentle, caressing Swazi lilt as she approached him. 'How early in life some of us must do so.' she softly sighed.

Katie stooped down to pick him up, and examined the offensive toe while pondering what she was to do next. She knew how things stood in the household: that he had been displaced with the arrival of his sister Verity, was suffering from acute separation anxiety, and had to fend for himself for the first time.

Africans had a social system whereby any orphaned waif was immediately adopted, and reared, if not as one's own, then most certainly in a close family, and extended family, environment. He had just been adopted. Katie's dilemma was how to do it without arousing his mum's negative sentiment, as his mum did not fully understand the ways of the African, for she was newly arrived from Wales in Britain, and therefor knew not.

Katie went in to see his mum and the two ladies agreed that he and John could be good friends, and could play with each other under Katie's watchful eye. That wasn't such a major arrangement, as they had been doing so for the previous year, but it was arranged that he could go up the hill every morning on Tuesdays, Thursdays, Saturdays and Sundays, and Katie and John would come to their house on the other days, which were washing days. It was all easy enough, because Katie's hut was within sight of the family home, and within his capabilities to walk there.

No-one thought anything more about it, least of all his father. That was when the reign of terror by two tiny boys, on an unsuspecting and innocent world, really began, as Mzenze and John started growing up. The two of them were mischief personified.

Katie, a fine, young Swazi woman from the royal kraal of Dlameni, a regal, gracious and dignified woman as ever can be imagined, had in reality, been his adoptive, and adopted, second mother, nanny and covert wet-nurse long before he had turned one year old, and had started to walk.

John and Nondwe were about two months older than Mzenze was. John's father Ndlovo, The Elephant, had come from the Zulu kraal of Gumede, which was the sub-tribe which raised Mzenze's father, and Ndlovo, and his father, were as one. His father and Ndlovo had lived, travelled, and worked together, from the time they were very small boys. They were an inseparable unit.

Ndlovo and his Zulu impi had gone on a marauding raid into Swaziland with the intent to rape, pillage and plunder as was the customary recreation for Zulu warriors in those days. Part of his booty was Katie, whom he abducted in a moment of lust and passion in the innocent raid, and, as best as Mzenze could understand, not reluctantly so. Ndlovo later paid twenty head of cattle, and forty goats, as dowry to keep honour and temporary peace between the two tribes intact, and a major tribal war was averted. John and Nondwe were peripheral consequences of the raid.

Ndlovo and Katie had come with Mzenze's family from Barberton on the Swaziland border. Mzenze had been conceived in Barberton, and later saw his first sunbeams in Sabie.

Katie had been his family's washerwoman from the time of the impi raid. Mzenze's parents also employed a Shangaan housemaid who did the housework, and basic cooking, which left his mum free to raise the children, and to make dresses and clothes for the wealthier people in the community in addition to their own.

When it came time to feed John and Nondwe, Katie would manoeuvre the blanket on her back around to the front, and, proffering one of her soft, melonous, naked breasts to each, they would drink as lustily as they cried out when they demanded to be fed, and they were very good at doing that. The African people breastfed their offspring far longer than Europeans did.

Mzenze often found himself being picked up and lobbed into Katie's blanket to join John and Nondwe, and they would scruffle and scuffle happily for hours on end, while Katie did the washing and ironing, and not so happily when it came time for them to be fed. Three into two didn't go, and it was very lonely being last, alone and left out.

Katie resolved this problem by feeding them one at a time. She would reach out behind her, grab the first one she laid her hands on, and feed it. Somehow, Mzenze always managed to also get a feed, even if it was last sometimes.

Katie and her family lived in a single-roomed, mud-walled hut, with a thatch roof and cow dung floor, about half a mile away up against the hill in which she raised John and Nondwe. She used to come down from the hill three times a week; to spend the whole morning bent over a galvanised iron tub washing clothes, and a never-ending supply of soiled nappies.

The tub was at ground level, and she would be on her very callused knees on the rough, concrete floor, her ample hips swaying to and fro all morning as her pink-palmed hands rubbed one part of the garment against the other, the home-made soap coloured blue with Rickett's Blue struggling to make a lather. Sunlight soap would have been much better, but they just couldn't afford it.

Little John, Mzenze and Nondwe, perched as they were on Katie's back, were rocked gently back and forth, and purred with the constant rocking. As each load was washed, she would rinse it out and then hang it up on the washing line to dry.

She would then spend the entire afternoon ironing the laundry in the lean-to shelter next to the kitchen. A blazing hot, old, coal-fired stove, which she constantly had to keep stoked up, kept a series of cast-iron irons hot to ensure a crisp feel to the flour bag shirts and bloomers, and the coarse khaki trousers. The fact that it was often over 100 degrees Fahrenheit in summer time didn't seem to matter. As she ironed away, little John, Mzenze and Nondwe kept on rocking, and Katie kept on singing lullabies to them all through the day.

Katie would stop only once during the day, and that was at lunchtime. Her, and the other servant's lunch, consisted of 'mieliepap', as it was known by its Boer name, or 'putu' in the Zulu vernacular. It was a maize meal porridge, cooked by the African servants in a three-legged cast iron pot over an open wood fire in the far corner of the back yard.

A batch sufficient to last for two days would be made, and the fire stoked periodically to keep it warm. The putu was, more often than not, supplemented by 'maroch', which was a sort of spinach made from the leaves of the blackjack weed, or sometimes from pumpkin leaves.

No child in sub-Saharan Africa knew the meaning of hunger, neglect, or the lack of love in those days. That was before the advent of Apartheid, before western decolonisation, and before the Commies came with their guns to recolonise, and to attempt to subdue an untameable Africa. African children can't eat bullets and live. Not even the white one's can.

Mzenze's father was the kindest, most gentle, and most compassionate person he ever knew. He and Ndlovo worked as underground miners in the gold mines in Sabie for ten hours a day, six days a week. For this, his father earned the princely sum of thirty pounds a month. It was nigh on impossible to raise a large family on that sort of income in those days.

His father did not mind the fact that Mzenze, his brother and himself spoke Zulu, Shangaan and Swazi amongst themselves, for they felt comfortable about it, and it therefore seemed natural to do so. He spoke to his mother and sisters in Shangaan, they in turn answered him in English, and everyone was happy. His maternal grandmother spoke to him in Welsh, which he understood, but could not speak.

He simply did not speak English at first, although he could understand it well enough. His mum made very sure of that. Whenever she put her foot down, which was often enough, she did so with a rather firm hand, and everybody knew it then.

Mzenze's parents gave up on him entirely very early in his life. He was glad that they did, for it provided him with the richest upbringing imaginable, steeped in the cultural, tribal, social and moral values, languages, mysteries and sensible superstitions of Africa, in addition to his Anglo-Saxon, colonial, African origin. Then came the Afrikaners - the White Tribe of Africa. That was followed by his later exposure and affiliation to, the Jewish and Cape Coloured peoples.

All this cultural absorption early in life however, spelt massive trouble for a boy growing up in post-World War II Apartheid South Africa. This was later to be supplemented by acceptance into the Indian, and Chinese, communities in South Africa in his twenties.

A further eleven years in the Antipodes brought an element of maturity, and the rich tapestry of Southeast Asia would further encloak and enrich him, when he worked in Indonesia, and in the jungles of Borneo, and then his acceptance into the Chinese community in Sydney.

The only philosophy of any value he acquired in the fifteen years that he lived in the cities was, sadly, that there appeared to be a misplaced notion that the ability to deceive others, was some form of elevated intellectual ability. He learned, in those morally bankrupt deserts, how to detect, and to counter it, for it was vital to do so. Searching for, and expressing the naked truth there, only served to confuse everyone.

Betrayal and assassination have been accepted art forms in society, and it has been so from time immemorial, but nothing as bad as he discovered in the cities. The African and Australian bush and deserts, the tropical jungles of Borneo, and the people living therein, and the solitude to be found in the vast expanses of the Pacific Ocean, were the major mitigating features which ameliorated his wealth of experience. He was in familiar territory, and back in his elements - the bush, the jungle, the desert and the sea.

The odd, true-blue Aussie mateship, such as he found in his friend Mike, who once saved him from certain death by drowning, and very nearly lost his own life in doing so, was a welcome rarity. It was comforting to know then, that real mates still existed.

The whole however, would confusingly conflict in the search for richer meaning in life, and indeed, for his very being, as he was to discover later, very much later, happily so, and eventually, in the Australian Outback, and in the African bush. Even then, he discovered that he still had a long way to go, his path and destiny quite unknown.

I knew then that he could tell the most incredible tall stories. Where he got them from, I couldn't begin to guess. There were more Lighty and other campfire stories to come - much more.

Chapter Seven

We spent two further days at Caulder's Lake. One night, we drove in a westerly direction from the camp and, using our spotlight for the first time, we were lucky to spot a tawny frogmouth owl from about two metres away up a gum tree, and the red eyes of a dingo lurking in the scrub nearby.

'This second batch of damper you cooked is a lot better than the first batch you tried; it is quite edible. Not using two spoons of salt with the dough, but two pinches thereof instead, makes all the difference' Jack cleverly observed. I cooked it in a billy can which I placed in a hole dug in the ground, filling it up with hot coals from the campfire, then covered it all with a layer of earth. It took Jack quite a while to dig a hole in the very hard clay ground.

By then, the mandatory after-lunch naps we had, ensured that we were up to the early hours of the morning, staring pensively into the campfire, and silently star-gazing into the cloudless night skies above while wondering what there was out there. We did very little and loved every minute of it.

We departed Lakefield National Park, calling in on Clare on our way out. We arrived just in time, as she was about to set out to come and find us. We had a marvellous shower on the front lawn of her office, taking turns to spray each other with the garden water-hose while we lathered up and rinsed the grime off ourselves. It felt good to be clean again after five days in blistering heat, sand, dust, flies and mosquitoes. We no longer smelt of five-day-old sweat and insect repellent.

We had in mind taking the more adventurous northern road via Marina Plains to Musgrave to join up with the main Peninsula Development Road. Clare however, told us that it was totally impassable due to mud and the run-off from the recent late rains, and she strongly advised us not to even contemplate it. Left with no other option, we set off for Laura to the south to fuel up and to take the dusty main track north with the rest of the mob. We discretely deposited a six-pack of Foster's Lager in Clare's Landcruiser as a token of our appreciation, quite sure that she would enjoy it later. Not many visitors, if any, did that sort of thing we knew, and it was all the more reason to do so.

It was to become a standard practice of ours for the rest of the trip to try, when we could get away with it, to show our appreciation to the Rangers from the National Parks and Wildlife in this way, and it was, we were sure, always much appreciated by the recipients. Indeed, it proved to be a decided advantage as we discovered later when we pulled up at Ranger Stations thereafter. Most of them already knew in advance of our pending arrival, and our reception was always warm and friendly. We were also directed to the best places in the particular area, and provided with abundant, useful information on things of interest.

When we got to Laura, another small settlement, at around midday, we headed straight for the bar for an ice-cold drink. We had previously heard a lot about the Quinkan Caves where there was an abundance of Aborigine rock paintings reputed to be very old. After a short search we managed to track down the Aborigine Ranger, who appeared to us to be a little troppo at the time. He, in turn, and quite rightly so, must have thought we were totally crazy wanting to stagger around the ridges in the midday heat.

Mad dogs and Englishmen we thought we heard him mutter. How very right he was on both counts, but we couldn't admit to it then. He gave us directions, maps, information pamphlets, and permission to top up our water supply from his tap. The latter completed, we set off for the caves some twenty kilometres southeast of Laura.

Equipped with our Akubra hats we scrambled the fifty minutes up to Turtle Rock and the galleries. Phew! We got very hot and frustrated despite the marvellous rock formations and views. The scenery from the top of the ridge was like something out of *Picnic at Hanging Rock*. There was, to us, a lack of signposts, and we initially took the track to the left, and again, naturally, headed off in the wrong direction.

'We have come this far, so we might as well continue until we find the gallery,' I gasped. Soldiering on in the blistering heat, we found to our great dismay that the track stopped. We knew something was amiss, so we back-tracked to where the path took its course down the mountain again. There was another path to the right, appropriately signposted that time we noted, so I decided to try that one, leaving Jack sitting on a rock in a shady spot again.

I headed along the track for about half a kilometre, and all of a sudden fell upon all sorts of paintings of emus, crocodiles, lizards, geckos, and lots of very genitaled-looking individuals in all sorts of poses. There were heaps of hand-prints in nooks and crannies, the ochre paint weathering away.

All alone, it was like discovering ancient treasures on my own. It was hot and still, not the faintest breath of a breeze about. I kept a vigilant look-out for snakes and other nasties but saw none. It had turned out to be a little adventure on my own.

On rejoining Jack again, we staggered back down to the Toyota where the air conditioning was most thankfully received. We had to get a move on to reach Hann River before nightfall. On our arrival there in the late afternoon, a rather large lady at The Restaurant served us hamburgers and a hot pot of tea.

'No chips I'm afraid. The fryer is broken. Spare parts will be here next week,' she told us cheerfully. We hadn't expected anything as civilised as hamburgers, let alone chips.

We were pointed in the direction of the Hann River where we found a superb camp spot, and I had a swim in the fast flowing creek. It was to become the standard bath along the way to Cape York, and the only way to stay clean, albeit for a very short while.

I was so proud of myself that night for I had cooked up dinner on a fire that I had made on my very own with no assistance whatsoever from Jack. He just sat there, contentedly contemplating his navel, slurping away on his can of Foster's Lager, and occasionally, merrily burping and farting away at the birds and the bees and anything else that bothered to get a fright.

'It is just as well for you that you are sitting down-wind from where I am preparing dinner. Heathenish bush habits you have,' I shouted at him. I must blushingly confess that I later acquired some of them, and a few additional, rather unique ones of my own.

Our original thoughts were that our diet was going to be bland and uninteresting. It fortunately turned out to be quite erroneously so. We took turns at cooking, the passive observer washing the dishes afterwards. Jack, using his concoction of spices, churned up the most delicious biryanis, vindaloos and rogan joshes that, at times, made my tummy rumble, and me grumble about how long it took to cook. I equalised by slaying him with al dente cuisine, accompanied by sauces that my mum had taught me to make. He started to get a bit beefier, and so did I.

The next day, bright and early, and soon after the then-customary dawn chorus of abundant birdlife, we set off for Musgrave, Coen and Rokeby National Park. It was to be a long, dry and dusty road.

Musgrave consisted of one house serving as roadside cafe, post office, bank, police station and pub. The obligatory hamburger was had there of course, and I managed to post some mail. I hadn't the faintest idea when the letters would reach their destinations though. There were many road trains, being large trucks consisting of a prime mover and three trailers, ferrying cattle south to Cairns. We counted forty six wheels on one of them. There was also a Royal Flying Doctor airstrip which was very well kept, a comforting sight.

We met a group of five young female backpackers who had been to the tip of Cape York with a tour operator from Cairns at breakneck speed in an eleven-seater vehicle. The whole lot of them looked thoroughly bored and miserable, and they didn't take long to tell us all about it. We told them what a whale of a time we were having which, unfortunately, seemed to make them even more miserable. They had a lot to learn about the bush.

We travelled over some quite rough, sandy and corrugated roads. I enjoyed my one and a half hour drive, finishing off with crossing the Stuart River, and again very nearly bogging the Toyota.

Some twenty seven kilometres south of Coen we decided to divert off the main track onto a side road. Our topographic map of the area indicated a track of unknown quality, which apparently, was the old road, which traversed, what appeared to be scenic and hilly countryside. It looked adventurous.

Jack and I had our first major verbal duel then. Jack was driving, and I was navigating. We approached a fork in the road, one track going north, the other going east.

'Go right,' I said. We did.

Some three kilometres further, the track turned south, and it appeared to continue in that direction indefinitely. I insisted that we continue. Jack stopped, looked at the detailed topographic map, and decided to turn around to take the left hand fork instead. On the way back to the junction there was much debate. I was very annoyed.

'How dare you question my judgment? Do you think I'm bloody useless?' I finally asked him, most indignantly.

'You can work that out for yourself. I'm not prepared to make any judgments about you,' he replied dryly.

The arrogant South African bastard! I'll get him yet. Just you wait and see!' I decided resolutely.

We took the other road and jollied along through very pleasant countryside. We came upon some alluvial gold mine diggings in a dry river bed. One of the miners there had built a very robust cottage from large stones he had carried by hand from the river bed. The cottage was perched halfway up a hill, overlooking the river. It looked very frontier-like, and was quite picturesque.

Jack observed that there didn't appear to be much mining activity taking place, nor were there any signs of the reputed gold boom which was supposed to be taking place in that area. Some of the alluvial gold mining claims had been trading for up to a million dollars in Pitt Street, Sydney. The reality was that it was a speculative shambles, and unwary, and gullible, investors had never left their air-conditioned ivory towers to make the effort to put their feet on the ground there. It was too much like hard work.

Coen was another settlement, this time a little larger than the others we had encountered thus far. The police station, post office, cafe, shops and pub were actually all housed in separate buildings. Coen had that forlorn, desolate look and feel about it as do most Australian Outback settlements have on a Sunday afternoon. There were very few people around.

The local pub had dubiously been renamed the *SEXCHANGE HOTEL* after someone had added a battered looking 'S' to the front of the *EXCHANGE HOTEL* sign originally bolted to the roof. We bought ice, replenished our depleted beer supplies from Pete's shop, and then went to refuel at Irene's fuel station.

The sun beat down ferociously and mercilessly in mid-afternoon as I phoned home to my parents whom I aroused at seven o'clock on a Sunday morning in Chichester.

Cape Tribulation Camp

1. *Bloomfield Falls*

2. *Caulder Lake*

3. *Old Laura Homestead*

Chapter Eight

We went to see Mike Delaney, the Chief Ranger for the Cape York Peninsula, before we went into Rokeby National Park. Mike was a super guy, and he gave us all the directions, instructions and information we needed. He suggested that, due to us probably arriving at the Ranger Station in the late evening, we stop for the night there where there was a hot shower, a kitchen and a bunkhouse in which to sleep.

Mike said that Wally, who was care-taking in the absence of Stewart, the regular Ranger, would take care of us, and would also value our company. Off we set for the hundred and twenty kilometre haul into Rokeby. We were the only human beings in the park then, apart from Wally.

On the way into Rokeby, Jack discovered that the fuel filler flap had not been closed. On closer examination, we discovered that the fuel cap had also not been replaced. It had, apparently, been left behind at Irene's shop one hundred kilometres away. We were nearly at Rokeby station when this was discovered, so we continued on. Mike had mentioned that he would see us some four days later, and we reasoned that we could contact him to see if he could affect a rescue.

Somehow, we had to ensure that no dust got into the fuel tank. Jack suggested that one of his old socks might remedy it, but he left it as it was because it also could serve as a very short fuse, and turn the fuel tank into a bomb.

We saw an old rogue water buffalo wandering close to the road, quietly minding his own business. Water buffalo were not native to Australia. They were imported from Asia in the late 1800's as domesticated beasts of burden. As time went by they, like the pigs, went feral - prolifically. It was environmentally undesirable as they competed with great advantage over the indigenous vegetarians.

On our arrival at the Rokeby Station, we were greeted by a mob of tame wallabies merrily hopping around and grazing quite peacefully. We went in search of Wally, and finally found him furiously engaged in mighty battle attempting to get the water pump next to the shed started. He was quite amazed to see the two of us unexpectedly coming around the corner. A huge grin appeared on his weather beaten face as we did.

Formalities were dispensed with in a hurry. Jack traded Wally a dozen warm beers for cold ones, and it was on!

Rokeby National Park was a big park, which, together with the adjoining Archer Bend National Park, was 457,000 hectares in, extend. It was a park that, according to the brochure, was 'for those seeking a quiet and intimate contact with nature'. Dead right for us it was.

Rokeby had formally been a very large cattle station. It had been converted into a National Park a short time before. The homestead was built on a large, elevated, open area with views over the tops of gum trees all around. It was built on elevated ground because the surrounds were flooded as far as the eye could see during the wet season.

The gum trees had been felled in a hundred metre radius around the homestead in order to offer protection against bushfires in the dry season. Australian bushfires can be very fierce. Gum trees, inherently containing vast amounts of eucalyptus oil, literally explode during an intense bushfire.

It appeared that very few people went to visit Rokeby. The reasons for this, apparently, were that, firstly, fishing was prohibited. Secondly, it was seventy seven kilometres west of the main Peninsula Development Road, and off the beaten track. The birdlife was prolific and therefore precisely our kind of place.

After a few beers, Wally called Mike up on the two-way radio to inform him that we had arrived. Mike said he would check out the fuel cap with Irene and, if unsuccessful, would make an alternative arrangement to solve our problem.

It was a calm, warm evening after a beautiful orange sunset. The flies disappeared, and the mosquito brigade arrived soon thereafter to torment us further. The birds softly nestling in the trees for the night, and little wallabies hopping about, made for one of those magic moments one all too rarely experiences. The tranquillity, and being in total harmony with nature at such a time, more than adequately compensated for any minor irritants. A languid euphoria gently swept over us, and a peaceful, blissful state prevailed.

I wonder what the poor people in cold, grey, wet and dismal suburbia are doing I allowed myself to think during one of the many silences. Conversation during such interludes was superfluous. It was indeed, invading. What delightful company and what better surrounds could one wish for?

We spent the night chatting away with Wally in his softly spoken, quaint, German-Australian accent. He had been a German prisoner of war in Cornwall during World War II. He used to be a crocodile hunter in the good old wild days when crocodiles were considered vermin in northern Australia. Wally had also become a fair dinkum, harum-scarum, boozing banana-bending Queenslander by then. We somehow managed, without apparent great difficulty, to wade our way through more than a modest number of beers that night.

I cooked up a good, hearty, pasta, bacon, onion and cheese dish in the bunkhouse kitchen for the lads. I did miss my campfire and damper though. Jack retired early, and with relative ease, taking himself and his very wobbly boot via the scenic route to bed after the long, six hour drive north from Hann River over some quite rough sand and corrugations.

Shortly after I went to sleep, I awoke with a start. Going into the kitchen to investigate the cause of the din, I found the place was crawling with green tree frogs! They were clambering over the cutlery, the crockery, up the walls - they were everywhere! I fumbled for the light-switch in the dark, only to put my hand on a cold, damp, but very alive object.

On returning to my room, I found that I was sharing it with, not only green tree frogs, but rats, mice and all of nature's other nocturnal creepy crawlies as well. It was too much trouble to erect the tent at that time of night, so I oozed myself quietly back into my bunk, and just let things be.

Let nature take care of itself, I thought. Who am I to argue or to judge? I am far too exhausted to spend the night chasing after rats and frogs. They never bothered me in the slightest for the rest of the night.

The next day we became quite domesticated and washed our laundry. The crystal clear water quickly turned pitch black. We put a fresh load of clean water in the washing machine and set it on its dutiful way again.

By then, the sun was getting hot, and Crocodile Hunter Wally was singing happily away to an audience of feeding galahs parked on the grass opposite. What a treat it was to have open views. I decided to stay out of the sun that day, as it was going to be extremely hot.

Mike kindly delivered the fuel cap to us that same day having had to bring forward his visit to Rokeby by three days. The fact that it was a two hundred and forty kilometre round trip didn't seemed to matter to him. He earned a six-pack of Foster's Lager in the process, and we were extremely grateful. We had sneaked the six-pack into his truck while he was not looking. As he was about to take his leave, his six year old son discovered it in his Toyota Landcruiser utility truck.

He promptly delayed his departure to tell us of his personal camp spot at the old Archer River crossing where he normally took his family on weekends. Definitely not to camp less than fifty metres from the water we were told, and definitely no fishing allowed.

'Crocodiles will drag you into the river if you camp to close to it,' he warned.

We then told Mike about the old rogue buffalo that we had seen the previous day. He was quite surprised, as he had thought that all the buffalo had been culled from Rokeby earlier. We promised to call in on him and his family on our way back to take good care of the six-pack, and to join them for a barbecue if we did not manage to get a berth on the landing barge sailing from Weipa to Karumba.

By late afternoon the temperature had cooled. Wally offered to take me on a trip around the station to show me the lagoons, while Jack busied himself checking out the Toyota and again applying liberal doses of WD40 water dispersant to the electrics for the watery run further north.

At one particular place that Wally and I had to cross, was a large tract of water, and I scored a piggy-back ride so as not to get too wet. The water reached up to Wally's chest as he waded through it with me precariously perched on his back and hanging on for dear life. I didn't even get my bum wet.

The birdlife was magnificent, and I added the barred cuckoo shrike to my already impressive list. The calm, lily-covered lagoons mirrored the gum trees all around their edges. Wally and I thoroughly enjoyed our jaunt. He did not often get the opportunity to escort, and piggy-back, young sheilas around the bush. He was a great guy, and one of nature's true gentlemen.

We spent three nights at Mike's magic spot at the Archer River Crossing beyond Langi Lagoon, thirty five kilometres due north along the old track from Rokeby Ranger Station. The track was wild, and got wilder the further we went. As we got close to the river, the vegetation thickened and it became really shady, a welcome change from the sparse gums.

We set up camp under a huge, shady tree on the river bank on the soft river sand. It would definitely not have been advisable during the wet season, because the river then became a raging torrent. The spot we camped on would have resulted with our tent, the Toyota and all our camping gear being washed into the Gulf of Carpentaria within half a day. The huge trees caught up in the branches above us told us that.

Unlike most of the other camping spots we had before, we remained cool at midday, and we welcomed our afternoon naps during which we could really sleep well.

On our return from an excursion to visit one of the many lagoons in the area, we met Wendy and Jamie who had set up camp up the road from us. She was *frightfully English*, and was trying to save the notorious Queensland cane toad, much to Jack's utter disbelief. She was actually doing research for a Ph.D. on the subject.

The Queensland cane toad was originally imported from Hawaii to reduce the cane rat population in the sugarcane fields in Northern Queensland. The first problem was that it found easier prey, and forgot to eat the cane rats. The next problem was that it had no predators. The larger birds of prey in particular, were vulnerable, as the cane toad had a unique defence system. It excreted a poison from its skin which killed its predator. It served no useful function in the food chain apart from annihilating both up and down.

Jamie was an American lad. Frightfully civilly, they offered us a cup of tea, which, we of course accepted. Our extraordinary large mugs were filled quarter full. They were having a good time, and it was good to see them do so.

The two of them took off and canoed up-river early one morning. I watched them depart, and return later that evening, quite envious that we had not thought of bringing along some form of water transport. They had seen heaps of crocodiles, and we had seen none.

It seemed that we were invading each other's space and, after a cordial beer around our campfire that evening, they decided to move on in their Suzuki Sierra. They packed up and left early the following morning. That again left us the only visitors in the park at the time.

I found a birdwatching spot by the river that was an ornithologist's dream. It was on a tree trunk, which had become uprooted during the wet season, and had fallen over a pool in the river. Yellow orioles and honey-eaters, redbrowed firetails, leaden flycatchers, bee-eaters having a sunbath, little cuckoo shrikes, barred finches - all having a nice swim and dust bath.

I was thrilled to see a bunch of lovely wrens with blue heads. A pair of red-eyed Papuan frogmouth owls stared intently at me from their daytime perch up a gumtree, while I sat on my log over the river watching them in return. It seemed to be a mutually rewarding experience.

While birdwatching up river and back down the track, I saw about forty new species. Jack was very patient and supportive of my time-consuming passion. He was quite content to while away the time messing about, doing things in the camp, burying his nose in topographic maps and doing fuel and distance calculations. In this way, we whiled away many pleasant hours in our independent preoccupations.

On the morning of our departure we got up super early at 6:30 am to the dawn chorus, had a huge mug of tea, and got to work immediately breaking camp and clearing the area. We had, by then, got clearing a campsite down to a fine art. While Jack packed the Toyota, I took a last wander up river to my fishing (oops!) and birdwatching spot to say good morning, and a last goodbye, to my friendly pair of Papuan frogmouth owls.

I sat balanced on my log right above the river watching the mist gradually lifting, and the early morning sun creeping up from behind the tree tops. It was pure magic. I kept an eye out for crocodiles, but again, they did not oblige.

A pair of dingoes silently, and surreptitiously, slithered down to the water on the far bank for a drink, both of them nervously listening for any sound of danger, and scouring the surface of the river for signs of crocodiles, their bodies tense as bent springsteel while they drank. Jack came along and caught me red-handed on the camera *not fishing*, with a perch dangling off my hand-line. We ate the fillets that night for dinner, which Jack prepared. I hope I don't go to jail. Sorry fish.

By eight o'clock, we were back on the track south out of Rokeby via Bob's Lagoon. There were so many beautiful lily-covered lagoons in the area. They overflowed in the wet season all the way down to Ten Mile Crossing, where the Archer and Baker Rivers converged. We watched for crocodiles, saw none, but we did see a mangrove heron, or better known as a bittern, which was not on the Rokeby National Park species list. One to me Stewart!

We headed out of the park via Wally at the Ranger Station, leaving a note for Stewart with Wally, telling Stewart about the bittern, and included a list of all the other birdlife I had seen. Wally was pleased to see us, and very happy to be able to have a yarn with someone. Apart from Wendy and Jamie, no-one had entered the park the preceding three days.

A hot shower and a mug of coffee were much appreciated. We poured our newly-cleaned bodies back into filthy dirty clothes again. How people could have stayed so clean, and as fresh as a daisy in the movies, will forever remain a mystery to me.

Chapter Nine

Seventy seven kilometres from the Ranger station we were back on the track again, and having to put up with the mad drivers. There was bulldust, sand, grit, corrugations, potholes and invisible dips; we had them all. It was little wonder that those adventurers, who raced up to Cape York and back again during their annual holiday, found it a painful experience at times.

Archer River was not the thriving metropolis we had deluded ourselves it to be. Our shopping list could not be expedited, but beer and ice were always available. The settlement consisted of a peaceful cafe, telephone box, camping area, liquor off-licence and petrol pump. Obviously, some good stories could be heard if one stayed around for long enough.

A mob of Hooray Henrys in a Nissan Patrol pulled up with a very broken steering system and terminally damaged front suspension. They had forgotten that Rule Number One is *Don't Break the Truck!* They looked a sad and sorry lot. The nearest garage and mechanic were six hundred kilometres to the south.

Big mugs of coffee and obligatory, world famous, Archer Burgers were hungrily devoured. The hamburgers sat about six inches high on the plate and were enough to keep us going for the rest of the day; if one could find place for it all. We did. We took on fuel and water and belched off heading further north.

On our arrival at the Wenlock River, we discovered that it was a surprisingly low one metre and a bit deep. This quite disappointed Jack who had been all keyed up for it from the time we left Cairns. We chose to use a rickety, Heath Robinson, make-shift raft onto which vehicles were driven, and then got pushed across to the other side by the passengers while the driver watched from inside the vehicle.

I stripped down to the appropriate dress, waded into the river and joined the mob that had combined to raft the previous vehicles across. Jack drove the Toyota onto the contraption, and we started pushing the raft across with him sitting inside the Toyota. He opened the driver's side window, looked down at me heaving my guts away directly below him, a wicked grin on his face.

'Get your back into it sheila!' he yelled, closed the window, and then sat back quite contentedly, in air-conditioned comfort, and enjoyed the rest of the voyage.

'All mining engineers should dig themselves into hell!' I yelled back at him lividly. The indignities that we women have to sometimes endure.

Knock me down with a feather if it didn't just so happen that we were the very last vehicle to cross for the day. Jack got off Scot-free. He didn't even get his toes wet!

North of the Wenlock River, I drove the forty kilometres to the North Alice river. I thought I drove surprisingly well, including fording the Dulhunty River, which was a very dicey crossing. We took the left-hand fork to follow the old, unmaintained Overland Telegraph Line road, rather than following the new graded road north.

Mike, the Chief Ranger, had warned us not to take the new road because all the Kamikaze pilots took it. He never used it, saying that he would rather have been bogged for a week on the old road than go on the new one. He had told us that there had been twelve head-on collisions, and one fatality, over the previous fortnight on that stretch of road. It, being the first two weeks that the road had been open, was an indication of what it was going to be like later in the dry season when the bulk of the Cape York adventurers went in. That was more than adequate reason for us to avoid it.

Besides that, the old Telegraph Road was really the 'Fun Run'. We were more than suitably equipped, and prepared, for anything we were to encounter. Fun was precisely the reason why we were there in the first instance, and we had no intention whatsoever of returning in the obituaries columns.

We set up camp on the south bank of North Alice Creek for the night. With the tent up, our dinner prepared ready for cooking, and a decent hardwood fire set ready to be lit, we treated ourselves to a well earned icy cold Foster's Lager. A hard-wood fire meant having good, hot coals for me to bake the damper. There was not another soul for miles around.

Clutching our beer cans firmly in our ever-grubby grabbers, we took a wander along to see what lay ahead of us the next morning. The *winch material* we were to cross was a hundred metres or so of wall-to-wall mud, and probably a metre deep at that.

God help us! I thought to myself. It was probably just as well that we were tackling it in the morning after a good nights sleep; that was, if I could get a good night's sleep what with my nerves being on edge from the time I first saw that ghastly sight. The three Hail Marys I said that night I found quite necessary. If He were going to lend us a hand, He would have to call up some formidable reinforcements.

The next morning we were into it - and out of it again before you could say *Jumping Jack Flash*. Once on the other side, Jack stood there wide-eyed, puzzled and perplexed as to how it all happened. One minute we were on the south side, and the next minute we were high and dry on the north.

'Well, those are the breaks you get in life,' I remarked to Jack, feeling a little annoyed with myself for being so overly-anxious all night.

'Accept the breaks when you get them,' Jack replied philosophically, equally relieved that it was behind us. He shook his head in disbelief at our good fortune.

From North Alice Creek, we continued up the old Telegraph Road. We happened to find a complete spare wheel lying in the road. We stopped to pick it up, tied it to the bullbar on the front of the Toyota and took it with us.

At most of the more adventurous crossings there were people around watching the goings-on. One in particular, Gunshot Creek, was definitely such an adventurous crossing.

Gunshot Creek was most certainly not on our itinerary. We had planned to avoid it at all costs on Mike's advice, as it was a real truck wrecker and all sane people avoided it. The New Road was a sandy track with three ruts in it. The middle rut was shared. When one tried to get out of the ruts to allow oncoming traffic to pass, one couldn't, and a head-on collision resulted.

We intended doing the sensible thing by taking the longer detour via Heathlands where we wanted to call in on the Ranger to get permits to camp in the Jardine River National Park, but it was not to be. I was navigating again, and we missed the Heathlands turn-off. Jack took a quick look around.

'It is frightening, and I don't scare very easily' he observed, and was back into his boring fuel and distance calculations again.

'We can't go back to the turnoff to Heathlands,' he said. 'Our fuel supply is critical as it is now. The additional distance we will have to cover to get to Bamaga, with what we have, is doubtful enough. This is the first time the Toyota has been in full-time four-wheel-drive. I really don't know how far we can push our luck for fuel. I'll check it all out again.' He did so.

The approach was a steep, sixty degree, slippery incline straight down to the metre-deep creek. The entry was about three metres measured vertically, and another metre of water. It was a real chassis bender and steering and suspension destroyer. The creek bed was sandy, but appeared to be firm and the exit sandy, but comparatively easy.

While Jack was there, he mentioned to the other people that we had found a complete wheel in the road. One bright, red-headed young man claimed it fell off his Nissan Patrol. Jack reluctantly let him have it and helped to unstrap it from the bullbar.

'It is going to cost you a six-pack,' Jack told him.

'I'll give it to you when we get to the tip,' promised Blue. All red-headed Australians were named Blue. Perhaps it had something to do with their fighting each other all the time.

'We are going in,' Jack said to me when he got back to the Toyota. 'Are you coming along?'

'No thanks. I'll watch. Make it spectacular, because I'll be taking photographs of this lot,' I replied, going down into the river to take up a vantage position. There was no way in the world a team of wild horses could have made me get into the vehicle with him!

He didn't disappoint me. He drove in low four-wheel-drive to the very edge of the drop to where the Toyota would nearly free-wheel by gravity. He stopped and pulled the handbrake on tightly, all the while keeping his right foot on the footbrake, and his left foot depressing the clutch pedal. A rather helpful fellow then started to call out directions to him to keep him on the very narrow entry.

The front wheels look much too far apart, and will probably get the Toyota jammed in the near vertical position, I thought.

'Left!' Helpful Fellow called while flailing his left arm about.

'Left it is,' said Jack, easing the footbrake and promptly going to the right. The right hand front wheel stayed on the level embankment, and the left front wheel went down into the gully.

'Back! Back! Go back!' about ten people standing in the river shouted in unison while madly waving their arms about. The children loved it; it was really funny to them.

What on earth are those jokers going on about? thought Jack to himself. He eased the brake further, and the Toyota started to take on a rather awkward angle. The right rear wheel lifted off the ground at the same time as the left front wheel also lost contact with terra firma.

Now, I'm in real trouble! Jack thought, finally waking up to himself, but it was too late. He tried to reverse back out again, but there was no traction whatsoever with one front wheel, and one back wheel, off the ground. Gravity had, by then, taken the upper hand.

Not quite the time to discover the real value of lockable differentials Jack mused to himself. He turned the steering wheel slightly to the left.

With an almighty bang the front right hand wheel fell more than a metre into the rut. The entire rear end of the Toyota took to the heavens with both the rear wheels in the air like an upside-down bucking Brisbane Bronco at a rodeo. Both rear wheels came back down to earth, accompanied by a heart-stopping thud throwing a cloud of dust into the air. What a spectacular sight it all was!

'Who wants to go to speedway with bunnies like that around to watch?' a ten year old lad asked no-one in particular. Who indeed?

'If he has broken the truck, I will have a thing or two to say to him that he won't like to hear,' I said to myself.

The Toyota slid down the gully by its own free will and accord. As the bullbar touched the water, it looked like some prehistoric animal having a drink from the creek. As the nose got submerged, Jack let out the handbrake, dropped the clutch, and drove through to the other side without further mishap.

We did a superficial damage assessment and thankfully found everything intact. I thoroughly enjoyed watching Jack literally throw himself, and his vehicle, into a river. The billy was boiled and we made lunch. We returned to watch the rest of the show with damper and jam in one hand, and a mug of steaming tea in the other.

'I didn't do at all well there, did I?' Jack asked me as we walked back to the creek.

'You have remarkable insight into your shortcomings,' I eagerly agreed. Touche!

Southbound vehicles all had to be winched out without exception. With winches grinding away, tyres madly spinning throwing out clouds of acrid smoke from burning rubber, drivers grim-faced, fearful that they may make a wrong move and become the bunny of the moment. The children shrieked with virtually non-stop laughter. They were all having a wonderful time. Gunshot was not to be the last of our fun, there was still a lot more to come.

We, more or less, started driving in convoy from the old Gunshot Creek together with Ding and Dong Battle-Bickering, a retired couple from somewhere Down South who had recently retired, and were driving around Australia for the hell of it.

Ding, he just was like that. And Dong, well, she just looked like one. They had been camping and fishing west of Cairns, and were about to set off for the Northern Territory when Ding took out a map, looked at it, and said:

'Let's go to Cape York, Dong!' Ding! As a result of that hasty decision, they were rather ill-equipped, found that they were short of fuel, and would probably not make it to Bamaga, the nearest fuel supply station.

The day progressed with wash-outs, potholes, bulldust, mud bogs, deep rivers and deep, treacherous sand. We lead the way and communicated by radio with Ding and Dong, warning them whenever hazards, obstacles and oncoming traffic was to be expected.

It was tortuous going, especially alert to oncoming traffic as we were going into a right hand bend and vegetation obscured visibility. We lost count of the number of times our hearts leapt to our throats at the sight of near out-of-control vehicles at bends in the road. We drove at a respectable and safe speed, constantly at the ready to dart into the scrub to avoid a head-on collision.

Cockatoo Creek got us stuck in a bog for the first time. The approach to the river was steep; with an innocent looking little bog just before the water. Jack gingerly, and slowly, entered, and was up to the axles and chassis in mud in no time at all. The wheels were in the mud and not making contact with firm ground. Ding pulled us out backwards with his vehicle using our Snatchum strap for the first time.

I was prepared to sit and watch, but Jack made me walk Cockatoo Creek to find the best way through it while he un-bogged the Toyota. The river was a metre deep and fast flowing.

This is real crocodile country! I kept repeating this to myself as I waded in. The salt water, man-eating variety was what I was greatly concerned about.

Once Jack had repositioned himself and the Toyota back on the high and dry side of the bog again, I pointed out to him the best and safest route.

'Walk it again. This time ahead of me so that I can see where you walked,' he said. I did as I was told.

He engaged low range four-wheel-drive, crashed into the bog, went whizzing out of it, right angle turn to the right, right angle turn to the left, plunged into the river, drove over the viciously sharp rocks on the river bed, roared out on the other side and, without stopping, and at full throttle, went up the steep, sandy rise of fifty metres or more without much difficulty.

'Let's check this out for a while,' Jack suggested with a glean in his eye after he had parked the Toyota out of harms way.

Climbing the sand rise at the north side caused a lot of red faces and extreme embarrassment to the less experienced drivers. Snatchum straps were the order of the day.

One right gentleman, a lawyer named Lex from Sydney, got halfway up the sand rise only to find that he was going nowhere in his Nissan Patrol. He spent over an hour there thrashing around with a Tirfor hand-winch getting nothing done, reversing back into the river time after time, and then having a few more almighty rushes at the rise only to drag his engine dead at the same place every time, all the while churning up the already loose sand even looser.

Jack had watched him letting him do his independent thing and offered our assistance if he felt the need for it, but a very independent sort was our Lex. He was holding up the traffic building up on both the north and south sides, and was starting to incur the subtle displeasure from a few of the less patient types...

At last, Jack, with our Snatchum strap tucked under his arm, approached him really closely.

'What do you want me to do next, Lex?' Jack asked him.

The beaten look on Lex's face said it all. He would learn, but not in a courtroom, and it would take him a while. In the bush it is never wise to refuse assistance when it is offered. The bush has no respect for foolish pride, and can be totally unforgiving. It does allow the dignity to remain intact provided one is prepared to bend a little. It is all a matter of dignified survival and interdependence. Snatchum strap in place, the pain was over in a matter of seconds.

The road becomes increasingly rougher and bendier. Every hundred metres or so, the road appeared to have a right angle bend. I had never, in all my life, been so badly shaken about. Jack did his very best as I desperately clung to the panic bar conveniently positioned on the dashboard in front of me, and I kept my feet firmly implanted on the footboard to keep me in my seat. My back was absolutely aching in the end - in fact, it was screaming at me very loudly. I couldn't tell Jack about it because he would probably have had me medi-vacced back to Cairns. I had my seatbelt on of course, but it had limited application under those conditions.

There were a few more rivers to cross after Cockatoo Creek. I had decided that there was not much future in wading through mud. Water and sand were enough to contend with. We warned Ding and Dong of any nasty looking potholes, wash-outs and on-coming traffic on the two-way radio. We were constantly on the lookout for hazards. Jack thankfully did all the driving that day.

The vegetation changed quite quickly, and the density and size of the gumtrees increased markedly. Fan palms and blackboys started to appear. The sand colour alternated between red and white and, when we were on the higher ranges, the views were terrific.

We joined the new road for a short while until it forked to the left for the Jardine River ferry crossing. We took the right hand fork being the Old Overland Telegraph Line road, followed that for some ten kilometres, and went straight into Jardine National Park.

Chapter Ten

We examined the main campsite at Twin Falls. It was crawling with people and tour groups, with noisy generator sets adding to the chaos. There was garbage strewn everywhere. It was not our sort of place. We saw Blue and his Nissan Patrol at the campsite.

'Don't forget that you still owe me a six-pack of beer for that wheel!' Jack called out to him as we were passing.

'What did you do that for?' I asked Jack. He could be so rude to people sometimes.

'We will never ever see that six-pack,' he explained. He was right because we never saw Blue again.

We spent two nights at Twin and Elliott Falls. Being a little more adventurous than the norm, we followed the river upstream and found a delightful waterfall with a natural, cold water, bubbling Jacuzzi on our doorstep. We had the place all to ourselves. Had someone earlier mentioned something about a Jacuzzi? Perhaps in Cairns?

Jardine River National Park was a true wilderness. It was 239,000 hectares in extent. We had a hard look at going to Captain Billy's Landing, as well as to Usher's Point Landing on the east coast. It looked too formidable, and besides, we would have to miss Iron Range National Park if we did go there. Jack gave me the options to decide on, and I had to compromise. We set up camp with Ding and Dong. It was the first time we had shared company from the time we left Cairns.

On the river banks grew pitcher plants with the quaintest carnivorous flowers on them. They were sort of snap-dragon like, if not in appearance, then certainly in dragon-like behaviour. They would open up in the morning and invite all sorts of insects to enter the parlour. Once in, the insects would sit on the slippery lids, slide down into the digestive juices cupped in the bottom, and bye-bye Louis the Fly and Adam the Ant.

Australia should really look into the matter of growing the plants on a national scale, teach them to select flies and mosquitoes and so take care of the scourges of the Outback. Is anyone out there listening?

There were very few birds around due to the presence of humans. Apart from a few lone geese that flew overhead, we saw very few birds of any real interest.

'I don't miss the birds too much' I said to Jack.

'You must be on birdwatch overload by now,' he diagnosed correctly.

Ding and Dong were the most delightful people, but only when they were not together. They were the world's champion bickerers. The constant bilateral criticising, condemning, complaining and contradicting was a textbook case of how to be married in total disharmony, and still think that it was normal. Jack and I tried really hard to let it all flow over our heads, but without success. We desperately wanted our peace, quiet, solitude and tranquillity back. Little did we know then, what lay in store for us as the black, stormy clouds of discontent started looming ominously on the horizon.

The waterfall compensated to an extent for the discomfort. We spent a lot of time lolling around our Jacuzzi. The damned eternal Australian Outback fly was an ever-present irritant in the daytime. No sooner had they gone to bed, than the mozzie brigade took up duty for the night shift to torment us further.

We sprayed each other profusely with 'Aveagoodweegend', a well known Australian personal insect repellent. We had rather foolishly decided not to drop the odd gumleaf into the tea billy. Eucalyptus oil was a natural insect repellent, but it took about two weeks to enter the system and for it to be effective. It was quite pleasant once we had acquired the taste.

We were looking over the river one afternoon when we saw a mob heading north along the old Telegraph line road to the old Jardine River crossing some forty kilometres distant. The Nissan Patrol short-wheel-base vehicle was very heavily loaded, and had an enormous heavy-duty steel roof-rack on top of it with heavy paraphernalia securely lashed to it.

'That,' Jack casually mentioned 'is a recipe for catastrophe if ever you saw one. Expect a rescue and recover appeal at any moment'

He had no sooner said that than the poor Patrol sighed, and went to lie down on its side, very sadly, and very reluctantly. We quietly sat and witnessed the spectacle with badly frightened bodies clambering out and scurrying to and fro doing a damage assessment.

Another party went to assist them, and we watched them all as they kicked the very expensive electro-mechanical winch mounted on the bullbar in front. It was quite useless in a roll-over situation. There were spades, hand-winches, chains, Snatchum straps and ropes all over the place with a bunch of troppo galahs thrashing around in the thirty five degree centigrade midday heat. They were most certainly not having fun, and they would have an interesting story to tell their grandchildren, if their dented egos and dignity would allow them to.

We spent a pleasant evening after dinner with a mob camped downstream from us. Jack and Peter, who worked for the Department of Primary Industries, had a lively, constructive discussion on the Ph.D. thesis on the benefits and advantages of the cane toad in Queensland which was being done by Wendy, the English lass we had met in Rokeby National Park. They drank to her health, ruining theirs in the process, and wished her well and everything of the best in her absence. She had chosen a tough assignment.

They were a well organised party of some ten people, and even had a deep-freeze driven by an unsilenced generating set all occupying an entire Toyota Hilux four-wheel-drive utility truck.

'We like our fresh vegetables,' we were told.

'Where has the pioneer spirit gone?' we asked ourselves.

Ironically, we were quite happy to leave our nice little campsite in Jardine National Park. The flies drove us away. I had been using very strong, un-convent-like language to describe their somewhat less than desirable attributes. They got into my ears, eyes, nostrils and sores. One even found its way into my mouth, and then to the back of my throat while I was talking. I inadvertently inhaled it, then tried to cough, spit and hack it out simultaneously and nearly vomited in the process. They were quite disgusting. I had found out why Outback people spoke with their teeth firmly clenched - it was not because they were angry.

The only reason the flies were there was because there were so many people, and not enough predators around. What with the flies, the mosquitoes, the people, and Ding and Dong constantly bickering, it was little wonder that both Jack and I had chronic headaches.

Jack gave Ding a twenty litre jerry can of fuel to get them to Bamaga. He helped Ding to siphon it out and copped a mouthful of petrol in the process before we finally saw them off. They had barely disappeared down the track, when we packed our gear and followed them to Bamaga. We drove slowly, constantly piercing the road ahead with our binoculars, ever-ready to dart into the thick scrub at the slightest indication of their vehicle.

It cost us twenty dollars to cross the Jardine River on the Aborigine-owned and operated ferry. It most certainly was a civilised way of doing things. The alternative was to continue on the Old Telegraph Line Road and to cross the Jardine in two metres of crocodile-infested water, which was about two hundred metres wide. We most certainly did not have suicidal tendencies.

On our arrival in Bamaga, we discovered that it was Sunday, and that the fuel station was closed. We staggered in the searing heat into Jacky Jacky's cafe instead and pigged out ravenously on chicken and chips. Jack did some more fuel and distance calculations and decided that we would go to Somerset Beach to see what there was to be seen.

Somerset, as best we understood, was partly-Aborigine owned, so we set out to obtain a permit to enter. Being Sunday afternoon it did not surprise us that there was no-one to be found to get one. To compound the problem, there were six or seven different Aboriginal communities involved, and we had not the faintest idea which of them Somerset might have belonged to, if any of them at all.

'What the hell!' said Jack. 'Let's go anyway. No disrespect intended, but there is nothing we can do about it now.'

We set off and drove through the most beautiful rainforest. It was what fairy tales were made of. Jack was driving, and I was supposed to be on traffic-alert to warn Jack of oncoming traffic whenever we approached a right-hand bend in limited visibility. There was just so much beauty passing by that I was somewhat less than alert when another vehicle came directly toward us as we were approaching one such right hand bend. We narrowly averted a head-on collision, and Jack made it quite clear that he was not amused.

Nearing Somerset, we came upon a very unstable looking timber bridge. The piles had gradually sunk about a metre below the original level and it appeared to be in very hazardous disrepair.

'If the bridge collapses, and we fall in, we simply winch ourselves out,' said Jack. I promptly got out of the vehicle, closed the door firmly behind me, and watched. The bridge sagged even further, swayed a lot, creaked, groaned and complained profusely, but miraculously stayed intact as Jack drove the Toyota to the other side.

'The topographic map indicates that there is a scenic drive south of here which we will take on our way back,' said Jack. 'We will not come back this way.' I agreed.

We arrived at Somerset late that afternoon to be greeted by a string of three beautiful beaches. There was fresh water available by digging out a pool by hand in the damp sand in a depression high up on the beach. The rocks separating the beaches were covered in oysters.

We had the whole place to ourselves. Not another soul in sight and solitude at last. We found an ideal campsite on a well-grassed patch above some rocks separating two of the beaches. A fresh easterly breeze ensured the absence of flies and mosquito. A few shady trees added to our comfort. What more could we have asked for? It was a welcome opportunity to rest after a quite successful fortnight of strenuous driving and over-socialising.

We had no sooner set up camp and taken a short walk to explore our surroundings before nightfall when, on our return, the wind veered to the southeast, and then increased in intensity - fiercely so. The tent pegs were torn out of the ground and the intact dome tent started tumbling away at high speed. Jack raced after it and, with an awesome, death defying, Springbok-like rugby crash-tackle, stopped it and brought it under control. We dragged it back to the camp and Jack held it down while I carted gas bottles, backpacks and anything else heavy enough to place inside it, including ourselves, as ballast to keep it from blowing away again.

The wind whipped the surf up into frenzy, and blew the heavy spray straight into our camp. Everything, including ourselves, got drenched in saltwater spray and rain. The framework of the tent miraculously remained intact throughout the ordeal even though the shape of the tent altered dramatically at times - alarmingly so. We spent the rest of that night in the tent hoping and praying that the storm would abate.

Jack told me another Lighty story to while away some of the time. It was difficult at times to hear what he was saying because the storm was very fierce.

Chapter Eleven

It all started at about the time when Lighty was in primary school. It was when he had mislaid his Afrikaans reading book, and had, for that, been given two cuts on the bum with the Indian cane soaked in saltwater by his teacher, Boggie, for not having his reader in class. Boggie never thought of giving him another one as he did with the Boer boys and girls who lost books. It was automatically assumed that, because Lighty was English, it was his way of defying Boer authority and supremacy.

When he finally retrieved it from the dog's kennel where it had served as a bounty to be playfully fought over, had lost some pages, and had acquired an unmistakable tell-tale doggy look about it, as well as a distinct wet-dog odour, he triumphantly presented it at the next reading class.

It was a hanging offence. He was off to The Principal, The Office again, led there by Boggie who was desperately trying to tear his ear off in his haste.

Boggie got his nick-name because he had very long arms, and used to bark like a baboon every so often to clear his throat when he wanted to speak. 'Boggom! Boggom!' he would bark all day long while pumping his elbows in and out as he did so. Very seriously too his very red face told everybody.

The Principal was Fiehla, a staunch Afrikaner purist and a prominent member of a secret organisation propagating white Afrikaner supremacy at the expense of all other race groups, especially the English and the black Africans, that one could wish upon one's self to have the displeasure of encountering.

They were always going to *chase the Engelse and the kaffirs into the sea.* He was also an elder of the Church and read a lot from the Bible at school assembly - very stern and sanctimonious he was too then. He had very recently arrived at the school to take over as the Principal.

Fiehla came by his native name because John said that he was very good at hiding things - especially the real truth the natives said. He was a very secretive man. He went white with rage at the sight of the sacrilege committed against his beloved Afrikaans Taal. Lighty knew that he was in deep trouble in more ways than one.

'Four cuts with the saltwater soaked cane! Bend!' Fiehla commanded. Boggie grabbed Lighty's head and thrust it underneath Fiehla's desk while shifting his weight from one foot to another very rapidly.

Two cuts were delivered to his, by then, savaged nine-year-old backside with pinpoint accuracy which came from extensive, and intensive, practice, and with an indignant fury and enthusiasm to match. The third stroke elicited a rather rude, and indiscreet, mousy sort of fart that squeaked out from Lighty's backside followed by a sudden roar of great delight from the two Afrikaners.

'Dis reg! Maak die klein donder nog 'n keer poep!' roared Boggie in a high pitched, near-orgasmic laugh urging Fiehla on to greater heights. Make the little thunder fart again. It was as funny as a circus to the two of them.

'I'll teach the little guttersnipe from Londonderry who has a kaffir boy who speaks English fluently for a friend, and who laughs and jokes with the *verdomde* kaffirs in a language that we cannot understand, to fart in my office!' roared fearless Fiehla, and with new-found vigour and venom, delivered the mightiest blow Lighty had ever known, deliberately striking in a downward motion connecting excessively high on the buttocks, an area known to be super-sensitive.

Lighty peed in his pants then, which drizzled down his legs, and then dripped onto Fiehla's zebra skin carpet. Lighty wasn't at all happy then that he had, at long last, found his Afrikaans reading book.

The blows then rained down on him incessantly in a frenzied fit of outraged zeal and vitality, and with a white-hot fury quite disproportionate to the severity of the crime, or so Lighty thought. They fell across his shoulders, and across his back, and across his kidneys, paralysing him so that he could not use his arms to protect himself. And they kept on raining all over him, as he lay prostrate on the floor, squirming and grovelling in his own urine. Dry-eyed - for when you have been hit in the kidneys, you cannot cry.

'Here! Jy sal hom dood slaan!' Boggie had yelled out in panic as a blow came dangerously close to his head. God! You'll beat him to death! The two men, Fiehla, short, fat and bald-headed and Boggie, big, and fat, and both very ugly, engaged in mighty battle - a really funny sight.

Lighty had managed to crawl under Fiehla's desk. Boggie came out on top of the scuffle having wrestled the cane away from Fiehla. They were both quite exhausted and were breathing very heavily. Lighty's pee had soaked into their clothing which, as indicated by their twitching noses, they didn't appear to like at all.

Two African annies who were related to John, and who worked at the school, found him near the boy's toilet block. They undressed him, washed, and ironed his clothes dry so that when Lighty got home, no-one could see what had happened.

When he got home he showed John what the two had done to him and they decided to keep it a secret. Lighty's father didn't like that sort of thing, and he was afraid that his father would really kill the two of them, and then get into trouble himself, so Lighty didn't tell him.

He was going to be expelled from ordinary school, and be sent to reform school, and that was really why Lighty couldn't tell his father. Reform school was where the really bad boys went. Nobody ever came back from reform school, or was ever heard of again.

Deliberately peeing on the Principal's zebra skin carpet with malicious intent was bad enough to be sent there. Lighty was going to be deprived of an education for the rest of his life. Lighty didn't know where you went to, and he knew that you didn't learn anything good there, if anything at all, and that was bad enough.

It also meant that he could no longer help John with his schoolwork as he had been doing to keep John's education on a par with his. John had been doing Lighty's homework with him so that John could stay ahead in his inferior black schooling. By that time, John was superior to his peers at the native school that he went to and was two years ahead of his age group. He was very clever, and learnt very fast and easily. Lighty also learnt a lot from John then.

It was just as well that Lighty didn't tell his father then because the very next day Boggie told him to go to Fiehla's office. Fiehla was very frightened. Fiehla told Lighty that he was going to be sent very far away to a place called Glenmore in Natal after the Easter holidays. It was three days ride on the steam train there.

So that was where reform school is, thought Lighty.

Fiehla then told Lighty that his son couldn't go to the seaside home for under-privileged Afrikaner children at Glenmore for the next school term and he and Boggie had arranged for him to go instead. Under-privileged sounded like a really bad word.

It was the Afrikaans newspaper *Die Vaderland* that ran it Fiehla said, and Lighty knew that they didn't like the English at all because he sometimes used to read 'Die Vaderland', and they didn't write any good things about the English at all. Fiehla told him that it was a privilege, and a great honour, for an English boy to go there and Lighty was to be the first ever.

That meant that he was really going to be in for it, and they were going to chase him into the sea there. Fiehla said that Lighty's sister Margaret could go too so that Lighty wouldn't be alone. Boggie's daughter suddenly couldn't go either he said.

That really frightened him. They had been plotting to send their own children to reform school, but, because Lighty was worse than they were, he was going instead. And his sister too, and she was a good girl who never hurt anyone. You didn't have to be too bad to go to reform school in those days.

That reform school must be chock-a-block full of really very bad children if their two children can't go! Lighty thought. They didn't have school there Fiehla said, but Lighty already knew that.

When Lighty got home that day he and John went straight to the mine adit where his father and Ndlovo worked. He had to be the first to tell him about it, because his father had long before told him that whenever Lighty was in real trouble, his father had to be the first to know. His father never ever beat him, and Lighty thought it was because he told his father about really big trouble early - especially trouble to other people. His father had told him that it was all right to get up to all sorts of mischief - but he had to stay out of trouble.

They sat there above the mine adit watching the mules pulling the cocopans out of the mine one after the other until four o'clock in the afternoon when his father and Ndlovo, at last, walked out of the mine.

Lighty told him right there and then that he was going to reform school and that they were going to chase him into the sea because he had peed on Fiehla's zebra skin carpet. His father at first laughed a lot about the carpet, but in a way that told Lighty that he didn't really want to laugh. He didn't think that the reform school was such a funny idea. His father didn't really want to know about him getting hidings at school because he always said that it was good for him when he was naughty, and when his father didn't know about it.

His father went to see Fiehla later that day and, when he came back afterwards, he told Lighty that Glenmore was not a reform school but a good place to go to after all, even if Lighty did pee on the carpet. He said Lighty would like it there. He told Lighty to go to the bathroom and to take all his clothes off. There, his father and Ndlovo looked at the welts on Lighty's body.

'No-one will beat you like this ever again. If anyone ever lays as much as a finger on you, you must tell me, otherwise I will beat you again, and ten times as bad as I will beat the person who did it,' his father said as he washed the blood off his hands, and then put some ointment on the cuts on his knuckles. It sounded then like a very sensible idea to Lighty to tell his father about things like that early.

His father then told Lighty that he and his sister were going to swim in the sea, play on the beach, and build sandcastles all day long for three whole months. His father told him also that no-one ever got hidings there, and the people there were very good and kind to everyone.

Lighty thought that perhaps it was a bit like Heaven, so he asked his father if God was the Big Boss there. His father answered no, but he said that God had told Fiehla, very loudly, all that night, that God was on Lighty's side. Lighty thought that it was about time that He was too. Lighty later wondered a lot about what the sea really looked like.

Reform school didn't sound like a very bad place after all. It sounded a bit like *The Star* Seaside Home where any old child could go, and there were English and Afrikaans children there. Lighty used to read 'The Star' newspaper every day from front to back, and he saw the photos there, every Saturday, of the children with English names laughing and having fun while playing on Durban beach and building sand castles.

Lighty had always wished that he could go there whenever he read *The Star*. He sort of wondered a bit why he couldn't go to *The Star* Seaside Home instead, but then he remembered that they were only allowed to stay there for two weeks, and he even saw photos of them sitting in classrooms going to school. That all sounded a lot worse than the reform school run by 'Die Vaderland' at Glenmore.

Lighty's father took him to the police station to see the police sergeant, and to show the sergeant what Fiehla had done to him. The sergeant took photographs of Lighty while he was naked, and then called the district surgeon to examine Lighty.

For more than a week Fiehla wore dark glasses to hide his eyes, but he had very fat and broken lips, which he couldn't hide. And he couldn't speak properly either, so Boggie had to read the Bible for him. Fiehla never came back to school after that week because the Department of Education suspended him forthwith in disgrace.

There was much jubilation at the prospect of a three month holiday, and much sadness and tears from both children and parents at parting. There were six boys allocated to a six berth, second-class compartment. The girls were organised in the same manner. There was a special coach attached to the Garrett steam engine for the occasion. There were children and suitcases everywhere and much confusion.

Mr and Mrs Bonnie Koeleman were in charge of the fifteen boys and fifteen girls. Bonnie was a teacher at the school and Mrs Koeleman was a nursing sister at the hospital. Bill Stringer was driving the Garrett engine that day, but he wouldn't let Lighty and John ride with him in it that time.

With seven mighty long toots of the steam whistle, which the whole town could hear, Bill set the steam engine in motion and slowly chugged off from the platform. Other than talking to his sister Margaret occasionally, perhaps once a week, Lighty had spoken his last words of English for three months. All the other children were Afrikaners. His cultural absorption was to be immense.

The train merrily choof-choofed its way along the thirty mile journey to Nelspruit through the mountains and pine forests. A lot of the boys and girls leaned out of the windows to look at where they were going to and got lumps of soot in their eyes which Mrs Koeleman had to extract. She was a very busy nursing sister that afternoon.

At Nelspruit the two coaches were shunted into a siding to wait for the Lourenco Marques main-line train to Middelburg, Witbank, Pretoria and Germiston. Bill came along the platform to the coach to wish Lighty and all the other children a happy holiday and promised them all a ride on the steam engine when they returned from Glenmore.

Dinner was being served in the dining coach at sunset when the coaches were hooked up. Everyone's plates of food went all over the floor like a dog's dinner with the first bump. It then rearranged the dog's dinners with the second bump. One could tell that it wasn't Bill who was driving the engine that time.

On the train choofed into the night to Pretoria. Some of the children cried for their mums that night, but the others who were boarding school brats, shed not a tear. Lighty had a little cry late that night when no-one was looking, because he was homesick, and didn't know where he was going to, and he didn't know what was going to happen to him when he got there.

They arrived at Germiston Station the following morning and were shunted into another siding to wait for the evening train to Durban by the sea. A big bus came along and took them away to visit the Big City of Gold, Johannesburg - Egoli, and then to the Johannesburg Zoo for the afternoon. They saw all the animals there and went for a ride on the elephants. Then they ate ice creams, candy floss and toffee apples until they were all very sick and had to go back to the train.

That evening it was train time again. Again they were having dinner in the dining car when their dinner went all over the place when they were hooked up to the Durban train. On they choofed all that night until they got to Durban the next morning.

Another bus was waiting for them there which took them to Durban Beach for a ricksha ride and to see the sea for the first time. Then on to the Valley of a Thousand Hills that afternoon to visit a Zulu kraal. There, he had a merry chat with the Zulus who took great delight in the little fellow who spoke Zulu fluently and who knew all the things that a little Zulu boy ought to know, and who even danced like a little Zulu.

They slept in the coach on the platform that night and the next morning they set off for Port Shepstone where the train line ended. They choofed throughout the banana plantations and sugar cane fields, with the sea and the waves constantly to the left of them. At Port Shepstone, there was again another bus to take them to Margate and then on to Glenmore Beach. They arrived at the Glenmore home at four o'clock in the afternoon and were ushered to their sixteen-boy dormitory.

Lighty got a top bunk in the furthest corner away from the door because he was very low in the pecking order. The bunk below him was empty because only fifteen boys from the school went to Glenmore so there was a spare bunk in the dormitory. To be a townie and not a hostel brat, counted against him. Being the only Englishman there counted against him totally.

The next evening another strange little seven-year-old Afrikaans boy was ushered in by Mr Koeleman. Because Mr Koeleman had discovered that Lighty had started to pee in his bed on the train ride, he moved Lighty to the bottom bunk and gave the top bunk to the new arrival. He did not come from any of the other schools. He seemed to come from nowhere.

He was a gaunt-faced, emaciated little fellow by the name of Willie van Rensburg. Bonnie asked Lighty to be his friend, and to look after him. He spoke to no-one, and no-one spoke to him. His face told the world that he wanted to cry, but he never did. He said very little to Lighty. He seemed to be too shy to ask anything. Even when he had to go for a pee, he just peed in his pants. That was when Lighty took him outside and showed him where the outside toilet block was.

That night, at bed-time, Willie took his clothes off to put his pyjamas on. Lighty saw what he saw. Willie was scarred from head to toe by savage beatings and abuse.

'Who beat you like that?' Lighty asked Willie. Willie just burst out crying and cried all night to himself.

Once in bed Lighty remembered. Lighty had religiously read in *The Star* newspaper, every day, all the evidence presented at the trial of Willie's parents on the east Rand. The locking up in crates and cupboards, tying them to table legs, not feeding them, beating them with a plastic electric cord until they bled, cigarette burns, boiling water...

Willie is singularly the most battered and scarred living human being Lighty has ever seen, physically as well as mentally, in all the years he has been on this planet and he never wants to see another like him.

Both Willie's parents died when he was at Glenmore. He knew the true meaning of being alone in this world. Lighty was proud to be his very first and only friend in the world then.

Willie's father got fifteen years of hard labour, but was bludgeoned, raped and battered to death by his fellow prisoners after serving only three months. He was lucky to have died so soon.

Willie's mother was hanged at dawn at Pretoria Central Prison for the battery, cruelty to and neglect of Willie and his five year old sister, and for the eventual murder of Willie's little sister. Willie's mother was hanged two weeks after Willie arrived at Glenmore. Willie was perhaps unlucky to have lived.

The week before Willie's mother was hanged, the other boys used to remind him every day that it was only so many more days to go. The night before they hanged Willie's mother, Willie slept not a wink, and Lighty lay awake with him all that night.

At dawn the next morning, when the eastern sky started to get lighter, Willie got up and went outside. Lighty followed him. They went to stand on a mound next to the path leading to the toilet. They looked east over the sea, and just stood in silence in their pyjamas. Willie had totally cried himself out by then.

The eastern sky got lighter and lighter. When the sun took its first peep at the world, Willie let out a blood curdling series of prolonged screams of terrible anguish and agony, followed by the closest to a long, guttural death rattle Lighty had ever heard before falling onto the ground and grovelling, and grunting, and giving spasmodic kicks and arm movements like a fatally wounded animal. The sight of his face haunts Lighty to this day and forever will.

'It is not you that is dying, but your mother that was hanged. Stand up and be a man!' the boys said to him as they were walking to the toilets for their early morning pee.

Lighty just hopes, with all his heart, that Willie made it safely through life and prospered. And he asks you please to do the same. And NEVER beat and neglect the children. The price you must pay is far too high.

Every day they saw many whales playing in the sea, and dolphins frolicking in the waves.

Thomas, the Zulu Lifesaver, was a very busy man indeed looking after 120 children all together, all at the same time, altogether at sea, and he all on his own. Nobody drowned, but many very nearly did, including Lighty many times.

Thomas was so fierce that not one of the children ever was eaten by a shark. Thomas and Lighty got along especially well as they could talk freely in Zulu for many hours every day. Thomas always accompanied them on their beach walks and excursions wherever they went, and Lighty and Willy were his constant companions.

The bigger boys made Lighty and Poekies van Zyl fight each other five times, all five draws, until the two of them decided to refuse to fight anymore. They became very good friends instead. Slowly Lighty started to make more and more Afrikaner friends as he went along. He even had Engela Venter as a girl friend.

Lighty later tried to recall, and to write, some of the other things, good and fun things, they did at Glenmore. And there were many good things, and no bad things. The best Lighty could do was to write a collection of four poems that he wrote for the all the children of the world. And for all the big people who are sensible enough to be big children sometimes, and to remember what it was like to be a child on a seaside holiday for the first time.

Sand Crabs

One bright and early sunny day,
I went to Glenmore Beach to play.
Sand crabs did I chase and say,
As they dug their holes to hide away.
'Don't be frightened sand crabs nay,
Hide and seek is what I want to play.'

Their little eyes peeped through the sand,
Watching for that fateful hand,
That would pick them up for a dinner ball,
To be gobbled up, claws, feet and all.
No future that for a crab so small,
A tiny fellow, not very tall.

Jellyfish.

The jellyfish, now he's a funny one,
Has no legs so he cannot run.
Just lies there drying in the sun,
Doesn't seem to have any fun.
But don't you mind the wobbly jelly,
As he lies there on his belly.
The tide will turn, it won't be long,
To wash him back to join the throng,
Of all the creatures where he does belong,
In the sea, so mighty and strong.
Where he will sing and will rejoice,
With his friends in cheerful voice.

Sandworms.

Sandworms they're a crafty lot,
They're good for bait but not the pot.
They hide away for you cannot spot,
Beneath the sand so very hot.
There they live and spend all day,
Waiting for a morsel, perchance to stray.

Fishermen like them, good bait they be,
To catch fishes from the sea.
Bream and grunter and whiting once free,
Bite the hook and get cooked for tea.
Worms can be caught, but before you go,
You must remember to be very slow.

Sandflies.

The sandfly small is a terrible thing,
Can't see the blighter, can't feel his sting.
He will bite you and great pain will bring,
You itch, you scratch, your hands you wring.
He knows best how to get a feed,
He will bite you, he'll make you bleed.
Insect repellent, Rid may work,
To keep away the pesky jerk.
You rub it on your skin and smirk,
'Try that for size, you nasty burk!'
But he will get you, no matter what you think,
When he is thirsty he will get his drink!

When Lighty came back from Glenmore, there was a new principal at the school. He was a Jewish man. His name was Mr Berelowitz and he was a very good man.

While Lighty was at Glenmore, Fiehla was caught red-handed by the police with two Bapedi maidens in Fiehla's car in the veldt late one night. He had no place to hide. It was rumoured that the dominie was also involved, but managed to extricate himself from his predicament and escape arrest in the nickers of time they said. It really wasn't a very proper thing to do in those days and the South African Police Force took a rather solemn and serious view of such goings-on.

They policed the Immorality Act as if it were a religion and indeed, with an unsurpassable passion. They had a lot of difficulty in understanding why Fiehla wasn't wearing the two pairs of trousers in his car, and why the dominie's wife took all her children to far-off Kuruman in remote Namaqualand the next day.

There was much talk amongst the people who thought that little children couldn't hear, or couldn't understand, such profound things, or something. It had a lot to do with sixpences so it was said. Lighty understood this to be so because the children at school used to ask Fiehla's children how many sixpences it would take to get him out of jail. Many times. There were some very badly frightened policemen for a while after that too.

Lighty one day asked his father what had happened to Fiehla. John and Ndlovo had told Lighty the full story, but Lighty still wanted to know the real truth.

'He came to a somewhat sticky end my son,' was what his father told Lighty, and then laughed until he cried so much that tears rolled down his cheeks and he spilt his beer on the floor. Lighty laughed a bit too, but it was a sort of slightly puzzled laugh. He was very cleverly funny was his father sometimes. Sometimes much too clever for Lighty.

Lighty also was a bit afraid after that to be too friendly with the black annies that he liked so much and who were always so good to him. Lighty didn't want to go to jail like Fiehla did, and very nearly the dominie too, for being too friendly with the black maidens.

Boggie never hit him again, and he was quite kind to him after that, but the bus he drove to and from school every day, somehow just didn't want to go any more. Lighty thought it just got tired. John and Ndlovo told Lighty that all the black people knew what Fiehla and Boggie had done to him. They said that it was for that reason that the black farmworkers on Boggie's farm also seemed to get tired, and when they did manage to do something, it was always the wrong thing. The black people had decided to play some dirty tricks on Boggie. Boggie also got too tired one day when he was at the athletic track at the Annual Inter-Primary School Athletic Meeting.

Boggie was entrusted with the very important task of starting all the races with his big revolver. The very first race was the girls under-six eighty yards dash. He was supposed to say 'Take your marks', then wait a while, then say 'Get set!' and then wait a while, and then fire the revolver into the air to start the race. Everybody's eyes were on him, and it was a very important, poignant and memorable moment for him as he stood there in his white ice-cream boy's coat with his 'Beampte - Official' badge stuck to it.

But instead, he pointed his revolver into the air, said 'Take your marks', clutched his chest with his left hand, just fell down, and then shot the revolver at the little girls instead. He had forgotten to buy blanks and was using live ammunition instead, but apparently he had forgotten to tell anyone about that.

It was the fastest start to a race as Lighty had ever seen as dust and pebbles flew all over the place when the Colt .45 roared, the bullet gouging a deep furrow in front of the little girl's bare feet, and the little girls running in every direction but to the finish line. It could have turned out to have been a terrible tragedy. The little diddums could have all been killed, innocently kneeling as they were at the starting line like ducks in a row. Screaming too they were. Loudly.

It seemed that Boggie had forgotten to breath or something. He was like that sometimes, especially when he got angry and exited and turned very red in the face and couldn't talk. He just died. Heart attack! Just like that! The athletic meeting was abandoned and everyone sadly got back onto the school buses and went home again.

'It was a jolly good thing that he could shoot straight,' the new dominie had solemnly said at his funereal farewell a few days later.

I told you he could tell the tallest of stories!

Chapter Twelve

By daybreak the storm had abated and we were greeted by a welcome sunrise in a cloudless sky. July had also discretely crept up on us.

How delightful it was to be sitting in the relative cool of Somerset Beach on the eastern Cape York Peninsula with the entire place to ourselves. There were no people, flies or mosquitoes to bother us, and we were much happier and contented. It must have been thirty five degrees centigrade in Bamaga that day.

We had not been bothered by a single fly or mosquito all the time we were there - sheer bliss. We were looking forward to being alone again. The two days in Jardine National Park with bickering Ding and Dong and the rest of the multitude was quite enough socialising thank you!

We had bush concerts in the evenings with Mozart, Mendelssohn, Vivaldi and Tchaikovsky, wine and nuts for nibbles and heaps of chat again. We hadn't been following this ritual for quite a while. The half-moon was bright and the neap tide surf gently rolling in, the severity of it broken by the Great Barrier Reef.

Perhaps we will catch some fish tomorrow, this is all positive stuff, I thought. I suddenly remembered that there was another world outside and that I should do some writing.

It has been a week since I telephoned home. I'm glad now that I phoned from Coen' I thought. My parents would have worried otherwise. The tranquillity however, was not to last for long, for things started to go very badly wrong between the two of us.

Jack was off to sleep in his chair again and responded to nothing I said. I hated it when he acted like that and ignored me. I didn't know what I had done wrong. The previous few days he had been putting me on the defensive.

'On purpose,' he told me. He gave me a two-hour talk on why he was doing it. Body language philosophy came into it. Now that was interesting. He told me that I was assuming all sorts of protective postures and setting up defensive barriers which made talking to me nigh on impossible.

'You do not make talking to you very easy,' he claimed. 'I have no intention of harming or hurting you. I have no idea why you are so defensive. Why don't you open up a little and let people in so that they can discover the beautiful, unique being that is you in there? Just be your bloody self for a change,' he asked me. I could safely say then that we were having very difficult times.

He then he spent the rest of the evening sitting in his chair next to the rear of the Toyota intently gazing far out to sea as usual. He was in a world of his own and totally ignored the fact that I existed.

He did a two litre cask of wine an enormous amount of damage getting quite inebriated while listening to Bob Dylan loudly and noisily whining and wailing away on the Toyota sound system. I left him there in peace to do his thing and went to bed. The horrible din kept me awake however, but he seemed to be enjoying it all immensely. He finally went to bed well after midnight.

The following morning I got up to find that he had left all the doors of the Toyota open all night. Being camped on the beach, with a strong easterly wind blowing, everything got soaked with dew and saltwater spray including the binoculars. That really got me annoyed.

'How the hell am I supposed to go birdwatching with fogged up binoculars?' I asked him angrily while he was groggily waking up. I proceeded to point out to him his shortcomings in no uncertain terms. I was quite miserable and very angry with him to the point of being very rude and aggressive.

'I may very well deserve this, but I don't think I need it right now,' Jack thought to himself. I was at my rampant, ropeable very best! He said nothing!

'There should be a law against picking on defenceless drunks!' I heard him yell out to me from inside the tent. He promptly went back to sleep again.

How on earth does he expect me to argue against such logic? And how are we supposed to build a peaceful planet with people like that in our midst?' I wondered. I stalked off on stiff knees, stiff upper lip firmly in place, and I took off on a birdwatch on my own.

Like all previous days, that day was special - nay, very special. To start with, I had found a pathway into the rainforest. Surrounded by lovely wrens and rufous fantails, I stalked what could have been a manucode (Bird of Paradise). The birds were generally hard to spot in the dense and high rainforest canopy. I found a delightful glade of palms off the main track into Somerset.

I shall show it to Jack, I thought. It was so peaceful there.

Quite suddenly, and unexpectedly, I heard a bushpig grunting behind me. Spinning around to where the sound was coming from, I saw a small black piglet foraging for roots and generally minding his own business. We both spotted each other simultaneously and, without hesitation, we both charged off in opposite directions at enormous speed with me yelling at the top of my voice and the piglet squealing 'Wee, wee, wee!' in discernible G Sharp. It raced off into the scrub and back to its mum. She *oink-oinked* loudly from nearby.

My legs had never carried me that swiftly before. With the binoculars grasped in my one hand, my Akubra hat firmly flattened to my head with the other, and my knees pumping ninety to the dozen whizzing past my ears, I must have looked a right frightful sight crashing headlong through the rainforest. I had hoped that Jack might have heard me yelling back at the camp a kilometre away and come charging to my rescue, rifle in hand, but alas, he did not.

Badly shaken, I decided that I would have to be more cautious in future. If the mother of that piglet had come anywhere near me the old sow would have torn me to shreds. They could be vicious things those pigs. There were many men who had some very nasty scars, and have even lost limbs, from being mauled by them. One could develop extraordinary tree-climbing skills in an exceptionally short period of time under those circumstances.

Sitting on a log by the roadside to catch my breath while contemplating my quivering upper lip, and while doing some serious cerebral gymnastics, I wisely decided that the pigs had got there first and that they too, were entitled to their territory. I thought that a safer past-time was to explore the old Somerset homestead ruins instead. There was very little left of it but a ramshackle shed, a few relics, coconut palms and swarms of hornets. It was quite an eerie place.

Somerset was settled by the Jardine family sometime in the last century. They had visions of it equalling Singapore as a busy port and major trading centre but that was not to be.

We went for a superb, refreshing swim at lunch time that day. The surf was calm and the water warm and clear. That was where the fun stopped very abruptly. A blackish-grey shark started to follow me. I instinctively put my hand out to protect myself and touched it. It brushed against my leg and its rough skin barked some skin off my calf. I screamed in panic and Jack, who was some ten metres away, quickly waded out to where I was. He reached out and, grabbing me by the wrist unceremoniously threw me in the general direction of the beach.

'Run for your life!' he yelled at me. I goose-stepped to the beach in thigh-deep water while Jack back-pedaled keeping a constant lookout for the shark in case it returned for another attempt. We eventually both made it to the safety of the beach, breathless, badly frightened, but enormously relieved. Our laughter was due more to shock and relief than from humour. We dug a small fresh-water pool in the sand high up on the beach and rinsed the salt water from ourselves.

Later that afternoon I left Jack at the camp, took the surf fishing rod, and sauntered down to the same beach to see what unfortunate marine life would pay the ultimate sacrifice. I hooked something quite large and worked away at beaching it, but it snapped the light line. The damn reel also kept wobbling and getting the line tangled. I tied another rig to the line and the bait was again taken after about twenty minutes, but the line again snapped.

On the third attempt I finally had it on the beach. I had caught the same shark that had given me trouble earlier that day. It was very satisfying to haul it in successfully. It was about a metre and a half long. I saw Jack at the camp about two hundred metres away intently gazing far out to sea again while gingerly nursing a hangover. I called out to him but he didn't seem to hear me again. I left the hook in the shark's mouth and started dragging it back to camp triumphantly.

As I approached camp, I was huffing and puffing away from dragging the live shark behind me. It was thrashing around trying to throw the hook from its mouth. I finally got into camp and, at last, got Jack's attention.

'Look what I've caught!' I roared at him. Jack slowly turned around and looked at the shark with some amazement.

'What on earth are you going to do with it now?' he asked me, quite bewildered he was.

'I'm going to kill it, gut it, skin it, fillet it, cook it and devour it!' I roared back at him.

'Count me out. I'll watch' said Jack.

Killing it was somewhat more difficult than I had anticipated. It was still very much alive and kept snapping its jaws at me when I came too close. I tried stabbing it with a sharp, pointed knife but the hide was tough and impenetrable. It still kept snapping away at me.

If she wants to learn how to survive in the bush, then now is a good a time as any to learn how to kill, for that is what she will have to do at times, Jack thought, and then silently handed me the hand-axe which was lying next to the campfire.

I finally bludgeoned the shark to death, first stunning it into submission with an almighty blow with the blunt end of the axe and continuing until all signs of resistance had ceased, and it finally lay lifeless at my feet. Jack sat quietly and calmly on his fold-up chair and looked on with mild amusement as he sipped away at a mug of wine.

Quite the worst job was gutting it. The stomach contents smelt absolutely ghastly! I gagged many times and came very close to throwing up my lunch but my determination kept me going until it was finally gutted. I then took it down to the water's edge and cleaned it in the brine.

Stripping the skin off was equally as difficult. At first I tried tearing the tough skin off with my bare hands, but I kept losing my grip. I then tried cutting the skin away with a knife, but that too proved equally unsuccessful.

Finally Jack handed me two pairs of stout pliers from the tool box, again silently. The skin came away quite easily with the pliers much to my surprise. The next job was to cut fillets from it, which proved to be easy. I then diced the flesh into cubes and cooked it with garlic, salt, pepper and wine. It was delicious, the flesh tender and delicate. Accompanied by a mug of wine I absolutely gorged myself. Jack had a can of bully beef for dinner - straight out of the tin. We had a nice camp fire at last and temporarily any hard feelings were forgotten. It had been one hell of a day, believe you me. One hell of a day!

The next morning I took off on one of my long walks alone, this time south along the beach. To my absolute surprise and delight I found a nautilus shell in pristine condition amongst the flotsam and jetsam washed up by a cyclone the previous March. We had intended to clear and burn the debris which polluted the beach but unfortunately never did get around to doing it.

The amount of blown-out rubber sandals amongst the debris was astonishing. There were some savage looking shark teeth marks on many of the plastic bottles also washed up on the beach. There was also a great deal of pumicestone on the beaches which had been spewed out of one of the underwater volcanoes somewhere in the South Pacific Ocean, had floated to the surface, and finally had been deposited on Somerset Beach carried there by sea currents and wind.

I found a superb spot back in the sand dunes with plenty of shade to while away the time. The honey-eaters in the mangroves, the butterflies and rainforest were all so close, and I continued to dream.

That afternoon we packed up camp with regret and departed Somerset, the very tip of Cape York our next destination. It was sad to leave Somerset after a week there, but we did want, and were indeed badly in need of, a cold beer and a hot shower in exactly that order.

I could have lasted at Somerset forever!

Chapter Thirteen

Before we took the beach drive to the south we had a quick shot at fishing a little further north opposite Albany Island. The hot sun, strong winds and extremely strong current perhaps had something to do with us catching nothing. We did manage to lose any amount of hooks, line and sinkers.

The views across to Albany Island and up to the tip were magnificent. A pair of large leatherback sea turtles lazily cruised by us giving us a good look every now and then. The previous day we had tried to find a cave with Aboriginal paintings in the area but unsuccessfully so.

We took the south scenic route in order to avoid the rickety bridge. At one stage we had to negotiate a particularly nasty stretch of large boulders which rearranged the Toyota's cosmetics and left a few 'crocodile bites' for us to remember them by.

En route to the tip the Toyota's engine spluttered and died - the fuel tank was bone dry. Emptying the fuel from our last remaining jerry can into the tank was a ghastly business. Jack made me hold the funnel steady while he poured petrol from the jerry can. I protested furiously, gagging, spluttering and spitting with the petrol fumes filling my mouth, nostrils and lungs. He made very sure that I was standing downwind.

'Real girls don't pump gas,' he said to me with a nasty looking grin on his face. How terribly right he was!

We drove as far north as the road allowed us to go and finally ended up at a campsite filled with group tours. Again there were people everywhere, which put paid to our visions of setting up camp there. The pies and tea served at the kiosk by an English lass was very civilised and much appreciated.

We set off on foot along the tortuous footpath to the very tip of Cape York, the most northerly point of Australia. It took us about twenty minutes through the rainforest to get to the beach. Gripping our Akubras in the fresh wind, we clambered up the rocky slope.

It was a breathtaking sight from on high. The most beautiful vista enfolded the higher we climbed. To the west was the longest, whitest, widest beach I had ever seen. To the south the distant hills wore a thick cloak of vegetation. We could see the northern tip of Albany Island to the east and

Papua New Guinea was only a hundred and fifty kilometres across the Torres Strait. To the north, some three hundred metres away, was the end of the line - Cape York.

We walked along the rocks to the very tip. Dipping our feet into the water we could walk no further. We had made it.

The only other person around was a German tourist who kindly took a photograph of the two of us. Wandering back to the Toyota we took a leisurely stroll along the beach and dipped our toes in the clear, warm water again. It was hot, the sea was glistening, and there was no-one else around. We stopped for another fill of tea at the kiosk before heading for Bamaga, and then on to Seisia, some six kilometres west of Bamaga. The road passed though magnificent thick rainforest.

We pulled up at Bamaga but, unfortunately, once again, it was Sunday. Except for the wet community canteen and Jacky Jacky's cafe everything, including the fuel station, was again closed. We dived into chicken and chips once more as before.

I phoned my mum from Bamaga. She was very glad to hear from me and we decided that the regular phone calls were no longer necessary. I was quite relieved about that. The annual family picnic was, at the time I called, in progress at home where the entire family gathered every year for the weekend - about 100 of them. I would have loved to have been there, but the adventure had to continue as long as Jack and I could resolve our differences.

Jack did some more fuel and distance calculations and shrugged his shoulders in resignation. We headed for Seisia.

What a dump it turned out to be compared to Somerset and the other places we had been to. Why couldn't they make civilised places civilised? We set up camp in the camping ground together with some hundred other people and three noisy, unsilenced electricity generating sets.

The hot shower that we had so eagerly been looking forward to turned out to be cold. It had been in Rokeby, two weeks previously, that we had last had a shower let alone a hot one. From the time we left Rokeby we had taken our baths in freshwater creeks and rivers. The red dust churned up by traffic soon settled on our bodies as trucks continually sped in and out of camp ferrying yet more people in.

We celebrated our reaching the tip of Cape York that night with two bottles of champagne we had nursed all the way from Cairns and we both got rather sozzled. I crawled into the tent just as everyone else was starting the evening's entertainment leaving Jack sitting by the campfire with his thoughts.

Then the nightmare of Seisia with its emotional turmoil began. Jack and I had an appalling divorce from the time of our arrival three days previously. I had decided to ignore his quiet and cutting comments by starting to laugh and sing and I tried to act normally to see what would happen.

The trouble was that I could never understand what he was thinking about which resulted in us going through a mass malcommunication phase. One evening he burst forth blaming his fatigue on my demanding character. I knew something was up, and I suspected that it was probably I that was upsetting him, but I didn't expect him to say it right out aloud. He did! I wish he had not kept his thoughts and feelings back from me for so long. He had changed so much from the time we arrived at Seisia.

All I could do was to apologise for the foul-mouthed, impatient, intolerant, interfering bitch I had been so that our plans to visit the Northern Territory and Kimberley would not be erased. He wanted to do it without me I guessed. I fully realised then, and bitterly regretted, how big and insufferable a bitch I had really been. He had been enduring it in tolerant, polite silence.

He had been keeping such a lot back from me. Suddenly I felt extremely lonely and all I wanted to do was to fly back to Cairns and to mingle with people who treated me for who I was.

How can we possibly survive each other another day? I repeatedly asked myself as I miserably crawled into my sleeping bag that night. Jack had shown not the slightest indication of remorse all that time. He was behaving totally out of his normal character. In fact, he had become an abominably unbearable, insufferable, unforgiving bastard. And he hadn't yet started working on my case, as I was to find out later.

Deep down I strongly suspected that he was curing my one-to-one relationship and spoilt brat problem that I had told him about, and which he had promised to fix. I didn't at all like the medicine he was dispensing in massive overdoses. This wasn't the real Jack that I knew he could be, and actually was. For the first time in my life I was utterly and completely powerless to do anything about a situation I didn't like.

The following morning we were sitting around the campfire having early morning coffee in stony silence. Jack was very deep in painful thought.

'Juliette, I believe the time has come for us to go our separate ways,' Jack said. 'I have carefully considered my position and responsibilities and I have decided that my obligation to you, with regard to getting to Cape York, has been fulfilled. We have been away for nearly four weeks and I feel that I now have a need to be totally alone and I wish to continue the journey accordingly. I have no idea at present what I will be doing or where I will be going to from here. I now want you to get your things together and I will take you to the air terminal to ensure that you are on your way back to Cairns and to the safety of civilisation.'

Never before in all my life had I felt so deeply hurt and totally shocked. I had just been dumped for the first time in my life! I had always been the dumper - many times.

We then drove to the airline office in Bamaga to check on flights and fares back to Cairns. Jack insisted that I had to pay for the airfare to which I objected strongly. The next flight was the following day - the fare was two hundred and fifty dollars. We drove back to Seisia in further stony silence.

On our arrival back at Seisia I inquired at the kiosk if any trading ships were due and bound for Cairns in the next few days. A vessel was due to arrive the next day I was told. I decided to approach the master then to ask if they had a vacant berth back to Cairns.

Jack had problems I couldn't help him with. If only I could have. I promised him that I wouldn't pout and throw temper tantrums anymore. I also told him that he could make all future decisions without my interference. Suddenly an excellent four weeks, that I most certainly didn't want to end, had lost its momentum and fun. We no longer laughed, I scowled, and he ignored me which made me even more livid.

Suddenly I remembered a vital piece of wisdom from a bereavement counselling course I had done:

Be there. Just be there, and give them all the space they need. I recalled. Jack simply slept through it all - sixteen hours and more a day.

At last I managed to get a bit of a birdwatch and I saw a mistletoe-bird. I had a nice walk along the beach at nightfall on my own and I was quite content as I had just started to enjoy Seisia. The locals fishing off the pier told me that crocodiles came up onto the beach at night.

That evening I witnessed the most peculiar event. A guy with super heavy fishing tackle hooked a monstrous twelve foot grey shark in the dorsal fin which took him an hour and a half to reel in to the surface off the pier. The poor shark was so exhausted it just limply hung there not even attempting to flick a fin.

The fisherman was in no better condition, although he did put up a brave front for the crowd of spectators. He worked the shark carefully around the pier, finally manoeuvring it almost onto the beach where a further struggle ensued. The shark made a last desperate bid for its life finally shaking the hook from its dorsal fin. It took some time to realise that it was free, and then slowly, and very tiredly, swam off.

'Why?' it must have thought as it disappeared beneath the surface grateful that it had secured its freedom at last.

I tried to enjoy the other company in Seisia so I spoke to the locals who were such a happy and contented people. I laughed for the first time in a long while at the pier at a very large bat that had been caught on a handline. The bat, with almost a metre of wingspan, had, in mid-air, taken the bait of a fisherman when it was being cast into the sea.

The children dived off the pier into shark and crocodile infested waters to harpoon squid for bait. The pier was where the locals all met, everyone including Granny and everyday socialising was done there. I noticed that the Torres Strait Islanders had a darker skin than mainland Australian Aborigines.

I threw in a line, had a few bites, but caught nothing. I had only seen four fish being caught, but there were masses of them out there as they jumped all over the place, They continued to be very elusive - far too elusive for me.

Jack simply continued to sleep through the first four days at Seisia. How he did it with the wind, rain, dust and generator noise as background totally amazed me - and didn't he sleep! On the fifth day I decided that enough was enough and I insisted we got out of Seisia.

We visited Punsand Bay further up the west coast with its magnificent shells on the beach and views of the Cape. It was a rough road for the Toyota on the relatively unused track but a paradise if ever there was one. Jack and I went for a long walk on the beach. We walked a long way apart.

On our return via Bamaga I posted a letter to my parents telling them that the trip had come to an end and that I was returning to Cairns the following day. We returned to Seisia in continued silence.

At last, that evening, I could bear the agony no longer. Jack was sitting in the driver's seat of the Toyota fiddling away on the two-way radio, more to isolate himself from me than for any other reason.

I went to the passenger side door, opened it, and then told him exactly how I felt about the sense of injustice I believed he was inflicting on me. I couldn't believe he wanted me to get the first plane or boat out of Seisia back to Cairns. I did this in a two minute soliloquy drawing on my most deepest and innermost feelings and emotions. When I had finished, I was utterly astounded at the amazingly eloquent manner I found that I had expressed myself.

Jack said nothing. He just sat in the Toyota listening to me quite impassively. He stared straight ahead of him into the darkness looking utterly miserable and dejected. There was no response from him whatsoever throughout my passionate pleadings. I had pleaded with him not to ruin what was for me the most incredible realisation of a never-to-be repeated odyssey - the most fascinating adventure of my life. It could, in all probability, have been my last.

He had so much hurt, grief and injustice dealt out to him, not only recently, but also throughout his lifetime. If only I could find a way to make him understand that I didn't want to hurt him.

The prolonged silence was deafening. Silently screaming with rage, frustration and anger I looked fiercely and intensely at him.

'Why? Why? Why?' I cried out, repeatedly beating the seat with my fists.

'You're a Pommie basher!' I shouted at him even though he never ever laid an angry hand on me.

Totally drained of all emotion, anger and frustration, and utterly exhausted, I threw my arms on the passenger seat and wept for the first time in two years and never so bitterly in all my life. Still Jack said nothing.

After what seemed an eternity, Jack slowly and deliberately climbed out and walked around the front of the vehicle until he stood next to me where I was hunched over the front seat still weeping bitterly. His mind was racing, searching for solutions. Alas, there were none.

He put his hands on my shoulders and turned me around to face him. He looked intently at my tear-stained face for a long time.

He took me in his arms as I again sobbed deeply and shaking to my very inner being. When my sobs had subsided he gently kissed me on the forehead. Taking the front of his shirt out he carefully wiped the tears and snot off my face. He then again put his arms around me and held me close to him as I continued to sob. When I had stopped sobbing it felt so very good.

I then determinedly demanded that we went for a cool drink in Bamaga. We drove the six or so kilometres into Bamaga, walked into the community canteen and took up position at the bar counter. Jack then ordered two beers from the Islander barmaid. Six local Aborigine and Islander lads apparently weren't too keen to stay up at the bar too close to us. They preferred to move to a table further away and to eye us from a distance. They then started playing pool.

The most wonderful transformation of our characters started happening as we chatted over several beers. It felt as if an enormous burden had been lifted off my shoulders. Jack revealed some more about himself and how he was still grieving the death of his daughter and said that he couldn't help it.

'What I need most of all is space and solitude. The last thing I need at the moment is a troublesome woman in my life. If we can't have a non-judgmental, non-demanding and harmonious companionship, then there is no point in continuing the journey together. The odd bit of affection and a bit of visible caring for my well-being would also be most welcome. If we have it otherwise, you fly back to Cairns first thing in the morning,' he said to me.

'Being the take-charge type, you should take charge of your destrudo', he also told me. I reflected momentarily.

'That sounds like the ancient, philosophical expression of hurting the ones that you love most dearly,' I replied.

'It is all one and the same thing. It is also the very thing that does one's self the most harm,' Jack said. The Bamaga locals looked on silently as they listened to this strange conversation.

I begged him to let my dream come true and pleaded with him to give me a chance. He gave no answers to those pleas. We continued to talk positively, effectively and openly far into the night about relationships and what made them work.

'Something else we will have to deal with is the fact that we are both exceptionally highly endowed with personal power, intelligence, integrity and forthrightness. This is something we can utilise in a positive and effective way such that we can both benefit from it enormously. If we don't recognise and accept this fact and we mismanage it, then it has the potential to totally destroy both of us,' he concluded.

We went to sleep feeling much better for it, but I was still totally uncertain as to the outcome. I didn't know whether Jack wanted me to go with him or not, or even if he was going anywhere at all.

I didn't think that he knew either. In fact, I now know that he didn't know then. I knew that he would, in all likelihood, head off alone without telling anyone, drive deep into the bush to some totally inaccessible place until he ran out of fuel, then go walkabout without water until he died like some terminally wounded animal. I couldn't allow that to happen to him.

Early the following morning I took the initiative to find out if I could return to Cairns on the cargo ship. Jack was still fast asleep as I arose, was dressed, and walked to the wharf. I first asked the second mate about the possibility of a berth to Cairns. He then went off to discuss the matter with the master.

'Yes,' was his thankful answer on his return. 'You can go as long as you didn't mind sleeping in the radio room and helping the crew out occasionally'. Miserably I organised a berth - it was to cost $240 for three nights to Cairns via Thursday Island.

It sounded like a great adventure and a definite alternative so I approached Jack with confidence. Arriving back at camp I found him sitting by the early morning campfire contemplatively drinking a mug of tea and staring intently into the fire.

'I have secured a berth on the ship that is departing tomorrow morning. You must now decide what was best for you,' I said to him, not knowing what he was going to say.

There was a long, painful silence.

'Do you know what occasionally helping the crew out might mean?' Jack asked me.

'No,' I replied innocently. I hadn't thought about that.

'Let's pack up and get the hell out of this miserable dump,' he eventually said and tossed the remains of his tea into the fire as he stood up. I was thrilled to hear those words. I threw my arms around him in delight and gave him a big hug. He didn't even give me one back so surprised he was.

We were packed and ready to go in ten minutes flat. We said goodbye, and thanks, to the second mate on the ship and the girls at the kiosk, and we were back on the track, very content, soon thereafter. A miracle had occurred!

In Bamaga we bought provisions and fuel for the six hundred and fifty kilometre haul to Iron Range National Park on the east coast. It was a long haul with no fuel supplies anywhere in between. We knew that the Toyota had a four hundred and fifty kilometre range in four-wheel-drive on a full tank. The forty litres in the jerry cans would get us to Lockhart River Aboriginal settlement with very little fuel to spare.

A short distance out of Bamaga we took the wrong turning. Jack, who was driving, mentioned that the terrain was vaguely unfamiliar to him and asked me to check my navigation.

'Straight ahead! Its O. K!' I cheerfully said with every confidence.

The next thing, horror of horrors, the Bamaga airport was in our way! Not only was that dreaded airstrip the last thing in the world I wanted to see, but my navigation skills had failed me yet again, this time on the most critical of all the destinations we had.

Will he change his mind? I thought, fearing that he might. We back-tracked to the junction and headed south into more familiar terrain. We saw a large, fat, lazy python called a carpet snake slithering across the road as well as a blue-tongued lizard basking in the sun.

At the Jardine River ferry crossing we were recognised by the ferryman who had been one of the chaps playing pool in the wet canteen in Bamaga the previous night. I had so wanted to talk to some Aboriginal people but they always appeared to be aloof when white people were nearby.

A short distance south of the ferry crossing, while Jack was driving, we accidentally ran over a small, black snake crossing the road. It was writhing in agony, had clearly been mortally wounded, and had to be put out of its misery.

Jack reversed the Toyota running over it again and then, from some thirty metres away, rushed at it locking the brakes as the wheels went over it a third time crushing and mangling it completely. We kept driving on. I spoke to Jack but there was no reply. I looked at him and saw tears running down his cheeks. He hated killing things needlessly.

We got to the junction of the Old Telegraph Line track fondly known as the *Fun Run* and the newly renamed *Death Alley* track where the lunatics play *chicken* and wipe themselves out. No major decisions were necessary there. A right hand turn onto the old track and on to Sailor's Creek we went. There was not much water flowing; a lot of mud and loose, wet sand, but Yea Gods! A one and a half metre near-vertical exit!

It will break the front end suspension to smithereens no matter which way we approached it, I thought. It wasn't like that when we were headed north, but the exit was an entry then. Jack took a wander upstream on foot, came back, drove upstream for a hundred metres or so where he had found a clear run, and we were through the creek and back on dry land in a jiffy.

We set up camp on the north bank of the by-now notorious Cockatoo Creek on a delightful shady patch not far from all the action. We arrived in time to watch the other jokers bog themselves in sand and mud.

We met Danny Chew, the Relief Ranger at the nearby Heathlands Ranger Station who was on his way home from a trip to the remote eastern part of the Jardine National Park. We invited him over to our camp for a cup of tea and a nosh that evening if, for any reason, the traffic prevented him from crossing that night.

Danny was a good laugh and started teasing me immediately, subtly probing and exposing sensitive aspects of my life. I found that it was a pleasant change, but it certainly got me to sit up and take note of a few things. He was a very sharp people observer was our Danny. He in turn invited, nay, insisted that we stop over at the Ranger Station at Heathlands on our way through. We had missed them on the way up due to missing the turn off and ending up at Gunshot Creek instead.

Swimming in Cockatoo Creek was so refreshing. The friar birds and parrots were doing their evensong - it was so good to be back with the birds again. Who would have believed it the day before?

A short ten metre walk from our campsite was a vantage point overlooking the river crossing where we had our meals while watching all the hilarious goings-on below us. One afternoon, while we were having a late lunch, a two vehicle party heading north fell into the south side bog.

The men were furiously thrashing about in knee-deep mud attempting to extract their vehicles. They were ably assisted by more than adequate technical expert advice from their middle-aged spouses. A short, but firm, verbal exchange followed and the two very muddy and somewhat disillusioned ladies then set themselves down on a rock across the river from us muttering veiled threats while generally contemplating their marital future.

Jack and I were discussing some other totally unrelated comedy at the time, laughing hilariously as we did, when one of the ladies took great exception to our apparent lack of sympathy to their plight. Standing on a rock across the river, with her hands on her ample hips and her feet firmly on the rock, she inquired as to the source of our mirth. This focused our full attention on what was happening down below us for the first time. The comedy of it all totally overcame us both and for a long time we were unable to respond to her irate inquiry.

Not long afterward a north bound party in a Land Rover arrived on the south side. The driver deflated his tyres in preparation for the deep, loose sand on the northern exit, got through the bog, plunged into the river and found that he had deflated his rear tyres too much. They both bumped through on the sharp, rocky river bed and the air fizzled and bubbled through the water and then stopped. He had to change the two rear wheels in knee-deep water before attempting, six times, to clear the sandy exit and blocking traffic all the while.

So the victims of Cockatoo Creek fell one after the other, dozens upon dozens of them. We saw Mike, the Chief Ranger, going through on his way south to Coen late one afternoon, but he had disappeared before we could talk to him. He didn't get bogged down. Pity though, we could otherwise have had a chat with him then.

We passed the days reading and taking our lunch down to the river to watch the other jokers. Our neighbours were delightful people and we spent a lot of time talking with them about their various trips around Australia. They were equipped with two dogs, a silenced Honda generating set and a deep-freeze. One of the men had worked in Papua New Guinea before and had some very interesting stories to tell.

One evening we were sitting around the campfire sipping a mug of tea and enjoying the sunset. It was so peaceful and tranquil. Jack quite unexpectedly started telling me another story in the life of Lighty.

'He stared down, one-eyed, at the still-life scene before him. It was a bitterly cold winter's morning, the sun yet come up over the horizon. His father had unexpectedly aroused him from a deep sleep at five o'clock that morning, had dressed him in his khaki school clothes, and had taken him, barefoot, by the hand, and led him in silence to the front lawn.

They had been friends for five years, from the time his father had brought a little warm, squirming, bundle of black and tan fluff home and had given it to him when he was two years old. The chubby little bundle had licked his face and kept on licking - slurp, slurp, slurp.

He sat down on his haunches and stroked the white frost off Tony's chest. Again, and again, and again, he stroked until his hand was painless from the cold and nearly as frozen stiff as the Alsatian dog was. Tony lay frozen, cold, still, stiff and dead on the white, frost-covered lawn.

'Don't touch the bone in his mouth. It probably has cyanide on it. It is probably those chicken thieves who did it,' his father told him. His father removed the bone from Tony's mouth and went to the shed to fetch a hessian sack to put Tony's body into.

He remembered then. He remembered a lot. He remembered all the snakes that Tony had killed to save him and John from harm and certain death. Those five years were a very, very long time, and they had gone along some long, dry, and dusty roads together. Many, many of them. And many, many happy ones too. More happy ones than the other kind. Many, many more.

And he knows that John, Tony and Jock of the Bushveld are *Up there* chasing puff adders, and night adders, and kudu, and impala. And running away from mambas, and cobra, and lion, and leopard. Very fast.

Tony was the best goddamn snake dog that ever lived. And Lighty knows that one day, one day'

My thoughts suddenly went out to my Labrador, Candy at home. She was starting to get along a bit and I hoped that she would still be there when I eventually got back to England sometime.

I then heard Jack murmur something, or was it a sob that I heard? I looked at him and there were tears pouring down his cheeks. He looked so sad. I asked him what was wrong, afraid of how he was going to respond. He took out his wallet and opened it. He took something out and slowly handed it to me. In my hand was a small, white baby's bootie.

'That is all I have left,' Jack said.

I had never in my life encountered any man experience such deep grief and express such uninhibited emotion. He cried for a long time on my shoulder until there were no tears left to shed. He then took the bootie back and carefully replaced it in his wallet. It was my turn to tidy up the snot and tears.

Jack then started opening up more and more as time went by. He told me more about his background and experiences in Africa, Australia, Indonesia and Borneo. I had a great deal of difficulty believing some of the things he told me initially.

Over a campfire late one night he told me that he was going to track down this happy little chappie he once knew named Lighty. He said that he would write about Lighty one day. I made him take a solemn, sworn oath that he would definitely do so.

As time went by I started to look very hard at this strange and silent man with an unshakeable belief in himself and his moral and social values. He had a deeply-seated, inseparable affinity with black people. His Swazi wet-nurse and nanny Katie had firmly entrenched that trait in him. He just looked very hard at a rock in the ground.

Chapter Fourteen

After three days of lazing around at Cockatoo Creek it was time to move on. We had a refreshing swim in a lovely section of Cockatoo Creek before setting off. Danny had warned us to beware of crocodiles in that particular tranquil section of the river below the crossing.

We broke camp between rain showers and then spent seven hours on the road from ten o'clock in the morning to five o'clock that afternoon. The drive was fun, especially around the Heathlands area, the alternative and safer route that avoided Gunshot Creek. The area was flat, wide, open and green. The wind howled in from the southeast, refreshing and invigorating.

We stopped in on the Ranger station to see Danny and Donna the Rangers. Danny was out on patrol again clearing the rubbish at the main campsite at Twin Falls in the Jardine National Park. We did not envy him this distasteful but necessary task. Donna was superb company and very chatty. She cheerfully made us a cup of tea and served up some of her home-made biscuits.

What a treat it all was. It all felt so peculiar to again be in a strange, orderly domestic environment. There were real chairs to sit on and a real table to sit at, all in a well-equipped kitchen. She then showed us the out-buildings and sheds once used by cattle drovers, but then used by occasional visitors. I had to persuade Jack to let us stay with Donna for as long as we possibly could as I knew it would be a lot of fun. They had lived there from 1985 for three and a half years and were relieving the Ranger who was away on annual leave at the time.

Donna talked a lot about the wet season when there were no people around. The only people who did arrive at the station in the wet season were in the mail plane which arrived once a week with mail and occasionally with spare vehicle parts, emergency groceries and medical supplies.

During the wet season Heathlands is perpetually shrouded in mist, the only variation to the weather being regular heavy downpours of rain. Very rarely does the sun shine there in the wet.

Before the wet starts an enormous grocery shopping list for a five month period is posted to Cairns some nine hundred kilometres away. The shopping list is processed and a massive delivery is trucked from Cairns - a four day trip. The larder is stocked until it is bulging at the seams. A five month supply of fuel is also trucked in.

They then prepare themselves mentally for the five month long hot and wet isolation. To venture out too far in a vehicle is virtually tantamount to suicide. Vehicles are garaged and walking is the primary means of transport. It is also the most dependable and reliable.

The only communication before the advent of microwave towers was the Royal Flying Doctor Service radios. The R. F. D. S. transceiver radio has a frequency that is used by the women during specific times of the day to have a chat with the other ladies in the area. The men have their turn to socialise in the evenings. The School of the Air is on during the daytime where the children take up position in the 'classroom' in the house, turn on the two-way radio, and say 'Good Morning Miss' to the teacher some one thousand kilometres away.

Donna so wanted us to stay over for a few days. She said that very rarely do people like us call in and it could be very lonely for her at times. Rarely did she have the company of another woman to discuss the things that women generally talk about. She told us that Danny had instructed her to ensure that we stayed so that he could also have some decent company and conversation when he returned. We really wanted to stop over for a while, but we stupidly deprived them of a single night of our company. We had a landing barge to catch in Weipa, some ten or twelve days away, and we still had to get into, and out of, Iron Range National Park.

The road into and out of Iron Range was known to be horrifying and we didn't know what to expect. We had met no-one who had been either in or out, and that was a fair reflection of the state of the track. Mike, the Chief Ranger at Coen, had advised us not to attempt the track from Archer River into Iron Range on our way north, but to assess the position on our return before going in. Sorry Danny and Donna. We too have deprived ourselves and, with hindsight, we profusely apologise for our folly.

I would have done anything to stay, and so would Jack have, but he was quite firm about it. It was the first time we had reason to feel a sense of urgency, as a ship would not delay departure for late arrivals. If we missed the boat, it would have meant a long, four day drive back down the track in the heat and the sand and the dust and the flies - one thousand, two hundred kilometres of it to Normanton. We had seen it all before and it was all more of the same.

Donna looked so sad and forlorn when we left. She couldn't understand our haste. She had to put up with so many demanding, ungrateful and downright rude tourists day in and day out. How little we seemed to appreciate the courageous, tenacious and resilient people who maintain a wilderness environment for our enjoyment. It must be soul destroying never to get as much as a thank you from anyone.

We were soon back on the old Telegraph Road again. The track south was now familiar as I drove through the dreadfully boggy Bertie and North Alice Creeks. Bertie Creek was a rather interesting crossing. The water was about a metre deep but we had to enter the creek, head downstream for a hundred or so metres in mud and soft river bed sand, all under water, and roar out the other end. Formidable.

There were about six north bound vehicles on the south side with an equal number of anxious looking men of all ages furiously pacing up and down the river sizing the situation up, and all looking for the best possible way to negotiate the monster. Their now-familiar over-anxious spouses ably assisted them.

I got out of the Toyota, took a quick look around, and then got back in. Jack just sat, unmoving and disinterested, in the passenger seat.

'Well, what are we waiting for? Let's go!' he barked at me.

'I will show him what I can do!' I determinedly reassured myself and turned off all ancillaries to obtain maximum power. Engaging low four wheel drive I plunged into the river. Water, mud and sand flew everywhere. Wind screen wipers flying at high speed, but rendered totally ineffectual with the deluge of mud and water.

'The rev counter reads four thousand revs per minute. Too high. Change up into second gear and drop the clutch. The gear lever disengaged - it had not engaged properly. We have no traction! The engine screams in protest. Depress the clutch. Gently ease the gear lever into second. Engage without as much as a grate.' I spoke to myself. Jack sitting quietly in the passenger seats observing passively. Not a murmur from him.

Blurred windscreen, three thousand five hundred revs per minute on the rev counter, leaping to the critical five thousand when we loose traction. Slipping and sliding sideways, but slowly forward, in mud towards the high south side bank. Correct with opposite lock. The steering and front wheels won't respond! Decelerate, the front tyres bite a mere half metre from the bank. Foot down gently - power on the ground. An over-correction with too much power. Correct left. Gently she comes around.

Back on line again. The windscreen clears for a second. I see the forty degree exit thirty metres away. It is two metres high and very slippery. It seems to have near vertical sides to it. Indentations of a vehicle in the bank where some unfortunate soul had lost it. Mother Mary don't desert me!

Get the speed and the approach angle right girl. If only I could see where I was going to, let alone see where I want to go! A swift left-hander. The rear wheels loose traction. The front wheels grip and drag us around. Square on approach! Power to the ground, gently, ever so gently. Nearly there.

The front wheels hit the bank with a mighty thud. The front suspension protests loudly. Hold, hold. Please don't break truck. The front wheels are in the air. The rear wheels hit the bank. They can go no further. The rubber buffers on the chassis absorb the rest of the impact. A horrifying, bone jarring, spine chilling shudder is transmitted through the whole vehicle. Please don't break truck!

The front wheels come to earth with a bang. They grip on some firm ground. Traction on all four wheels. Gentle with the accelerator. Not too much power or we slide into oblivion. The wheels slip, and then bite, and the Toyota slews drunkenly from side to side.

You need to be a multi-dexterous octopus to drive this beast what with hands and feet flailing around as if I was having a violent catatonic fit. The front wheels bite on hard ground near the top of the rise and the Toyota comes rocketing out like a cork from a champagne bottle. I have made it!'

I parked under a shady tree leaving the engine running to dry out the electrics before resuming my breathing. The men came over to the driver's side presumably to inquire of us how we did it. As we jumped out to stretch our legs I got some dazed, stunned, amazed and utter disbelieving stares from the men who had been pacing up and down the bank for hours trying to work out a route through the quagmire.

'A sheila driving in that? That is supposed to be a man's job! She is only knee high to a grasshopper. Her feet couldn't possibly reach the pedals,' I hear them mutter.

'Have you guys got a problem?' I asked casually as they dispersed without as much as a 'G'dayhowyegoin'mate?'

We laughed a lot, especially at the couples whose divorces had been suddenly accelerated and indeed, appeared to be imminent! The ladies were not backward in coming forward with new-found confidence. The language and tone was enough to curdle the milk.

I felt absolutely elated, the adrenalin still roaring in my ears. Giggling like a schoolgirl due to the adrenalin overdose I pretended that this was an everyday event. My head held high, I was ten feet tall!

Further down the road, while Jack was driving, some lunatic in a Nissan Patrol came hurtling around a bend at breakneck speed and headed directly toward us on a very narrow section of track. The stretch was clear enough for them to see us approaching from afar. He, no doubt, was suffering the wrath of his spouse due to his excessive speed at the time and not paying much attention to what was ahead of him.

They were both probably wanting to get the nightmare over and done with as soon as possible. Jack slowed down to a crawl anticipating an event and prepared to take evasive action. The wife was doing an extraordinary amount of arm-waving and making her thoughts known in no uncertain terms. Suddenly the driver saw us, panicked, locked the brakes while going around the corner, lost control, and the Patrol took to the bush spectacularly and at very high speed.

How they managed to keep the vehicle upright without over-turning it no-one will ever know. Badly shaken and very frightened the two of them got out of the vehicle. We then witnessed the most ghastly spectacle as the wife who, in reality turned out to be the proverbial *Dreadful Boiler*, then really expressed her sentiments. The husband just stood feebly flapping his arms in the breeze but his anger, frustration, fright and sheer desperation was clearly apparent. Had he had a tyre lever in his hands we would have, without doubt, witnessed the bloodiest of murders. The same prediction similarly applied to the wife.

'Some astute divorce lawyer, marriage guidance counsellor and a psychotherapist should set up practices in Bamaga during the dry season. They would have their own mint and would be able to retire permanently, and in great comfort, within five years,' Jack casually observed once we were on the track again.

On our arrival at the Wenlock River late that afternoon we found heaps of people camping on the north bank. There were no vehicles crossing and the makeshift raft was unattended on the south side. We had planned to set up camp at the Wenlock but, on seeing all the people camped there, immediately decided against it. Without bothering to get out of the Toyota Jack engaged low four-wheel-drive.

'We'll go wide to the right where the sand has accumulated to form a bar,' Jack said and plunged in. The water splashed over the bonnet again.

'If we flood the engine now, it is all over' said Jack.

We groped our way out on the south side without mishap. Jack parked the Toyota and left the motor running. It gave a cough and a splutter but kept on idling. We got out to stretch our legs for a while and then continued south.

Near Batavia Downs we found the almost obscure turnoff to the left to Lockhart River and Iron Range National Park on the east coast of the peninsula. Until then we had not encountered, nor heard of, any party that had either gone in or out. We had no way of knowing what the track conditions were other than Mike's sage advice that it was dreadful, treacherous, and to exercise extreme caution. He had advised us to first wait for word of a successful exit - there had been none that we knew of. Jack examined the track for some hundred metres.

'Are you sure you want to proceed with this?' Jack asked me. 'Once we do a left hand turn here we are in the lap of the gods. We have enough fuel to reach Lockhart River, but only just so. There is even less to spare now than we had going from Archer River to Bamaga. Once in there is no turning back. There is no sign of any tracks going in, or out, at all, and certainly not any for at least a week. Weipa to the west is the alternative. I'm listening.'

'Hard left!' I said firmly, my stomach lurching as I said it without further thought. I was not going to be deprived of the magnificent birdlife in the Iron Ranges come hell or high water. We got all three of them in massive lumps.

The track to the upper reaches of the Wenlock River was comparatively easy going. We crossed the Wenlock for a third time. Fortunately the water was about seventy centimetres deep and the quantity was half of what it was at the previous crossing.

Once across, we set up camp for the night on the sandy riverbed. It was late in the afternoon and we were quite tired after a long seven hours on the road. The bird evensong was again magnificent. We boiled the billy for a well-earned mug of tea and listened to our feathered friends until it was well past dark.

The following morning we decided to extend our stay for another night to see if anyone would come through from Iron Range. There was an outside chance that another party might have been as silly as we were, and we optimistically thought that we might convoy with them. We were mistaken, for we saw no-one that day, nor the following morning.

'We have nowhere else to go now,' Jack said finally. 'We might as well go in for the slaughter. There is no point in delaying our fate,' he added between sips of early morning tea from our sleeping bags. We broke camp and went in. We had hardly gone twenty kilometres when Jack stopped the Toyota.

'She's not handling properly,' he said. The left rear tyre was flat and we had our first puncture, one that had bumped through rather than nailed. We had previously deflated all the tyres to twenty five pounds per square inch to better be enabled to maintain traction in loose sand. We changed wheels and continued.

Another five kilometres further, with the early morning sun in our eyes, and with a dirty windscreen, we hit a vicious bump in the road. The front wheels took to the air followed by the rear wheels and we were airborne. The entire Toyota was a metre and a half off the ground at one stage. We came down to earth with a mighty bang, the poor suspension taking another hammering and transferring the rest of the shock through to the bodywork.

It felt not dissimilar to dropping a few thousand feet in a light aircraft when hitting an air pocket. The only difference was that ours was a hard landing. Examining for mechanical damage we thankfully found all to be intact. Marvellous things they are Toyotas.

'Oh! What a feeling!' as the Toyota advertisements would lead us to believe was not quite the sort of soaring feeling we were meant to feel. We most certainly did identify with the badly ruffled choke in the television advertisements!

The interior was an utter shambles and in total disarray, ourselves included. One of us had loosely stacked a carton of a dozen eggs on top of one of the containers and the inevitable had happened. Everything in the back of the Toyota was covered in soggy egg. It was the most ghastly mess.

'I never carry eggs around,' said Jack. 'I don't know what made us do it this time.'

Onward ho we continued eventually meeting a single-vehicle party coming out of Iron Range. We were elated to see one such vehicle and hoped to get some information from them about road conditions ahead. They flagged us down and stopped to talk to us.

'We went in from Archer River,' the gentleman told us sadly. 'We got past Mount Tozer, did some dreadful crossings, and then came upon about ten other vehicles, all coming out of Iron Range, and all bogged up to their armpits trying to come up a two hundred metre rise. There was no way we were going to venture in so we decided to give it all a big miss' he explained.

'Where to now?' I asked Jack.

'To the Archer River junction and another hard left into it all to Iron Range. Where else do we have to go?' he concluded.

The scenery from the Wenlock towards the hills of the Iron Range National Park was superb. We actually went up a real hill for the first time since we left Cooktown and we took in the wide panorama while we boiled the billy for a cuppa.

We then drove along a sort of plateau with views of bush-clad hills all around us. The thick, black, ominous cloud and rain falling on the Iron Ranges ahead of us was a warning of what lay ahead. It always rained in the Iron Ranges come wet or dry season. The task ahead looked decidedly daunting.

At the Archer River junction we headed east toward Mount Tozer which was so obscured by cloud and rain that we never saw it from a kilometre away. The track was wet but reasonably good. We then came upon the first really nasty crossing. Forty degrees in, forty degrees out, and five or six metres deep - all soaking wet with some very large strategically placed boulders scattered all around. It was bucketing down relentlessly.

'No vehicles other than that mob we met earlier have crossed here in days,' Jack said. 'I'm not looking forward to thrashing around with an egg-soaked hand-winch in this lot!'

We went in, got out, and went on again.

A few kilometres further we encountered the dismally sad sight we had been warned about. Fourteen vehicles by then, including a two-wheel-drive, antiquated Bedford truck belonging to some alternate lifestyle hippies from Chilly Beach, were there. It was all in total disarray and catastrophic looking.

Sitting on the back of the old Bedford were about four pre-school children drenched to the bone, crying, and very unhappy with their pitiful lot in life. The hippies had been stuck there for two days and were running short of supplies.

'See what you can find for the children in the back of the vehicle,' Jack recommended to me. I scrambled up a generous hamper for them and left it in the cab of the Bedford.

We were going downhill, this mob were going uphill. We were looking good.

'We were stranded at Chilly Beach for fourteen days,' the leader of one party told us woefully. 'The track out was four kilometres of deep mud. It took us a day and a half to cover those four kilometres after three dry days. I was supposed to start work again in Brisbane a week ago. No chance of that for at least another week. I have probably been fired by now' he continued sadly.

It all looked bleak and futile as there was not a single soul making any attempt whatsoever to extract themselves from the morass. Everyone had taken refuge from the deluge under haphazardly erected tarpaulin shelters.

We walked the two hundred metres down the hill. A dozen or more sad, dismal, frightened faces staring, not at us, but after us. We reached the bottom where there was a lone Nissan Patrol parked. It was the only one not yet bogged. They were recent arrivals and were in our way.

'Can you back up out of harm's way mate?' Jack politely asked him.

'Are you going in?' someone with a quavering voice asked from under a tarpaulin on the side of the track.

'Nowhere else to go,' I admitted to him.

'You're mad! Stark raving mad! Both of you!' came back from gaunt-eyed Quavering Voice.

'Fools rush in where wise men fear to tread...' someone else sang out to us as we passed by.

'All men are fools, many born to remain untouched they say. Wise men are created, for they know no other way,' Jack melodiously filled in as we walked on.

We strolled back up the hill all the while mentally picking our path and at the same time deluding ourselves that we were going to have some sort of control over what lay ahead of us.

'A man's got to do what a man's got to do,' said Jack. 'Coming for the ride?' he asked me.

'Girls also have their moments when they have to stand up and be counted,' I replied. We got into the Toyota and strapped ourselves in. Deep down I was regretting that we hadn't stopped over with Danny and Donna at Heathlands instead.

'Lets shake, rattle and rock 'n roll!' said Jack as we took off.

It was the understatement of the year. It was nigh on impossible to pick the deeper mud - it was purely a question of depth rather than a choice of either wet or dry. Picking our way through the deep mud holes, which we couldn't see, the string of stranded vehicles, and the boulders, was a nightmare.

We managed to miss all the vehicles but hit all the deep holes and a great many of the boulders. The crunching and grinding underneath the Toyota, as the rocks rearranged the cosmetics and ground off chunks of metal, was a very unpleasant sound indeed.

We reached the bottom of the hill, pulled up, and did a damage assessment as best we could. The thick coating of mud didn't make the job any easier. We could see nothing, so could find nothing wrong other than mudflaps at awkward angles and the right hand side running board bent like a banana. No oil leaks were evident. We were still looking good.

Another hundred metres further there were a second two hundred metres of downhill into a creek. It looked solid enough but very slippery. We slithered down the two hundred metres to the creek bed, snaked our way ever so gingerly into it, and roared out on the opposite bank.

We were going along merrily a little later, Jack and I chatting away, our confidence high, when Jack turned around to say something to me. He misjudged the right hand bend ahead of us. Turning too late, as well as perhaps going a bit too fast, we skidded out of control, crashed through a deep ditch, and stacked the Toyota into a metre and a half of soft, muddy embankment. He lost it completely.

1. *Ornithologist's Dream - Rokeby*
2. *Friendly Papuan Frogmouth Owls*
3. *Bob's Lagoon*

1. *Self-explanatory*

2. *Wally and Jack at Rokeby*

3. *Frog*

1. *Anthill*
2. *Tame Creek Crossing*
3. *Wenlock River*

1. *Gunshot Creek*

2. *Bogged It !*

3. *Jacuzzi*

4. *Carnivores*

154

1. *Near the Jardine River*

2. *Jardine River Ferry*

3. *Somerset*

1. *A long way apart*

2. *The Tip*

3. *We made it !*

1. *Upper Wenlock Camp*

2. *Having Fun*

1. *Happy Jack at Portland Roads*

2. *Palm Cockatoo*

3. *The Children - Lockhart River*

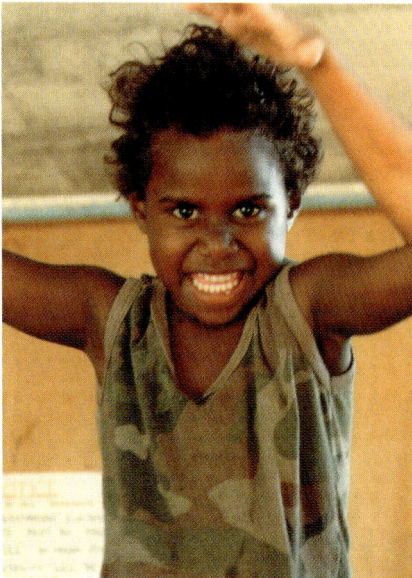

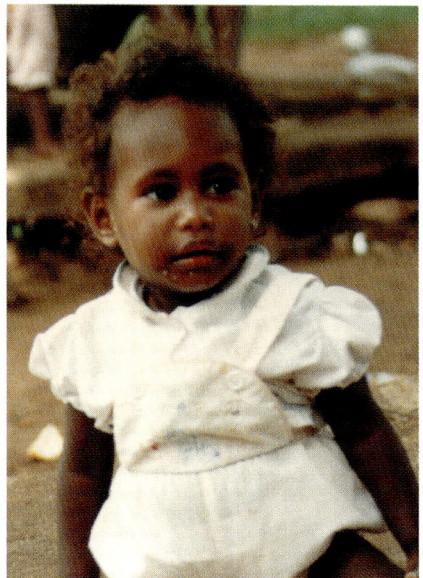

Chapter Fifteen

We got out to assess the sad situation. The Toyota was up to the axles and chassis in the dreadful mess. There was no traction whatsoever and no hope of backing out. There was no sense either trying to back out - the creek bed was twenty metres in front of us and that was the only way we could go. Twenty metres of one and a half metre deep filthy slosh to dig. It was late in the afternoon by then and raining bloody cats and dogs.

Jack took out the spade and began to dig, and dig, and dig, and dig. The slush kept falling back into the hole already dug. There were tree roots and stumps in the mud. It was back-lashing with the spade to make room for the real mud. It poured incessantly.

When a half-decent sized space was dug out the Toyota lunged forward at Jack. Jack was knee deep in mud and his legs were firmly implanted in the mud. His heart stopped and so did the Toyota - a centimetre away from his knees.

His heart started beating again, this time racing out of control. He dragged his left foot out of his boot and out of the mud. He embedded it again seven centimetres further away and the Toyota inched forward. He extracted his right leg, again bootless, and implanted it further down again. And he dug, and he dug. And the Toyota inched ever-forward.

I asked him how he was doing. He assured me that he was having a really fun time. And he dug. I took a photograph of him. He told me to stay well clear of, and behind, the Toyota. He told me to be prepared to put out a May Day call on the radio. The left front wheel came to rest against a tree root and the vehicle stopped sliding. And he dug. His heartbeat slowed down a little and he got further away from the vehicle. Then his legs were embedded up to his calves.

He stopped digging, got into the Toyota, and drove it out lurching, roaring, sliding, bucking, nearly rolling, down into the creek and out of it onto firm ground on the other side. He walked back to the creek where I joined him.

'Remember this patch for the return journey,' he said as we did our best to rinse the mud off ourselves. We were so badly frightened and shaken that we had forgotten that we had a winch on board and that it would have been far quicker, and safer, to have winched ourselves into the creek.

As we were about to continue, a Landcruiser utility truck with three Aborigines in it arrived from Lockhart River. They were on their way to Coen.

'We'll wait and see if we are needed,' said Jack. We were. They drove through the creek and bogged completely on the other side. We reversed the Toyota back into the creek and then pulled them out with the Snatchum strap. Three times they bogged, and three times we snatched them back out again. On the fourth attempt they made it out to the other bank. The *bossman* gave us a useful contact in Lockhart River to look at our punctured tyre.

We took our leave and continued on to Lockhart River. The patches of rainforest bog we encountered were also very exciting. I trusted Jack's confidence and competence totally and completely. He was so cheerful while I remained silent, kept my eyes closed, and held on tightly to the panic bar. My back was very sore.

It was late in the afternoon when we arrived at the shop at Lockhart River. We were tired, muddy, dripping wet and concerned about where to stay for the night. We were just in time to buy fuel which cost us $1.30 a litre. It cost us 80 cents on the track and in Bamaga, and $0.52 cents back in civilisation. It was shipped to Lockhart River in twenty litre drums by landing barge from Cairns.

Again we had to decant petrol from the drums into the Toyota. This time Jack diplomatically remained silent as we tried to prevent the rain from also getting into the fuel tank. I thoroughly detested the filthy job and Jack managed to pour a liberal amount onto my arms and hands. Some of it splashed onto my body and legs as I again held the funnel in position.

We bought some vital supplies and replaced the eggs, which went all over the countryside when we hit that big bump. One of the ladies at the shop informed us that there was a guesthouse where we could stop over.

We wearily proceeded to check the guesthouse out. We had to see the policeman Bruce Kuhn's wife Louise first about staying there as she was running the guesthouse. We had the whole place to ourselves for $30 each for the night. It was very well equipped with a washing machine, microwave oven, television, chairs, tables and clean sheets on real beds.

Finally, at long last, and none too soon, a piping hot, gas heated, never-ending supply of hot water shower. How terribly appropriate and timely for us two grubs covered in mud and stinking of fuel. It was a great place to clean up after a month on the road. We were very badly in need of it.

We then braved visiting the canteen, the local watering hole, that night. Jack had warned me beforehand that they were lively places at times. By the time we arrived their tensions were already running high. It was Pension Night, the time to settle political squabbles and domestic disputes over a few beers.

A chair and a full can of beer were thrown at me in quick and rapid succession from clear across the hall by a very large Aborigine lady. One, or some of the lads, had made remarks about the white sheila at the bar, and it had been overheard by the ladies. Both missiles narrowly, but thankfully, missed their target, if I was the intended target.

There were a few white locals standing around the bar having a *quiet* Friday night beer. We were surrounded by hundreds of Aborigines getting very drunk, loud and potentially violent. About five ghettoblasters were independently hard at work adding to the confused chaos. We had to shout at the top of our voices to make ourselves heard above the din.

We talked to Jim who told us a little about the area. It was to become self-governing with the white management withdrawn and the local council taking over full management of the settlement. Bitumen roads and a lot of new houses were to be built by the end of that year.

The Australian government had, by then, spent fourteen million dollars in five years towards housing. A nice Aborigine fellow pushed Jack to the front of the bar and collared his brother, the barman, to serve us, otherwise our intent of having a beer would have been futile.

Jim advised us to keep well out of the way of certain of the ladies. They were the worst he said. We had, by then, good enough reason to heed his advice. Jack would only let us stay for half an hour at the canteen as he sensed further trouble brewing.

We went back to the guesthouse and watched a good British movie on television. When the canteen closed the party continued into the streets for the rest of the night. We were fast asleep when, suddenly, we heard that the canteen had closed. The shouting, fighting and Phil Collins and Dire Straits emanating from a powerful ghettoblaster piercing the night air from across the road continued all night. The music was in good taste but somewhat unhourly.

'I'll kill you! I'll kill you!' came from a young man down the street.

'Oh God! Put that knife away! Put that knife away!' an older woman's voice followed. Then we heard a man scream.

They were still disputing, loudly and with beer in hand, when we woke the following morning at eight thirty. We decided to go to the canteen earlier that evening as it was not a pay day.

Jack went along to the mechanic's garage to see about getting the punctured tyre fixed where he met Phil the mechanic. The two of them discovered that they had both been born in Africa and had a lot in common including malaria and other tropical nasties. We were invited to their house for dinner one evening for the two of them to sort Africa out and to put Africa on the right road forever.

'There is the garage mate. Fix your own bloody tyre!' Phil said. 'If you find anything else that needs to be done, go for your life. All the equipment is there for you if you need it.' Jack fixed the tyre and washed off bundles of mud from under the Toyota to examine more closely for damage. Miraculously there was none to be found.

'A few crocodile bites. All superficial damage,' he said on his return. 'Pity about the eggs though.'

It was great having the guesthouse to ourselves. We would have a beer on the verandah of an evening and say *Gidday* to everyone passing by. The locals used a path running alongside the guesthouse as a short cut to the shop. We were fast becoming two of the locals.

We joined Phil and his wife Jenny for dinner after a few cold beers on their verandah with their two gorgeous children. Jack and Phil were deep into discussing Africa. And the deep sense of belonging they both felt for Africa, and the sometimes painful sense of loss of being elsewhere.

'I learnt somewhere, a long time ago, that Nature has implanted in the breast of every person an affinity and sense of belonging to the land from which they gained their birth and infant nurture,' Jack said to Phil. They stared far out across the horizon to the sun setting in the west, thinking African things. For a long time. In silence. The call of Africa. Homesick.

The following day Barry from the shop kindly let us have some of his own ice for the Esky. The shop did not sell ice. Jan, also from the shop, and I, had a good chat. She couldn't stand Lockhart River. It wasn't everyone's cup of tea.

On another occasion Jan took us to her house at lunchtime to dig out some ice for us from her deep freeze. When we arrived there we found a hen that had got herself badly entangled and entwined in a light nylon fishing net left drying on a rack in the back yard. Jack took pity on her, disentangled the poor entrapped creature, and set her free again. She wonderingly waltzed away on wobbly legs in search of her brood, ruffled and squawking, but with her dignity intact.

We really did have some lovely and memorable experiences at Lockhart River. The Royal Flying Doctor and the Community Health nursing sister joined us at the guest house together with their aircraft pilot. Dave and Vicky, who were part Tongan and part Maori, also arrived at the guesthouse. They had been commissioned by the Queensland Arts Council to put on shows for children in Outback schools. They invited us to attend their performance and we gladly accepted.

We watched their Polynesian floor show about the geography, traditional, ceremonial and warrior dress, songs and dances of the islands of the South Pacific Ocean and thoroughly enjoyed it all. It was superb and the children laughed their little heads off. We met all the school teachers and managed to photograph some of the children at the school playing fun games.

We set about unpacking the Toyota two days after we arrived. It was two days too late. The stench from the decaying eggs made us stagger back in disgust after we had opened a door. There were blowfly maggots crawling everywhere. What a dreadful job it was unpacking and cleaning it all up. Squirming, squelching maggots were not fun. We had learned never to carry eggs in a vehicle ever again.

All our clothes had to be laundered and we had to wash every single thing in the vehicle including the tarpaulin. Fortunately we had spread a large tarpaulin in the back before we packed anything else in Cairns. This prevented the maggots and the stench from penetrating the rest of the vehicle.

After the rowdy Friday pension night everything was pleasantly quiet - exhausted would more aptly describe the peace. We were walking along the path from the shop past some Aborigine women one morning when we heard some awful language apparently directed at us. It was impossible to pretend we just didn't see, hear or feel. The venom bit deeply and took the appropriate effect.

It was to be eighteen months later that the Brisbane media strongly critisised Bruce the policeman after he had accidentally driven over an Aborigine woman and she had died. Another six weeks after that Bruce was attacked by a mob outside the canteen and suffered severe injuries.

He had told us at length of the impossibility of applying the white man's law to indigenous people who had their own forms of social discipline and cultural norms which were being eroded. We understood perfectly Bruce's dilemma and the dichotomy of his duties. Two conflicting cultures and never the twain shall meet? Alcohol, in many instances, completes the continuing disintegration of a once dignified and noble people.

One night after dinner Jack and the Royal Flying Doctor were having a chat. It was summarised perfectly - diabetes, gangrene, amputations, dipsomania, delirium tremens, alcoholic dementia, shortened lifespan, batterings, stabbings - nothing improved but seemed to worsen. The futility of it all was almost overwhelming to us. The young doctor and Islander nurse were in tears by the time he had concluded his outrage. The hopeless, but not helpless, tragedy continues.

Those affected will regain their dignity - they must. The only way for them to do so is to take it back, for no amount of anything will ever buy it back for them. And there is no-one on God's Earth who ever will, or even can, give it back to them.

The enhancement of the dignity of the individual must, at all times, take precedence over all other things. Every provision should be made to create circumstances for all individuals to strive for, and to achieve, their highest potential. No amount of political correctness will achieve these practically possible ideals.

Chapter Sixteen

Our having the guesthouse to ourselves was unfortunately short-lived; it was just too good to last. The place was getting quite full so we decide to forgo the luxuries. When we left the guesthouse on the Monday morning we were desperate to go bush again and to get away from the other guests. The rain had ceased and it was starting to dry up at last.

A contingent of Aborigines had some years previously abandoned the Lockhart River settlement and had resettled further south on the coast where they had established a Mission. It was an alcohol-free community and accessible only by sea. We inquired about visiting them but unfortunately could not find anyone to take us there.

A landing barge from Cairns arrived bringing fuel and supplies for the shop as well as beer for the canteen. We went down to the wharf with the intent of getting some idea of the voyage we were to go on from Weipa to Karumba. It looked pretty civilised enough.

We went to see Mark Geyle, the Ranger at the Ranger Station and we had a good, long yarn with him. He knew all about us and directed us to the best birdwatching campsite. He seemed to take kindly to us. Mark was an avid birdwatcher.

He had the skin of a two metre long carpet snake python, which had been killed by one of the local Aborigines. It was drying out, stretched and pinned out in a board on the front verandah. A small wallaby was hop-hop-hopping around us but wouldn't have a bar of us getting too close to him (or her). Jack taught me to approach him without scaring him.

'Approach him with the palms of both your hands clearly exposed, slowly and deliberately,' Jack explained. 'Your exposed palms tell him two things. Firstly, he can see that you have no weapons in them which puts fears for his safety to rest.

'Secondly, he thinks that you may have something to offer him. He is inquisitive and will come forward to examine more closely. Lastly, he can sense if you have malicious thoughts in your mind and can read the intent on your face like an open book. Clear your mind of all vain, unbecoming and unkind thoughts,' he said.

Incredibly it worked. The little fellow allowed me to get close enough to touch him, but I didn't. Perhaps next time.

'It works with most animals, especially humans. It is not guaranteed to work on lion, leopard, tiger and crocodile however' he warned.

Mark was a bachelor and was thoroughly enjoying being at Iron Range. We invited him to join us around our campfire one night and he accepted our invitation.

Iron Range National Park covered some 34,600 hectares and conserved the largest area of lowland rainforest in Australia. It was home to some totally unique birdlife and other fauna and flora.

Our camp spot in the rainforest, which Mark had assigned us, was perfect and large. A large mango tree planted many years before provided total shade for the camp. Large fruit bats flapped around above us at night.

At the back of the campsite were several old roads leading to abandoned gold mine adits. For two of the mornings we had a bunch of geologists driving their trucks into our camp at sunrise to have a look at them.

On the first occasion they invited us to accompany them and it was fun. We clambered down the Iron Range River during which time I was filled in on a lot of local information by Alan (I think), the local patriarch who lived at Portland Roads. He was the geologists' guide.

I bravely ventured into a mine adit to have a look at the small red-bodied bats, which had made their home there. There were so many bats that it seemed that the warm, musty air was short of oxygen and I had a claustrophobic attack. Jack led me out of the mine back to daylight again and I felt a bit better.

We returned to the camp where they made a fire with our firewood, boiled a billy, and had their lunch. One poor lad who had emigrated from the UK with his wife and baby some months previously was having an awful lot of difficulty communicating with the rest of the Australians he was with. He had worked in the South African gold mines previously and, as soon as he discovered that Jack was a mining engineer who had also worked in the mines in South Africa, he unceremoniously abandoned his mates to join us.

'You don't know how pleasant it is to have an intelligent and sensible conversation for a change,' he exploded with purple-face frustration.

'Culture shock is your problem. Australianize as fast as you can!' Jack advised him.

Alan was deeply engrossed in espousing his views of their unwelcome invasion. He had a captive audience and made full use of the opportunity by literally, and liberally, bending their ears.

He was anti-mining in, or anywhere near, the Iron Range National Park, anti a proposed luxury holiday resort to be built nearby, and vehemently opposed to a potential space launching station to be built somewhere to the north. We totally agreed with everything he said. The Cape York Peninsula must be left alone forever.

On the second occasion the geologists arrived at seven o'clock in the morning while we were still sleeping. There was not a 'please, thank you, by your leave' or even an acknowledgment of our presence as they invaded our camp uninvited and unheralded. They simply parked their trucks and took to the bush for the day without as much as a 'boo, bah, or bless my soul'. It was extremely rude we thought.

The following morning I crawled out of the tent not long after the dawn chorus. The riflebird and the manucode were duelling. The rifle bird is a vain lady's perfect pet. It wolf whistles!

I had not walked very far up the road when I spotted a yellow oriole. He had been the one making a hell of a racket earlier that morning. I saw a figbird, a white eye, a mistletoebird and a manucode, all in fifteen minutes. I had yet to see the palm cockatoo from close up. We had seen two of them in flight over the camp the previous day. I had clocked up about 110 species by that time. Mark the Ranger, dropped into camp late one afternoon for a cup of tea. He was most impressed with the bird count I had chalked up.

On my late afternoon birdwatch I saw a red-cheeked parrot. I will never see it anywhere else in Australia, or the rest of the world for that matter. It was without doubt the most exciting birdwatching day of the trip thus far. They just seemed to get better by the day.

Our camp was ever so civilised and organised. Jack had found a stout plank, which he had suspended from the mango tree branch that we used as a table. We had used the tailgate of the vehicle as a table before that. Our canvas water bag was suspended from the tree for easy use. We had been eating extremely well and it was good to be back in the bush again.

We drove over to Portland Roads one afternoon. It was the end of the road with a handful of houses, mangroves and a few fishing boats bobbing about. It was very beautiful and peaceful with hovering frigatebirds to keep us company. It was apparently a good place for crayfishing. The drive was

167

through magnificent scenery - rainforest clad hills and sea.

On our way back we took a look at the road into Chilly Beach. We decided that it would have to wait until the next time we came around. Nothing could entice us into that quagmire.

That evening I came racing back into camp from my birdwatch. I was quite breathless and completely beside myself.

'Your favourite position' Jack told me.

'Guess what?' I said to Jack. 'I've just seen my first palm cockatoo from close up - it is magnificent. Now I can go home!'

'If that is what you really want to do, but I doubt it,' said Jack with a knowing smile on his face. 'Let me tap you a mug of wine and you can tell me all about it.'

When I had told him all about it at great length we set the campfire alight. Later that night, nearing bed time, he told me yet another story about how difficult it was to educate Lighty.

Chapter Seventeen

Lighty was educated with the greatest difficulty. As it so happily turned out, and perhaps somewhat miraculously so, Lighty had gone on to high school. It was another fortunate stroke, or strokes, of luck that came his way. That was when Lighty was nearing the end of the next-to-last term of his last year in primary school.

The innocence of the young is so easily, and so early, lost in life, alas. And the supreme innocence, to the very, very few, is never realised to the, if ever achieved, very, very end.

Lighty thought that it was a bit of a pity that his school didn't teach English children in English passed standard five but catered only for the Afrikaans children. It only went to Standard Eight for the Afrikaners and did not do the last two years of school so that one could matriculate. All that Afrikaner farmers needed in those days was to achieve the legal age of sixteen to abandon school and to revert to the family farm. Everything looked very bad and sad to Lighty for his father was not a farmer but a poor miner.

His father had said to Lighty that Standard Eight was a good enough education for a start and that Lighty could be an apprentice fitter and turner, or a blacksmith, on the mine when he finished his schooling and could then work his way in life up from there to be an engineer later. Lighty knew that his father really couldn't afford to send him to boarding school, as much as he would dearly have liked to, but he knew that his father just couldn't bring himself to say so, and it hurt Lighty deeply to know that.

Lighty didn't think that they would run a one-person class for two years especially, and only, for him, at the local secondary school so that he could complete his matric. and go on to university to become a doctor, or a lawyer, or a teacher, or something really honestly worthwhile in life, even if the classes were perhaps in Afrikaans, so he had to make other plans - and fast.

He also worried for a while about how John was going to get educated, as his black school only went to Standard Five, and he had to go to another school on the other side of town where he had to walk for ten miles there, and ten miles back home again, every day, to go to a high school.

The nearest high school for Lighty which went to matric. was a hundred miles away, and the school bus didn't go that far. Bill Stringer and his big

Garrett steam railway engine did go there, but it left in the morning at six o'clock, and arrived back every afternoon at two o'clock. That, however, suited John well, as he could go to the new Bantu high school on the other side of town with Bill on the Garrett, and that new school had started teaching to matric, but the white school didn't. And they wouldn't allow Lighty to go to the black school.

The only way out for Lighty to get a good education was at boarding school, and that cost a lot of money which his father didn't have. Answers had to be found, and easy answers were few and far between in those days.

Then Lighty had it all planned in an inspirational moment on the school bus one day. He would get a job to earn money to pay to go to boarding school. But who on earth would give him a job that paid money? He was only eleven years old then.

One day, when Lighty had caught the steam engine with Bill to the big town one day, and spent time there looking at the school of his dreams, he just stood there for a long time.

Yokkie Shilling, a good Jewish man who owned a big general trading store in town, lived across the road from the school of Lighty's dreams. The real reason Lighty was standing in front of Yokkie's house looking at the school of his dreams was because he was making an unobtrusive reconnaissance of Yokkie's fruit orchard with the eyes in the back of his head.

He remembered that Yokkie had a big shop, so, taking a very long chance, as he was wont to do in those days, he went to Yokkie's shop and asked the lady shop assistant if he could speak to him. She looked down at his clothes and his bare feet, raised an eyebrow, and took off in search of Yokkie.

Yokkie, as patiently as a Rabbi as was his Jewish father, listened to Lighty's request for a job. A smile played around Yokkie's lips when he asked why Lighty wanted a job, and what Lighty intended doing with the money he earned. Lighty told Yokkie about his high school dreams, and his many difficulties, and how the two didn't go, and that a job was the only way out of his jam.

Yokkie's smile gradually faded and he became more serious about what Lighty's plans were, and what his name was, who his father was, and where he went to school. Lighty asked Yokkie to please not tell his father about his asking for the job as his father might think that people would say that they were too poor, and his father might get angry at Lighty.

Yokkie said yes, he had a job for him during school time at boarding school in town, and he would pay him five shillings a day and Lighty could get his school uniform and clothes for half price. He had to work for one hour every day except when Lighty had sport practice and competition play days as well as perhaps Saturdays and Sundays.

Yokkie said he would talk to the concession store owner near to where Lighty lived so that he could work there during school holidays as well. Yokkie said that the owners were also Jewish and that they were very good people. Yokkie said that he would also talk to the Head Master of the town high school and put in a good word for him because he once was the Head Prefect there.

Yokkie asked Lighty how he was going to get to and from boarding school if he lived so far away, so Lighty told him about Bill Stringer and the Garrett, and how Bill was just OK. Yokkie just shook his head and said 'Jesus!', a strange thing for a Jew to say Lighty thought, but he understood the things that men sometimes said they didn't really mean.

A week later, one playtime, Lighty saw the town high school Head Master coming out of Mr Berelowitz' office. They were laughing a lot and saying that Yokkie was a really good fellow.

The next day Mr Berelowitz called Lighty to his office. Mrs Mentz, the teacher, said that there was another man there from the Schools Inspectorate or something that wanted to talk to him.

'Now I'm really in deep trouble!' Lighty sadly thought as he again walked to Mr Berelowitz' office. He didn't know what he had done wrong that time. Being sent to see the school inspector was even worse than being sent to see the Principal. It was far worse than being sent to detention.

Maybe it was because he had had to go to detention, all too often, to Mrs Mentz' house after school because of not doing his homework, or because of plain non-malicious mischief. Mrs Mentz never ever beat him, or even rowed with him, but gave him plenty of detention instead. Mrs Mentz had a special detention room at her house right next door to the school where all errant pupils in her class went to from one o'clock to two o'clock in the afternoon.

He had to miss Mrs Barrett's Ford bus home then when he had to do his homework in detention, as did his two best friends Frank Barrett and George Baynes. Frank was Mrs Barrett's very own son. And when Lighty didn't arrive home in the bus in the afternoon, his mother would either know, or his sisters or brother would tell her that he was really in for it because he had not done his homework again and was in detention after school. Fortunately, Frank Barrett was always in detention with Lighty so Frank's mother had no complaint.

Frank's mother owned and operated a local greengrocer shop in town. She bought in some of her vegetables and fruit from Lighty's mum and drove the school bus. She had a lot of time and tolerance for plenty of trouble because Frank, George and Lighty were holy terrors in the extreme. George's mum owned and operated a hairdressing and beautician shop right next door to Frank's mum's greengrocer shop. All three mothers and Mrs Mentz played tennis together every Saturday.

Lighty, Frank and George's mothers discovered that Mrs Mentz was more than just keen to keep them in detention at her house after school for an hour to make them do their homework. All quite unknown to the three boys, it was made into a semi-permanent arrangement.

The after school detention was really bad, even if Mrs Mentz saw them off to the railway line a hundred yards from her house in time for them to be picked up by Bill in his Garrett steam engine, and then to be dropped off near their homes five miles away. Bill always looked out for them then. Luckily for them it was still early enough to get to play in the veldt before the sun went down.

'Be home before the sun sets,' was the ultimate command to the three boys.

Frank and George, when they had been bad at home, had to walk to their mothers' shops where they had to just sit and behave, and were taken home afterwards when the shops closed. Lighty just caught Bill's Garrett home where he would await whatever was in store for him there.

The very worst part really was when the ladies discussed their misbehaviour, trials, tribulations and many shortcomings at tennis on a Saturday afternoon when the whole town would find out and laugh.

Later, after much protestation and very good behaviour, Mrs Mentz agreed that detention was no longer necessary, but if only one of them did not do his homework, then all three got detention together.

'All for one, and one for all. That is what you are, and that is what you will be,' she said.

Mrs Mentz was the wife of the manager of the Barclays Overseas and Dominion Bank, and they were the most trusted pillars of society., Her husband played golf with Dr Ovendale the local medical practitioner who delivered Lighty, Mr Potgieter the local lawyer, and the mayor Mr Killian, a business man and forester. The town and townsfolk were run and managed from the golf course every Wednesday and Saturday afternoon.

As far as the boys were concerned, nothing was amiss until many, many, years afterward when the full benevolent conspiracy amongst mothers was exposed; and only then did they fully realise the implications of that beautiful conspiracy that kept them together, and also made them do their homework.

When the boys were on to a very rare good behaviour run, and they were big enough to do so, their mothers agreed that they could walk the five miles home after school - but only if they went to detention to do their homework first.

School bags strapped to backs, barefoot, shoe laces tied together and the shoes slung over their necks and dangling down their chests, khaki clad, green school caps on head, loaded catapults in hand, eyes ever-piercing for something to shoot at, and on the lookout for snakes and scorpions, and for a difficult tree to climb, was a sight everyone feared with great anticipation of disaster.

Lighty believed that the real cause of the confusion was his fascination of the opposite sex at the time, namely his total fascination of initially Gloria Glass, or perhaps Elizabeth Kapp, both then equally threatening his academic male superiority. Or maybe the Simmonds twins Margaret and Heather, who had by then publicly disclosed that the *Bees have stung us* while looking down at their newly swollen, but very visible fresh breasts. Boys aren't blind.

Maybe it was because they had found out that Lighty wanted to go to boarding school to do his matric, and they didn't want him to go. Very funny things could happen in life so Lighty had discovered, and many things could happen which prevented one from doing the things one wanted to do.

Maybe it was because they had been seen stuffing a potato up the school bus' exhaust pipe with a broomstick one night and it wouldn't start the next day. Nobody went to school that day, and Lighty spent the whole day with Frank and George in a terrified state fearing being found out and punished.

Maybe it was because Frank, George and he had been found out about the other thing. Frank hadn't told, and George hadn't told for sure. And Lighty certainly hadn't. Maybe Mr Grumpy Greyling had seen them stealing his Katova grapes one midnight and reported them to the police sergeant, but their vehemently innocent denials to their fathers cancelled that one out.

173

Not that their fathers minded too much, because they had unwittingly eaten some of the grapes.

They were shot at twice with a shotgun that night as they ran away, and Frank had copped a salt pellet in the bum, but no-one knew about that - not even his mum. He told her that it was a barb from a barbed wire fence that got him there when he was crawling through it.

It was the fastest that George and Lighty had ever seen Frank run that night. He never could run faster than George and Lighty, but that night, he ran like the wind, howling as loudly too. Far in front of them he was. He didn't really mind being called Fast Frank after that.

Grumpy also certainly did not see them the night when they later got even when they all took turns poohing in a paper bag, then setting it alight when they knocked on his front door and ran away and then went to hide in the bushes.

He opened the front door and started stamping the fire out with his bare feet. First he tried stamping out the fire with his short leg that was six inches shorter than the long one, but it wouldn't touch the ground. Then he stood on his short leg and started stamping out the flames with his long leg. Up and down he danced - up and down. The language he used was a totally new education for them.

Haai kona! No! Grumpy had heard them laughing from the bushes for sure, but he didn't see them. They knew he also wouldn't tell such a story to anyone ever, because everybody would have laughed at him. If he had his shotgun in his hand that night, he would have blasted them to Kingdom Come. He didn't like them after that, and they never ever went near his house again.

It most certainly wasn't because the three of them had put a dead puff adder they had killed on top of the sun-visor in the young, new police sergeant's 1949 Ford V8. Directly above the steering wheel it was so that, when he was driving into the sun and he pulled the visor down to keep the sun out of his eyes, the dead snake dropped onto his lap.

Oom Willie Pretoors was very angry with Sergeant Hough because the sergeant had deliberately driven off the dirt road at high speed, through the barbed wire fence, and had killed one of Oom Willie's prize-winning Friesland cows stone dead. Oom Willie was of the firm conviction that the new sergeant had it in for him, and needed some of his priorities realigned.

Oom Willie was a very fierce man with red hair. He was also very big, with a big, wide, red nose, he was not known to avoid saying, and doing, what he thought was always right. He very quickly put a lot of things right in the district. He stood seven foot tall in his socks and without his hat on. Nobody ever argued with Oom Willie.

The whole school even went to see the rogue lion he had killed with his bare hands when they brought it into town on a Diamond T lorry one day. The lion didn't have a single hole in it. It had been eating the natives and the cattle on his farm. Oom Willie wasn't too worried about the eaten natives they said, because he could get any number of them from anywhere, but he was very worried about his eaten cattle.

The lion had jumped on him from an ambush and had knocked his rifle out of his hands. He had then killed it by putting his legs around the lion's chest and stomach in a scissor grip squeezing the life out of it, and he had wrenched it's jaws apart with his bare hands at the same time. It was the biggest lion seen in those parts ever.

Oom Willie was taken to the hospital where the doctor patched him up and let him go home again on the same day; only because Oom Willie wasn't the kind of man to take orders from anyone.

But however, because the police sergeant was the police sergeant, there was nothing Oom Willie could really do about the dead cow other than to have a stern word or two with the sergeant at the time of the crime. The sergeant even threw the puff adder at Oom Willie that day he said.

'One can never be too careful about new police sergeants,' he told everyone in town for a long time after. 'Especially the young ones from Johannesburg' he said.

There was no malicious intent on the boys' part about the puff adder mind you. It was dead anyway, and couldn't kill anyone anymore. They did it just because they agreed with Oom Willie that new police sergeants could be somewhat over-enthusiastic sometimes, and a bit of taming really did no harm. They got to know him quite well a bit later on when he had suddenly, and without any justifiable reason, made it his very serious business to get to know them better.

He wasn't a bad guy after all they found out, but maybe it was because he was a bit tamer by then. Whenever the sergeant used to see them walking along, he would stop and give them a lift to wherever they were going. Very friendly fellow he was.

The police sergeant took quite a while to citizen himself into the community. It was only after he had been to his first policeman's ball in Nelspruit did this finally occur, and he gradually become as one with the people.

When he was driving home after the policeman's dance he saw a limping leopard near his house, and he had crashed his Black Maria police van into Doctor Ovendale's gatepost. He immediately called up all the men he knew with guns to arrange a party to hunt it down - long past midnight it was.

Everybody knew that it was Oom Willie's mampoer, a very powerful peach brandy that he distilled in a very secret and highly illegal distillery on his farm from his peach crop, that was doing funny things to the police sergeant's eyes. Even Oom Willie said that he couldn't drive properly at any time anyway.

Nobody however, could fully explain why a lot of chickens and goats suddenly started disappearing thereafter. The local Umfundis Ezekiel, the African Zionist Christian Church preacher, was blamed for a long time because everybody knew it was he, but the sergeant would never arrest him. Ezekiel was not even apprehended and questioned on suspicion. The sergeant just let things be generally, which was a sensible thing for him to do at the time.

It was only after the police sergeant had shot and killed him in his fowl run one night did the chickens and goats stop disappearing. The police sergeant gave the leopard skin to Ezekiel. Ezekiel preached a lot better after that, especially about *Thy shalt not steal*, but more especially about *Thy shalt not kill*. He became very holy after that, and even stopped sacrificing goats on top of the hill they said.

Oom Willie even let the sergeant get married to his daughter, but only a very long time afterwards. They said it was only after the sergeant had made certain casual but discreet inquiries about the distillery that Oom Willie had by then, not very discreetly, nor secretly, been using to make his mampoer.

They said that Oom Willie's distillery took up a lot of his time, which they also said was a very good thing because his mampoer was the best in the whole district by far and was much sought after far and wide. They said that when you threw a tot of Oom Willie's mampoer toward a fire, it would burn long before it got to the fire. The police sergeant started to grow a big, red nose after the wedding, and even started to look like Oom Willie.

By the time Lighty got to The Office, his head was so full of things that he forgot to go in, and walked past, fast, very fast, right past The Office, and beyond it. Lighty always did that. Fast I mean. Passed it. Looking down at his feet all the time. Lighty went to the boy's for a pee instead because his teeth felt as if they were floating, and it was there that he remembered why he was there in the first place. It became a very big pee then. And it took a long time.

The School's Inspectorate man was not a bad fellow at all, and he was quite a gentle man really. A gentleman. He was waiting outside The Office door for Lighty, looking around a lot, with a worried kind of look on his face as if he had lost something very important. Doctor Danie Smuts was his name he said, shaking Lighty's hand firmly like a real man should shake hands.

Lighty told him that he wasn't sick and looking for a doctor, but he was looking for the schools inspector. Doctor Danie laughed and said that he wasn't that kind of doctor - the kind that fixed sick people he said. They then spoke for a long time about the things boys did. Even stealing fruit at night is what he had done once he told Lighty, but Lighty could just tell from the twinkling in his eyes that it was more than just once. He knew a lot about what boys did - nearly everything.

Then Doctor Danie started asking him questions about all the things Lighty had been reading in *The Star* newspaper, and they spoke about that for a while. Lighty was very surprised that he spoke English very well, because that was a bit strange for an Afrikaner. He even spoke better English than the English did. Lighty was also very surprised that he knew so much about what was in *The Star*. He even knew about little Willie van Rensburg from Glenmore. He was very clever for Boer Lighty thought. And very kind.

He made Lighty sit down at a table and said that we were going to play some games to see how clever Lighty was. Lighty played all the games, and Doctor Danie just sat there with a clock in his hand. He smiled a lot, and more so the longer Lighty played games with the blocks and stuff. Then he put some tests in front of Lighty and told him to answer the questions, and to stop when he told him to. They were all very easy to do, and he was never told to stop - not even once.

Doctor Danie let him go back to his classroom and Lighty wondered what it was all about. Doctor Danie didn't tell him anything, and Lighty never saw him again. It was a pity, because he was a hell of a good guy.

Lighty heard that he later became Director of Education for the whole of the Transvaal. Those children didn't know how lucky they really were to have him as The Director. He even, much later, let black children go to white children's schools, and he got himself into a lot of trouble because of it.

177

A week or so later, Lighty was again sent to The Principal's Office by Mrs Mentz because he was *wanted there*. *Wanted* in the cowboy movies meant that The Law was after him. He was getting a bit tired of this. I mean, what were the other pupils going to think if he was always going to The Office because he was 'wanted'?

When Lighty got there, Mr Berelowitz told him that he could go to any government boarding school he chose to the following year. Anywhere in the whole of the Transvaal he said. Doctor Danie had recommended him for a scholarship or something, which he said meant that his school fees, books and boarding school fees were paid for in full until Lighty matriculated.

Lighty was in a hell of a fix. His loyalties were being put to the test to the ultimate extreme. Lighty had a real proper job to go to with Yokkie and he couldn't let him down. He also had a real school to go to where Yokkie's uncle was the Headmaster, and where he could do his matric in English. Lighty could also go to boarding school at Jeppe Boy's High in Johannesburg, or to Pretoria Boy's High even Mr Berelowitz said.

Mister Berelowitz then said that there was also another scholarship that Yokkie had arranged within the Jewish community, and that Lighty should perhaps go to the King David School in Johannesburg where all the very clever and rich Jewish boys went to, but Lighty said that he already knew that they couldn't, and didn't, play rugby very well there.

Mister Berelowitz said that he could also go to St. John's College, or Christian Brothers College, or one of those other posh private Christian schools where all the Larnie Dah rich blokes went to, or Queen's College, or Bishop's in the Cape, or Michael House or Hilton in Natal, or Grey College in Bloemfontein in the Orange Free State. Mr Berelowitz said that they were all the very best schools in the country.

Lighty didn't have a job there in those places, and said so, and he wouldn't be able to buy his school uniform and clothes, nor could he get money to pay for the train fare home and back to school again. And he wouldn't be able to go home very often even if he had the train fare, and he would get very homesick like he did at Glenmore.

'You have done exceedingly well for yourself Lighty. If anyone deserves a good break in life, it is you, for you have earned it. You must tell your father that the time has now come for me to talk to him about your further education. Everything is going to be all right for you now.' Mr Berelowitz said.

'All these problems will be solved in due course. You must not be afraid of going far away to boarding school, because it will be good for you in the long run. Leave matters in our hands for the moment and all will be well,' he said.

Lighty didn't want to go on any long runs to the Cape or Natal or Bloemfontein, or anywhere else. He was in real trouble. He was terribly at sixes and sevens, because he knew that now was the time to tell his father, because he had no choice, and that real big trouble had turned up. That kind of trouble.

He told his father that afternoon that his father would have to pay for all his clothes and train fares until matric if he didn't go to the town school. He could not go anywhere else, and he really had to go there.

Lighty's parents went to see Mr Berelowitz and Yokkie the next day at The Office. They appeared to resolve matters in a satisfactory manner after a long discussion while Lighty waited in the car outside.

'We have decided that you, and you alone, will decide where you are going to go to boarding school,' his father told him.

'You must do as you think best for yourself, and we will all support you in that decision. The Jewish people have arranged to pay for your rail fares, and if you go to Natal, or the Free State, or the Cape Province, they will pay for your airfares as well. All your clothes will be paid for, and your pocket money will even be provided if you choose to go to a private school. You won't need a job now. I don't like the idea of a job anyway.'

His mother then sent a telegram to his uncle and godfather in England to tell him about the good news. He swiftly telegrammed back to say that he thought it would be a very good idea if Lighty went to school at a place called Harrow in England where he had gone to school before, and where he would look after him.

He said that they had the best rugby players in all of England, and the entire world, and that it would be a good place for him to start and to make his mark in life or something. He also stressed the vital importance of getting a proper English education in real England instead of a second class colonial one, and that one day Lighty could play Rugby for England and the British Lions.

Lighty didn't think that playing winger for the British Lions against the Springboks was such a good idea. They might just win like they did when his father took him to see his first rugby Test match when Jackie van der Schyff missed that two point conversion against the Lions in the first test in 1955 at Ellis Park in Johannesburg.

It missed the right hand post by not even inches, just then the referee blew that long, shrill and sad final whistle. The final score was 23 points to The Lions and 22 points to the Springboks. Lighty also knew that there were no real lions in England, but only pretend ones.

Old Jackie was the best full-back Lighty has ever seen, even better than J.P.R. Williams and Don Clarke. Lighty was very sad for Jackie that day, but he thinks that he was even more sad when he read in 'The Star' that they wouldn't let him play for the Springboks anymore because they said that he was a Cape Coloured. He wasn't All White they said. Not All White - Not All Right *The Star* wrote one day that next week. Not even to play against the All Blacks.

Even Tom van Vollenhoven, the mightiest Springbok rugby winger ever to have lived, told Lighty one day when they were playing golf at Vereeniging a long time afterwards, that those two things were also the two saddest things in his life.

It was that kick that Jackie missed, and the Coloured kick that didn't miss Jackie, who was Tom's best friend then. It was Tom's first Test and Jackie was an old Springbok hand by then. They roomed together before the game. Jackie looked after Tom before, during and after the game to calm his nerves. All the newspapers, and all the people, blamed Tom and Jackie for losing that Test. Tom said that the Lions wouldn't let him score a try. Jackie was dropped from the Springbok side forever.

Tom said that, because he was so angry about it all, he knew not how to react to being selected for the second Test at Cape Town. He swore to his young self that he would play that game, and it would be the game of his life, and it would be just for old Jackie. He did, and became the first Springbok ever to score three brilliant tries in a Test match in South Africa and so immortalised himself.

Tom never ever played better rugby again after that. He later went to England to play rugby league for Saint Helens. Tom and Lighty were very sad that day in Vereeniging, and their golf wasn't very good either for the rest of that day. They drank a lot of beer instead.

No. Those English Harrow blokes, and England, and the British Lions, would have to get along without him. Lighty just couldn't play for them. His little Springbok heart just wouldn't let him.

Lighty then went to see Kobe's Koekemoer. Kobus was in Standard Nine and a boarder at the town high school where Yokkie's uncle was the Headmaster. Kobus had played on the flank in the Rugby First Fifteen that year. It was the year that they won the Administrator's Cup for the very first time ever. They were the Transvaal School's Rugby Champions and had beaten Helpmekaar, the previous and almost perpetual champions, by nine points to eight that year.

Lighty and Kobus spent a lot of time talking about the town high school, what was good, and what was bad there. Kobus told Lighty that they had a skivvy system there where each Standard Sixer was a skivvy and had to have a skivvy boss. The skivvy had to make the skivvy boss' bed in the morning, wash his socks, press his long trousers, and polish his shoes, rugby boots, and cadet boots. If the skivvy were bad or disobedient, the skivvy boss would cane him.

Kobus said that Lighty would be all right there, because Kobus would be his skivvy boss, and because Kobus would have many skivvies, Lighty wouldn't have to do too much. Kobus promised never to cane him or punish him because they had already been friends for a long time. Kobus told Lighty that if ever another senior told him to do skivvy work, Lighty was to refuse and report it to him immediately.

There were initiation ceremonies and other antics Kobus said. One of the first was called 'bakoond' or The Gauntlet in English. All the seniors lined up one behind the other, and the skivvies had to crawl between their legs as fast as they could because the seniors helped them along by beating them on the backside with the palms of their hands. There were to be some twenty five seniors each one getting in three to five bum smacks per skivvy. Lighty didn't think that a hundred smacks on the bum in one go was very funny. Especially for not having done anything wrong.

Another initiation ceremony was the Drain Crawl where the skivvies had to go down a manhole, one by one, in rapid succession and then crawl for a hundred yards uphill along a 24 inch diameter concrete storm- water pipe. At the end, the skivvies had no skin left on their knees, elbows and toes, and had to be bodily lifted out at the other end so exhausted and frightened were they. There was a skivvy night on a Saturday at the school hall where the teachers were also in attendance. There, the skivvies had to perform a creative piece by singing, reciting poetry, or enacting some original dramatics.

They also had to wear their blazers inside out during playtime at school as well as whenever they wore them at the hostel and to town. That didn't seem too bad to Lighty as it was quite painless, if perhaps humiliating.

They spoke a lot about rugby, and Kobus told Lighty many times how they had beaten Helpmekaar that year. It got more heroic each time Kobus told the story, and Lighty wanted it to be more heroic each time.

Lighty had a proper job to go to too, and he could also buy his school uniform and his clothes from Yokkie's shop. He could also go home on Friday or Saturday afternoons with Bill on the Garret steam engine, and then go back to boarding school on Sunday afternoons for free. Kobus' father was a ganger on the railway, and he and Bill Stringer were good friends. Kobus used to ride with Bill on Sundays to boarding school, and home on some weekends. All in all, that was good enough for Lighty.

So, he went to boarding school where Yokkie's uncle was the headmaster. *The Chief,* he was called there, and with very good reason. The school was dual medium, which meant that both English and Afrikaans boys went there. It had a reputation of being a very fine character-building sort of school.

Lighty managed to get up to every trick and lark in the schoolboy book bar none. Despite the fact that it was very well known, far and wide, that he was always the naughtiest boy in town, he somehow, inexplicably, managed to stay out of trouble a lot.

One midnight, when they were in Standard Seven, Lighty, Spotty Losper, Wayne Cooper, Ivor Isaacs, David Goldenstein and Peter Moolman stole peaches at a doctor's house near the hospital. It started to rain so they jumped into a nearby Chev van parked in the street. Lighty was in the drivers seat, looked at the very long downhill in front of him, took the van out of gear, let the handbrake off, and down they hill they went. They parked the van outside the Technical High School's boys' hostel and ran back to their High School hostel seven blocks away. For the next week the Tech was crawling with policemen. Sorry Techies.

I must not forget The Tech Principal Mac McDougall who was also a lay preacher of the Methodist Church. Mac, no matter how hard you looked at me in church, it really wasn't me that threw Jeye's Fluid all over your Vauxhall Velox for all the Duco to peel off. It was Des and George. I know that, because you later made them sand your car back and respray it from top to toe instead of sending them to reform school.

Mother Theresa from the St Thomas of Aquina Convent must get recognition for her kindness and compassion by calling off her three Dobermans one night. She called for the ambulance instead. We were all up a tree looking at the senior girls in prep when Gary Angelos lost his grip, fell out of the tree, and broke his legs. Gary's legs mended well enough for him to represent the Eastern Transvaal Province at field hockey. Charlie Andrew was the only one to stick with Gary throughout the ordeal. Gary came a very close second to Lighty for being the naughtiest boy in town.

At high school Lighty was to be perceived to be a soft target by most by the less than gentlemanly scholars at first, but initially Kobus soon took care of them for him. Kobus was the Head Prefect that year and also captain of the Rugby First Fifteen. Lighty had a very charmed life that year compared to the other skivvies

He soon discovered that it was not what you knew, but whom you knew, that made the big differences in life. Knowing and cooperating with the right people helped one no end. As for the initiation ceremonies, Lighty shirked not in the least, for to be caught slipping a ceremony meant a 'bakoond' and disgrace in full public view on the lawn before the evening meal.

The schoolmasters were all very decent sorts and very good to him. In his first year at high school Lighty had difficulty excelling on the sports fields as he was so young, underdeveloped and underaged. The school had a firm and inviolable rule and that was to participate in a physically demanding sport at all times no matter what the season.

It also had a similar rule to participate in non-physical activities such as chess and debating. Boy Scouts for the English and Voortrekkers for the Afrikaans were mandatory. The buying of a Scout uniform placed a further burden on Lighty's limited financial resources that he overcame with Yokkie's assistance. Yokkie granted him a credit facility that he could gradually work for, and pay off, as he did with his other clothes and needs that he got from the shop.

He was far too small and skinny to play team sports such as under fourteen rugby, and the under fourteen athletics boys were much bigger, stronger and faster than he was. He just wasn't there yet physically, so he searched around to find something at which he could at least do, preferably something in team sports, but initially to no avail. His little heart was nearly broken as he gradually was rejected and excluded that summer from athletics, cricket, wrestling and boxing because of his size.

He was in any case excluded from boxing as he had only one eye and, as such, couldn't see a cricket ball bowled at him for apples. His dexterity with a cricket bat matched that of a spastic spider. His exclusion that autumn from the under fourteen Rugby D side hurt him no end. They wouldn't let him play rugby at all because there was no E side, and he was too small.

Finally, under the helping hands of Carl Wilkie, the under fourteen rugby coach and Tarzan Jacobs, the physical education teacher, Lighty discovered gymnastics. It was a sport that took into account none of the major attributes required by the other sports. A high strength-to-bodyweight ratio and physical coordination were the real criteria. Size didn't matter with gymnastics, but agility did, vitally important so. That was right up Lighty's alley.

Gymnastics gave him the opportunity to cover the physical sporting requirements throughout the seasons that year - come winter or summer. He was constantly under the instruction of Tarzan and mostly worked alone, but he didn't mind. He knew that, one day, he would grow up to be good enough for the under fourteen Rugby team, even if he had to wait another two years and be in Standard Eight to do it. His dreams of winning the Administrator's Cup and playing for Northern Transvaal and the Springboks, were very much, much too far away.

One Friday afternoon, soon after his admission to high school, Wilks found him wandering aimlessly about the athletic field bruised, battered, bloodied and crying, his new school uniform torn. He was homesick and very confused.

'Who did this to you?' demanded Wilks. Lighty refused to tell him of how the four Standard Seven bullies beat and tormented him for fear of retribution and revenge which he knew a lot about by that time. Wilks immediately took him to Tarzan. Wilks said to Tarzan:

'This fellow is hopeless when it come to taking care of himself. He is only eleven and does not know how things really are. Teach him something to take care of himself before some bully more than adequately *takes care* of him once too often.'

'If we don't look after him, no-one else will,' agreed Tarzan.

Lighty had, from then, and over the years, been instructed in gymnastics and the art of self-defence in the name of Ju Jitsu by Tarzan, and later, in addition, by Lighty's sister's boyfriend during school holidays, but he never revealed this skill to anyone. Ju Jitsu was not on the physical education curriculum explained Tarzan, but he would instruct Lighty for his own good anyway.

184

The combination of gymnastics and Ju Jitsu worked very well for Lighty for Tarzan taught Lighty the initial basics of warding off unwanted attention as well as fending off attack with devastating results.

'Don't bother warning the boys who try to bully you, just tumble them onto their heads, backs, necks and arses. If they come at you again, throw them even harder until they stop. Don't ever use these skills when you have no need to,' he warned.

Lighty did so, and the bullying stopped abruptly after a number of such encounters where his assailants were left painfully bleeding and crying. The bullies only seemed to get bigger and bigger until the tormenting and bullying, at last, came to an end.

'It was Lighty who hit me like this!' was a complaint that only evoked uproarious laughter and ridicule thereafter. Lighty made friends with Derek Gavshon, a very small Jewish chappie who also was being bullied, and Derek joined the Ju Jitsu classes. Tarzan was happy that there were two of them as they had each other to practice on. Derek also took up gymnastics.

Lighty found the change from primary school classroom to big boy's high school very hard. His mathematics progressed well under the tutelage of Wilks. Miss Jill Edwards, in her frightfully proper Cambridge English, did her utmost best for Lighty's English and Lighty had to work hard at his grammar, figures of speech and poetry. Latin somehow came easy to him.

He hated History with a passion, as Lighty found the text books to be biased against the English and the black people and taught only the glory of the defeat of the two in battle by the Boers. The English never seemed to get things right, nor did the natives.

Lighty represented the Eastern Transvaal province at gymnastics in his third year at high school at the age of thirteen in Standard Eight. It was for that achievement that he was the youngest sportsman ever to be awarded the school's Full Colours blazer.

In Standard Eight he also excelled in age-group athletics winning a Gold Medal at the National Athletic Championship in the under fourteen 4 x 110 yard relay race.

He was forced to miss the National Championships, and indeed all sporting activities and a lot of schooling, while very early in Standard Nine as he had fallen off a motor cycle over the Christmas holidays and had broken his collar bone, his hip and his right thigh. It took a whole year for him to fully recover and to become competitive again.

185

In his matric year at the National Athletic Championships he won the under sixteen Gold Medal for the 220 yards sprint and a bronze medal in the 4 x 110 yard relay. He had a brief two years to compete there missing one full season.

He eventually, in his matric year, for a very short time at the end of the season, played for the Rugby First Fifteen on the left wing. In the penultimate game of the season they again beat Helpmekaar 3-0 in a do-or-die game in the quarter-final of the Administrator's Cup.

He played again in the semi-final. He had run across to the right hand side of field in desperate last-man cover defence, and had been wrong-footed and comprehensively beaten by the opposition's full back two minutes from the final whistle. The opposition's full back took all of those agonising last two minutes to prepare for the successful two point conversion of his own try. Lighty's team lost the game by a sad 18 points to 16.

He finally went on to win the National Gymnastics Championships title a year after he left school. The eternal flame of the Olympic Games did not shine for him, for he was forever barred because of his race and the colour of his white skin.

He started by going to the Methodist Church every Sunday night because he had been baptised a Methodist. He continued to do so until he had completed his three months of confirmation classes. On the Thursday before the confirmation Sunday, the padre had declared that all the candidates were spiritually fully prepared except for Lighty. He said, in front of all the candidates, that he wanted Lighty to spend the next few days before the Sunday to decide for himself if he was going to attend the confirmation ceremony. Lighty was a spiritual and Christian reject.

Lighty attended his confirmation because he believed that only God could make decisions like that, and that God had told him no such thing. He never ever again went to the Methodist Church.

The problem was not that Lighty had, from his first year at high school, been taken in by the Jewish community and that most of his friends were Jewish. The Jewish people had fetched him from the boy's hostel every Friday evening, had taken him to the synagogue, and then for the Friday night Sabbath family meal at one of the Jewish homes. The real problem was that the synagogue was virtually opposite the Methodist manse. The other problem was that he was also a very good friend of the Presbyterian minister.

In his confirmation year, Lighty had this innocent thing going with the Presbyterian minister's daughter. On a Sunday afternoon, when her parents went to spend the afternoon at a faraway native mission in a Bantustan, and returned home late at night, and as often as they could get away with it, and until they got caught, the two of them used to go to the vestry, steal a bottle of sacramental wine and then kill it. Seven or eight of the Ten Commandments on the Sabbath, in the vestal vestry, in one fell swoop.

Bulletjie, the Little Bull, was the ultimate hurdle at high school. He was a twenty two year old new Physical Education instructor of magnificent physical proportions. He had replaced Tarzan, and was somewhat over-enthusiastic about disciplining English boys, in particular him, it seemed. It was the first time that Bulletjie actually was a teacher having finished Teachers Training College the previous year. He had played on the wing for the Western Transvaal Rugby side while he was there.

He was as thick as a brick and couldn't string two words of intelligible English together. *El Supremo* Afrikaners never spoke the Rooi Taal, 'die verdomde Ingelse taal', if they could help it. He refused to instruct Lighty and Derek in the art of Ju Jitsu as it wasn't on the curriculum.

'Wrestling is a proper Boeresport, and you will learn that. We will have no fancypants coolie activities here,' he had told an astonished Lighty and Derick in Afrikaans when they inquired about continuing their Ju Jitsu instruction at the beginning of the year.

Bulletjie had developed a rather nasty habit of walking up and down the queue to the dining room before meals, and ridiculing, pinching, punching and taunting the little English fellows. One day, as he was approaching Lighty, Lighty stepped out of line and away from his reach. He lunged out at Lighty grabbing him by the front of the shirt and then hurled him back into line. Lighty fell down on the rough concrete slab barking skin off his hands, knees and elbows.

Wilks was observing events from nearby with disgust. He had been quite vocal for some time about his desire to see this sort of practice cease but, being only five feet tall and as light as a fairy feather, he was physically powerless to do anything about it. He got by with a brilliant mathematical brain and a matching skill to teach it, the likes of which Lighty since then never came across.

Bulletjie again came at him, but this time Lighty was prepared and had the moral high ground together with the wounds to support it. He knew he had

Wilks unswerving backing. Using Bulletjie's own momentum Lighty hurled him effortlessly through the air with a hip roll onto the steps leading up to the dining room. Bulletjie hit the steps upside down and just lay there for a long time. He painfully, but bravely, denied that he had been hurt. Just as well thought Lighty.

Bulletjie reported Lighty to The Chief with deliberate and almost indecent haste demanding that Lighty be expelled forthwith.

The Chief, a fair, just and honest a man as ever existed, was aware that such a distasteful event was bound to occur sooner or later. Lighty was summoned to report to The Chief. Wilks accompanied him and, leaving Lighty outside The Chief's office, Wilks gave his account to The Chief.

Lighty went in and gave his account. He didn't mention the Ju Jitsu. Lighty told the Chief that he was trying to get out of the way. The Chief was a Marquis of Queensbury Rules man and not known to delay settling disputes. He was also somewhat punctual about correcting wrongs.

He called Wilks and Bulletjie in. No fool was The Chief, and he liked Lighty a lot - about as much as a headmaster could like the brightest pupil in the school, and one who was two years younger than his peers.

'Three rounds in the boxing ring! I will be the referee and judge. Select your seconds and report to the gym in half an hour,' he commanded. 'Tell Lighty that the rules of boxing will apply, and only those rules,' he told Wilks.

He was up to something was the Chief. He was always good to Lighty, but Christ, thought Lighty, he had just turned sixteen, weighed a hundred and ten pounds, couldn't see a punch coming because, having only one eye to see out of and lacking stereo vision and depth perception, he couldn't anticipate anything let alone exhibit a survival reflex.

Bulletjie was twenty two years old, weighed one hundred and fifty odd pounds, and was a perfect physical specimen. Two good eyes too. Wilks said that he would be Lighty's second, but Lighty knew that even with his brilliant brain it wasn't going to stop him from bloody well getting murdered.

The gong sounded for the beginning of the first round.

'Towel! Towel! Throw in the bloody towel!' a terrified Lighty desperately screamed to Wilks.

'Leave his head! Work his body! Work his body!' Wilks shouted back at him. Wilks didn't even have a bloody towel in his hand.

Lighty walked across to Bulletjie where he was standing in his corner pleading with the Chief to stop the fight because he was afraid that he was going to hurt Lighty.

The Chief just said 'Box on!'

Bulletjie never laid a glove on him, he hardly tried, but he squealed, hurt and bled a lot for three rounds, and a lot more after that. He was too dumb to take a dive. He hardly ever took his hands out of his trouser pockets after the fight. Nor did he talk to anyone. The fifty or so boys who saw the fight in the gymnasium that night swore blind, even to this day, that it was Lighty who hit him like that. They said that Lighty's first straight left did the damage as his fist buried itself deep into Bulletjie's rib-cage.

Bulletjie retired prematurely, permanently and unceremoniously two months later - he just forgot to come back to school after the holidays without telling anyone. Very unhappily so Lighty understood.

His ribs breaking had sounded like a rifle shot as he fell on the steps and could be heard a mile away, but no-one ever mentioned it. Everyone knows that with broken ribs, one can hardly breathe, and one cannot even handle a powder puff in anger let alone throw a punch.'

'Herman Charles Bosman would have liked the story about Oom Willie and the police sergeant,' Jack said. He had some of the late Herman's short story books in the Toyota and had started to read some of the funny Bushveld stories from them. Herman is a South African short story legend.

The story about the Afrikaner Bushveld congregation singing the whole of Psalm 119, all of Sunday morning and deep into the afternoon, was an absolute scream. *Cold Stone Jug*, which he wrote while waiting in his cell on Death Row at Pretoria Central Prison to be hanged for murder, was a bone chiller. Herman lived to tell the tale and wrote *Cold Stone Jug*. His death sentence was commuted to a life sentence at the eleventh hour.

Jack also read stories to me from a collection of Outback short stories by Henry Lawson, the Australian literary legend. The one I remembered best was the story of Little 'Arvey, the eleven year old boy who was worked to death in a Sydney factory leaving his mother and younger siblings without money to live on.

Henry Lawson had spent many of his last years as a hopelessly derelict drunk living between lying in the gutters and in prison for drunkenness and vagrancy. He died an ignomious, inglorious, impoverished death in someone's back yard, and was then given an elaborate State funeral. Fat lot of good that did him. Short story telling and campfire earning didn't seem to me to be a career with good prospects.

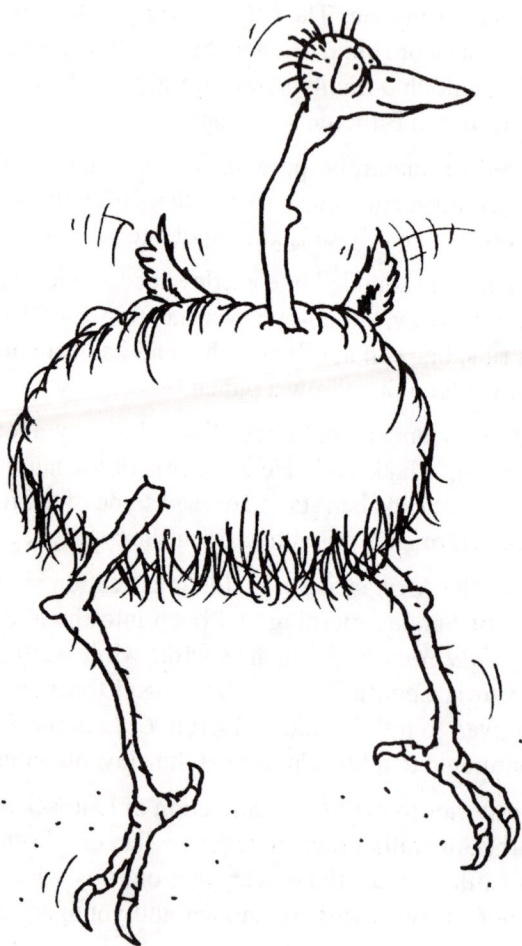

Chapter Eighteen

Jack had to go to the clinic at Lockhart River one morning. The nurse diagnosed a throat infection and dispensed aspirin along with a mouthwash to gargle with. We sat in the waiting area of the clinic fascinated by all the goings-on.

There was a video playing on Aboriginal welfare and some horrifying facts came to light. There was a clip on advice for Aborigine woman who suffered domestic violence - more often than not as a direct result of alcohol abuse.

'He can hit me with the flat hand, but if he uses his closed fist then there is big trouble,' said one Aborigine woman to another as they were watching the video. Yet, everyone appeared to be outwardly happy. We had some difficulty understanding things.

We drove down to the Claudie River for the afternoon for Jack to do some fishing and for me to be on the lookout for crocodiles as well as chase after the elusive eclectus parrot. The birds of course, were being very sensible and taking it quietly, while I thrashed around in the early afternoon heat.

We had expected to have a superb fish nosh but we caught nothing edible. I caught four catfish and a turtle, losing my weights and hooks three times, one to something huge, and another to a catfish which I subsequently caught red-handed - my old hook and weight was still in its mouth. Jack was starting to get a bit miffed because he was having somewhat less luck than I was having with fishing. He did, to his credit, land a small catfish.

The sunset was pure magic despite our failure to land any edible fish. Jack was somewhat alarmed to find me knee deep in the water at the concrete boat launching ramp washing my hands.

'Get out of there at once!' he commanded sternly. 'Mark told me that the biggest crocodile in the whole of the Cape York peninsular lives here and is probably watching you right now!' he yelled while racing over to again throw me around. That was the closest I have ever come to being killed by a crocodile, and I don't ever want to get any closer. It just slowly swam away.

'Snakes, bushpigs, sharks, crocodiles! What the hell are you going to get up to next woman?' Jack bellowed at me, and then calmly returned to his fishing.

I must have eaten something that Jack hadn't, and I had been constantly plagued by the trots. Jack had his cold and a sore throat instead. What a crock pair we turned out to be.

We were tired and a bit ill, but didn't want to waste a moment of our precious time in that paradise. Bird watching had almost become an engulfing obsession by then. It was exhausting, but fun, chasing after the eclectus parrot between frantic races into the bush with a shovel in one hand, toilet roll in the other, and binoculars around my neck swinging to and fro.

On the Thursday we had our dinner party at the guest house for Phil and Jenny. Louise had kindly prepared a roast leg of lamb and a trifle for us. Poor Phil had been laid low with a recurrent bout of malaria and couldn't be there. He was baby sitting instead.

The Royal Flying Doctor, the Community Health nurse and their pilot joined us. We really tucked into Louise's delicious lamb and trifle. I hadn't had anything to eat for three days and my sore tummy disappeared completely as I waded into the first home-cooked dinner in more than a month. Jack's sore throat didn't seem to bother him in the least.

We had planned to leave Iron Range on the Saturday morning. However, on the Friday, just before lunchtime, large, ominous rain clouds rapidly started building up. It then started to rain very heavily and our little rainforest spot suddenly became very dark, and not very desirable any longer. Our six days of fine weather was up.

'This rain won't stop for another week. Another hour of this, and we can forget about making the landing barge at Weipa in three days time. Time to shake, rattle and rock 'n roll again. Look sharp!' Jack said

We got the right, ruddy hell out of the place. Within twenty minutes we were on our way. I never thought that either of us had the energy to break camp and make for anywhere - especially Jack. His cold and sore throat had knocked him about very badly.

We began the boggy exit out of the park. What a nightmare! The road was ghastly after half an hour of rain. I thought we would never make it out except for Jack's positive go-for-it attitude and grim determination. I was not very happy, still having stomach cramps, and making desperate excursions into the scrub.

I hung on for dear life as we slid around hitting rocks, ruts, mud holes, embankments and generally giving the Toyota a far worse beating than it took when going in. I also reckoned that it would do Jack's cold no good at all. Amazingly my sore tummy held out during the vitally critical moments.

The only place we had any real trouble was going up that first two hundred metre stretch with the solid, but very slippery, surface. It had taken us an hour and a half to cover the first one hundred and ninety metres. We had ten metres to go to reach hard, firm ground again.

Jack had started to take out the shovel to cut ruts across the track, which would have given us the desired traction we so desperately needed. Suddenly, two new Nissan Patrols came hurtling down the hill toward us. As soon as they saw us they braked hard. One Patrol went slithering to their right into the scrub, and the other, in the rear, managed to stay on the track.

'Here is trouble!' predicted Jack.

'What is the problem?' I asked him.

'Bloody Toorak Tractors from Melbourne,' he replied.

The one on the track tried to back up but got nowhere. His wheels just spun. That was when the trouble really started.

'Back up down to the other side of the creek so that we can get through and reach Lockhart River by tonight!' yelled one of the heroes wearing, would you believe, white shoes.

Jack stared at him in utter disbelief. Jack was sodden, soaked through, covered in mud from head to toe, and shivering from a high temperature. He walked up to White Shoes and his mate.

'I've come from there,' he said, pointing his thumb back over his shoulder. 'And I'm going there! ' he concluded punching his index finger in front of him and nearly knocking White Shoes over.

'But my truck is in the way! I can't back up,' said White Shoes.

'Then pull it off the road and park it there!' said Jack and pointing to a horrible looking metre deep ditch to his right.

White Shoes got into his Patrol and drove it into the ditch with his wife screaming blue bloody murder at him. The road was clear but the Nissan was terminally bogged. Mrs White Shoes could not open her door as it was lying against the embankment. The Nissan was lying on its side at an awkward forty five degree angle.

'Do you guys want to winch me out, or do you want to watch and wait until I winch myself out with my Tirfor hand winch?' Jack asked White Shoes' mate who had a power winch on his bullbar.

'No problem,' said helpful Mate and wound his winch cable out in a great hurry while Jack held the hook and dragged it closer to our vehicle. It was too short. Jack took out our Snatchum strap, joined, and hitched it to our tow hook.

As he was about to get back into the vehicle, Mrs White Shoes yelled out something indecipherable to him. Wearily, he walked up to her to inquire what her problem was.

'Turn you radio on and I'll talk you through it,' she tells Jack.

Jack had a quick talk to Mate the winch driver, got back into the vehicle, and switched the radio off. Mate started the winch up and we slowly crept up the hill past Mrs White Shoes who was screaming at the top of her squeaky voice into a dead microphone while lying at forty five degrees with her nose up against the windscreen.

'Don't come too close! You might hit us!' we heard her scream shrilly in wild-eyed terror.

The front wheels bit on firm ground and we were out. Jack unhooked the gear and recovered our Snatchum strap.

'Do you need some help to get out of there?' Jack asked White Shoes.

'No thanks. We will manage. You get along now,' White Shoes replied.

We went on our way - straight into the next two hundred metres of hell. It was the place where the fourteen vehicles had been bogged on our way in. Fortunately there were no vehicles bogged there then.

We hit it at a more than respectable speed and incredibly kept on going. It was no different from the first time. Slowly, we progressed until we reached terra firma again at the top of it. We stopped to catch our breath and to marvel at our incredible good fortune. We knew that the rest of it was comparatively easy going.

We reached Mount Tozer, which was where we finally knew we were safe. The mountain was misty with gentle, steady drizzle falling - it was a magnificent sight. We had so wanted to climb it but, it too, would have to wait.

'Never mind,' I said to Jack. 'We made it out. Been there, done that, got all the tee shirts, had a great time and met heaps of lovely people,' He didn't disagree. It had taken us five hours to cover fifteen kilometres! We could have walked twice as fast as that!

We reached the Wenlock River just before dark and set up a nice camp at the same spot we did going in. No sooner had we done that, than we were invaded by two families going into Lockhart River who set up camp next to us. We were so exhausted, and feeling so ill, that we did not even hear the feathered evensong, nor did we wake for the dawn chorus the following morning.

Having the sun shine on us the following morning was marvellous and it quickly dried ourselves and our gear out. We were in no particular hurry so we walked about in our swimming togs with sun-warmed sand between our toes. We pulled the Toyota into the middle of the river and gave it, and ourselves, a thorough wash-down.

It was fun, but we constantly had to be on the lookout for crocodiles. We both felt lousy but we did not let this deter us from having fun. During the course of the morning passing vehicles going towards Iron Range occasionally disturbed us.

'The poor sods!' I said to Jack. One vehicle came out from the east. The driver, a Northern Territorial, told us about the sorry party of Victorians who had spent the night in the scrub with both their Patrols in the ditch and both quite un-extractable. It had rained all night.

'They were very muddy, very wet, very unhappy and very vocal about it,' he said. We told him about our episode with them the previous day. He laughed until his sides ached and tears were rolling down his cheeks soaking his big, bushy, black beard. It must have been an hilariously funny sight that he had seen.

That night at the campfire was confessional time, and Jack told me about Lighty's life and times at college. Wait for it.

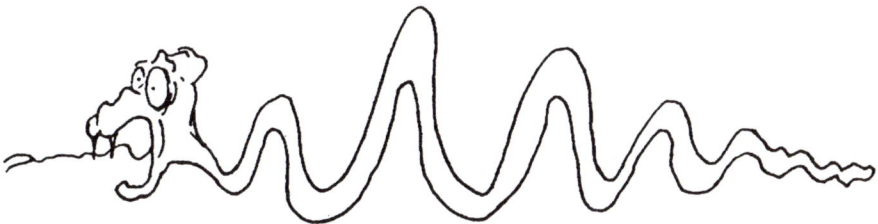

Chapter Nineteen

Lighty had left school after matriculating at the age of sixteen. He managed to get a job as a surveyor on a mine, but, because he had only one eye, he couldn't pass the medical examination for miners so he had to look elsewhere for a job. He started working in the administration functions of coal mines, a job organised by his father's friends in order to place him in a protected environment, supposedly because he had only one eye and was as light as fairy floss. He had progressed to becoming a hot-shot accounting desk-jockey six years later, and had one more promotion to look forward to for the rest of his life.

'Sitting around counting beans and getting paid peanuts is for monkeys,' he had figured. 'Similarly, drinking tea and smelling farts in an office all day is not my idea of living.' Suffice it is to say that, at the delicate age of twenty two, Lighty had his first major career crisis.

He again went for the miner's medical examination and cheated the doddering old medic by reading the eye test chart with his right eye both times. He became a learner miner then in a coal mine near Witbank. Everyone said that he was quite mad to abandon his highly successful career as an accountant.

His family, who had high hopes for him, disowned him for a while. His father was very disappointed as his father was of the learned opinion that underground mining was not a proper profession for his son. He wasn't at all vocal about it, but Lighty could see that his father was more than somewhat displeased.

He started work as a spanner boy on the rail gang bolting fish-plates to rails, and frogs, and turn-offs, and making rail tracks for the cocopans to run on. It was quite a change of occupation from accounting in an office and his hands soon developed calluses, and his back and legs got a lot stronger from carrying rails around with the Inyanbane rail-workers from Mozambique.

Some four weeks later, he had been handed a ten pound sledge-hammer to install timber props to support the roof in unsafe places. The conversion from pen to sledge-hammer often had Lighty wondering about the wisdom of his decision to change occupations. He thought then not with his head, but with his arms, shoulders and back. He did this for the fifty four hours he spent every week underground, forty eight of which he spent swinging a sledge-hammer.

He then spent another month being a trammer assisting two Xhoza coal shovellers to load and push fifty one-ton cocopans of coal every day. He no longer had to wonder about how hard-labour convicts got by.

That was also where he had first innocently encountered an affable character by the name of Nickers Olwagen. Nickers took Lighty under his protective wing. Lighty knew that his real name was Nickerless, as he had been born and babtised as such. He had, as time went by, lost the latter part of his name and people just called him Nickers. It didn't really matter too much which way one looked at him anyway. Deep inside he was one and the same man.

Nickers was also a learner miner then, had been awarded a scholarship from African American to study mining engineering, and was waiting for college to start. Little did Lighty realise then that his real education in life had just begun. With Nickers' devious assistance, and with the benevolent assistance of Lighty's father's connections, Lighty had then also been awarded a scholarship to study mining engineering.

It was late in his fourth academic year that life for Lighty started to go very badly wrong, and his fate took a turn for the worse. His grades deteriorated rapidly, and his room-mate Mike Poultney was convinced that his doing a valve-grind on his Austin Mini, aptly named *The Bomb* every third week in the room that they shared, was not a very good thing to do.

The fact that The Bomb used to burn valves regularly because the air-fuel mixture was wrong, was not the real cause of the problem. It was because Lighty did not know then, that he knew not.

Lighty started to believe that he had lost his marbles. He simply could not understand what was happening to him, and why it was happening. Nickers helped him to telephone the college counsellor and they made an appointment to see her with the idea that she would rectify the matter once and for all.

Now psychologists do not have easy jobs. Lighty's problem was in particular extremely difficult because the psychologist could find nothing wrong with him at first. Good looking for a shrink she was too.

It took quite some time for her to finally figure out what was happening and what the real problem was. It was all a question of innocent guilt, and still is to this day.

It was not Lighty's fault. Life takes some weird and wonderful twists and turns as one learns as one goes along the way. The psychologist couldn't help but laugh a lot, and loudly so, when she finally wrung the truth out of him and discovered what the real problem was.

She said that it was not Edna Plumstead's fault for scrambling his brain. Lighty had, in his second year, been blessed with the fortune to have Plummy *plum-in-the-mouth Oxfordian* Dr Plumstead for a geology lecturer. After many lengthy heated confrontations, when Plummy refused to initially accept the fact that lecturers could state the then known facts, and it was the prerogative of the student to question those facts, that Plummy finally started to understand the state of affairs of this planet.

Unexpectedly one day, after a heated two person debate at lectures, Lighty was discreetly, after the lecture, invited for dinner at the Plumstead's house. None of the others students were invited, just Lighty. It was the first of many such visits to the Plumstead's home over many subsequent years.

On his arrival there, man alone, a very charming and attractive elderly lady who asked Lighty to address her as Edna met him at the front door. Lighty, being the barbarian that he was at the time, knew not who she was, as did the rest of the world then.

Edna was a lecturer in geophysics and was busy completing her doctoral thesis. Formalities and niceties followed where Lighty did his very best to impress a really nice lady. Lighty fiddled his Lion Lager a lot. Plummy said very little but took a hard look at, and listened to, the discourse and conversation between his attractive wife and his very problem student.

Edna, with glass of very expensive scotch in hand, invited Lighty to her study in the rear of the massive Hyde Park mansion. Lighty followed her not knowing what was in store for him there. Elderly ladies were not exactly his style, but he went to have a look at what Edna asked him to have a look at.

On their arrival in her study, Lighty observed a collection of blocklike objects resembling the continents of Earth lying on a table. The objects were lying around close together. Edna said nothing at all but she watched Lighty intently. He walked up to the table and systematically re-arranged them in their proper order as he knew them to be thinking it was some sort of intellectual game at which he was being tested.

'That is how things are today, Lighty. We all know that. But how did they get there from where you first found them?' Edna asked.

'From where?' asked Lighty beer in hand.

Edna silently put them in the positions they first were and then stood back. Lighty then again put them in their proper positions.

'Plate tectonics, continental drift and Gondwanaland Lighty, is what this exercise is all about,' said Edna. 'You and I, with your inquiring mind, will tonight satisfy ourselves as to how this planet evolved. If we are agreed, then I will submit my thesis on this subject for my doctorate with total confidence in its ultimate success'

So ensued the most interesting and informative evening Lighty had ever experienced in all his life. He forgot what happened for dinner, if it happened. Long after sunrise the next morning a place called Gondwanaland was finally born, shifting continents became a reality, vulcanology became a predictable and known science, and earthquakes became better understood and partially predictable.

'I submit my thesis this week then Lighty. We are in total agreement. You must come to see me more often Lighty. If all I teach you is the ability to think, it will be reward enough for me,' she very tiredly said to Lighty that morning at breakfast table before he departed for Palm Villa and then on to lectures.

'The vast majority of past famous inventors, discoverers and philosophers were astronomers Lighty,' she once said to him. 'They are a unique and elite club. You must join them one day. I know you will,' Edna never in her lifetime admitted to being one of them. She is; and forevermore will remain so.

This profound enlightenment of the evolution of Earth, and his early exposure to the conception of its development, has never left Lighty. His ongoing study of astrophysics continues to this day. His deep love for, and appreciation of, Dr Edna Plumstead, the most profound geophysicist this world has ever known, has never diminished. She also opened up the science of astrophysics, and never in her lifetime did she graciously ever admit to that fact.

The Nobel Prize eluded Edna, and Lighty will never know why. The Plumsteads took him in as a son.

'Now Palm Villa is totally another matter,' the shrink said to Lighty. Palm Villa was not really a planned event in the lives of ten innocent, upright, law abiding, bright, innovative, self-respecting and self-determined young mining students. Palm Villa was a turn-of-the-century double storey colonial mansion built on a very spacious block of land in Houghton Heights in Johannesburg for some unknown mining tycoon shortly after the Anglo-Boer war.

It came equipped with five double bedrooms each with en-suite bathroom, a banquet hall, a billiards room, a swimming pool, a tennis court, four garages, six carports, a non-resident Matron named Mrs Meyer, a chef, two housemaids cum kitchen hands and waitresses, two gardeners and a night security guard. All was paid for by the mining houses. There were locks on the doors, but cleverly no keys for them.

Palm Villa was an unfortunate and expensive, but very necessary, acquisition on the part of the mining benefactors of the Terrible Ten. It had previously been a home for wayward boys, had been purchased by a collection of mining houses, and then refurbished and converted into a residence for them. This was only after a perfectly understandable innocent caper which had been going on for perhaps longer than was possibly tolerable, and which had been exposed, that they were relocated to Palm Villa.

The reason for the relocation was that the ten had been sprung. Ian 'Soutie' Foster, a Pommie immigrant fresh from England, had late in the first year, with great cunning and devious intent, conned one of the black workers in the kitchen of the Men's Main Residence to make impressions of all the keys to the doors leading to the kitchen as well as keys for all the larders and cool room doors. The impressions, made in window putty supplied to the paid, witting accomplice, were soon converted into a set of keys.

Soutie got his name having been wrongfully blamed for having one foot in England and one foot in South Africa. With legs stretched so far apart, and with an unmentionable part of his anatomy, his middle stump really, dangling in the salt waters of the Atlantic Ocean, Soutpiel was the appropriate reference to him. It was, in the vernacular, duly abbreviated to Soutie.

One night, early in their second year, at two thirty on a Saturday morning, on wearily and hungrily returning from the Devonshire pub in Braamfontein with an overload of beer, the ten made their surreptitious entry to the kitchen and commenced frying steaks, eggs and onions. It was not the first time this had happened but perhaps the tenth time that year. Nickers swore blind that it was the smell of onions frying that got them sprung to which Tannie Knor, (Aunty Growl), the Chief Residence Matron, eagerly agreed to.

The cooking was in full swing when the South African Police Force loudly made their entry accompanied by Barnie Barnard, the official Residence Housemaster together with Tannie Knor along with three police sniffer dogs.

'It's Lighty!' Tannie Knor cried out in triumph and pointing at Lighty as he was lifting his steak out of the frying pan.

Immediate expulsion was the order of the day and the boys took up temporary residence at The Springbok Hotel near Park Station that day and continued their studies as usual. The former was done with the eager approval of Barnie together with the vehement approval of Tannie Knor. They apparently had sound reason to do so it was said.

When Palm Villa became habitable and ready for occupation two weeks later the various mining houses paying for their education promptly relocated The Ten there from The Springbok.

Now it might be said, with an element of truth, that the mining students were a somewhat lively and socially active bunch of mixed smalls. They were also known to be somewhat disruptive in their general behaviour. Not that Barnie and Tannie Knor had any objection to their being so inclined, just provided that it was done off campus and not on their domain.

The expulsion and relocation did not later deter Barnie and Tannie Knor from paying the occasional social visit to Palm Villa in their unofficial capacities. Nor did it deter them from using Palm Villa as an escape from the boringly booze-free, women-free, sin-free, orderly and uninteresting Main Men's Residence.

Barnie had, during the first of his many visits, started to enjoy the odd game of poker and a few cold beers and laughs with the boys. Tannie Knor also had a place to go to where she could laughingly relax amongst sincere friends and kindred spirits with a rather large and soothing gin and tonic to calm her forever shattered nerves.

Palm Villa started off by not having any rules or regulations - none at all. The ensuing much-discussed chaos was a sight to behold until the boys all realised, after some four weeks, that the situation could not continue as it had until then.

'If we are to enjoy the privileges of Palm Villa and the best mining education somebody else's money is buying for us, then we had better do something to properly secure our very frail, fragile and fallible position,' Joao Texeira, in his advanced sober Portuguese wisdom proclaimed one Monday morning at breakfast before going off to lectures.

After much discussion, reflection and soul searching that day a Council Of War Against Wrongdoing And Drunkenness (COWARD) was called, and held. Some basic and inviolable rules evolved.

Mondays were to be held sacrosanct and reserved for study only. No errant capers were allowed, and all had to report to Palm Villa directly after lectures for studies for the rest of the Monday.

Tuesdays and Thursdays were rugby practice afternoons. Following rugby practice, all were to report in totally sober state for studies for the rest of those two days. On completion of studies at 9:30 pm each Monday, Tuesday and Thursday, all were allowed four beers apiece as a sleepytime sendoff to the eventful day.

Anyone who appeared to be lacking, or slacking, in any subject was immediately placed in the care and tutorship of the top boffin on that subject. Expulsion from Palm Villa included the omitting to hand assignments in on time, plagiarism and failing a test or an examination for whatever reason. Wednesday nights were reserved for external student bonding and general mayhem.

Palm Villa was women-free from Mondays to Thursdays. Wednesday nights were discussed at length with regard to women. Mrs Meyer's appeals for responsible moderation in morality won the day on that occasion. From Friday afternoon after lectures, and after Mrs Meyer had gone home, it was open slather until Monday morning.

'The very worst of us should be elected as a four man Coward Tribunal with no recourse for appeal,' Rudi Dutchke proposed. Rudi's real name was Eric Dillon, whose mother came from Ireland and he sported an unmistakably wild carrot-top hairdo. His endless intellectual bulldust on socialism was frowned upon and his Russian nickname stuck to him like glue sticks to an army blanket.

A democratic vote was arranged with each listing who was believed to be the four very worst on a very worst, second, third and fourth worst basis. The ensuing secret ballot revealed, by an overwhelming majority, that Nickers, Tex, Chris and Lighty, elected in that order, were to be the first Coward Tribunal.

At the beginning of each quarter a new election would be held and the make-up of the tribunal realigned accordingly. The withholding of beer privileges on Mondays, Tuesdays and Thursdays was the key to the success of Dutchke proposal, and the only measure necessary to maintain a regularly ordered lifestyle.

All their college expenses were paid for. The upkeep of Palm Villa cost them not a cent including their meals, which Mrs Meyer prepared for them and kept in the warming drawers for later consumption when so required. Each was paid a non-taxable allowance of a princely two hundred and fifty rand a month to spend on women, booze and motor cars - a fortune in those days.

A second-hand bar counter, complete with a fridge which could hold ten cases of beer soon materialised in the billiard room. A monthly fifty rand contribution from each ensured that a mountainous supply of beer was always to hand and they lacked for nothing. At ninety six cents for a six-pack of beer, the world was forever right.

The all-weekend parties held at Palm Villa once a month, from the braaivleis on the Friday evenings to the sad and sorry dispersal on the Monday mornings, were legendary and memorable events each with its own evolution, progression and conclusion. The lady students who were invited there for the weekend knew why they had been invited there, and none had reason to complaint. There were those who did, and there were those who didn't, and those who didn't soon did.

On those weekends, Mrs Meyer and her staff were given a long weekend off. She knew not what transpired and, for her own moral safety, did not want to know. Mrs Meyer and her husband, together with Barney and his wife, and Tannie Knor and her boyfriend of the time, were, on many occasions, guests of honour at some of the parties they threw. The shrink, who had been to a few of the parties that the boys used to throw from time to time, but never stayed overnight, said that she knew that Lighty's problem wasn't really Palm Villa. Who said that crime doesn't pay?

What had really happened was that, one day after lectures, the mining boys had gone on the regular pub-crawl in preparation for a party that was being held at the Berea Women's Residence that night. They had decided to make it their business to get themselves extra-specially prepared and ready for the big social event.

As it was on a Wednesday, they could start early as lectures ended early on that day. It was not exactly true that lectures officially ended early on Wednesdays as such, it was because they had decided not to attend Archie Park's boring Mining Plant lectures, and to let him feel lonely, neglected and abandoned.

Archie had taken them on a ten day field tour over the Easter vacation to visit mines of specific interest. He apparently had not enjoyed the tour at all, and had reported the mining students to the Baron von Maltitz for gross

204

disorderly misconduct. The Baron was Director of the School of Mining and Metallurgy.

God only knows why, but Archie had accused Mike Poultney of being the ringleader of the most heinous activities. The co-accuseds were Lighty, Chris le Roux, Johnny Texeira, CP Wissekerke, Nickers Olwagen and Bilious Bentley. In reality, Mike was a relative innocent in the overall scheme of things there really being no-one who could be accused as a ringleader as all were equally capable and culpable, if that is an appropriate term to use.

Archie's sense of humour had abandoned him very early on the tour, and it appeared that he did not enjoy the tour as much as he could have, or perhaps would like to have. In fact, it was on the very first night of the tour that Archie's nightmare started. There was hard evidence to prove that perhaps Archie had enjoyed the tour a bit too much on that first night, but had failed to bring that to The Baron's, or anyone else's, attention, including his wife's.

The undisclosed evidence consisted of numerous photographs of Archie dressed in his night-dress and with his night-cap on. He was sitting upright in bed alongside a pretty young bare-breasted lady, a bewilderingly startled look on his face. Archie was happily married, sixty six years old, and a staid and dour a Scotsman as can be imagined.

Archie really was not guilty, as it clearly was a set-up, and everyone else was equally to blame including Delectable Dulcie who had kindly colluded with the plot to ensure that Archie had a good time on the tour.

After the Baron had lightly reprimanded the five co-accused, with a rather benevolently understanding and paternal sermon in a cultured German accent, the boys sort of wondered about things for a bit.

The mine managers who were host to the students on the tour were discreetly informed that there was a *no booze* stipulation that Archie had imposed on the chartered bus. Being men of great experience, understanding and compassion, they equally discreetly arranged for many, many gallons of beer to be secreted in the bus as well as on the roof-rack while it was left unattended.

When it came time for everyone to board the bus for the next journey, Archie stood at the door for roll-call and to ensure that no booze was being taken on board. Roll-call completed, he would take up his seat of privilege on the very front seat near the driver. He had great difficulty understanding why Lighty kept on shouting for a comfort stop very often - far too often for Archie's liking.

'Pee, pee, or I'll pee in the bus!' Lighty kept on shouting whenever any-one felt the need for one.

Bilious Bentley didn't think it was his fault for having Lighty as his first friend on his arrival at college. Bilious was a fresh-faced, raw kid then and had still not learnt how to drink beer properly. His uproariously chunderous chucks were to become college legend. He reticently admitted in mitigation then that he had smoked pot once in his last year at boarding school, but that was no excuse and Bilious it remained forever afterwards.

'I am not going to pee over here, I'm going to pee over theeeeeere!' he kept on telling people whenever he had a bellyful of beer and a swollen bladder to match.

He had won the prestigious, dubious double in the college beer-drinking championships and the long-distance peeing knockout competition for three years in a straight row. His downing of 26 pints of Lion Lager in the space of four hours was a never-to-be-repeated feat of the most incredible endurance, and loudly proclaimed to be the eighth marvel of the modern age.

Bilious' rugby prowess in kicking a three point penalty from midway between the halfway line and his own three-quarter line and a metre in from touch in a match against Goldfields was considered to be a ninth modern day wonder. He next went on a death defying, bone breaking barge of epic proportions to score a try from fifty yards out. His attempt at converting the try shaved the upright, bounced on the cross bar and then bounced over.

Bilious collapsed from sheer exhaustion when the final whistle eventually shrilled to call an end to the mighty battle of Titans. The score in that game was tenaciously tied at eight-all for the last seventy five minutes of playing time. Whenever those feats were mentioned thereafter, they commanded a reverend silence, and inspired many dreams of great green and gold Springbok glory while intently staring glassy-eyed deep into the amber liquid.

Lighty swiftly administered a pint of Lion Lager to Bilious while he was still lying near-mortally incapacitated on the field of battle. A faint flicker of the left nostril reassured Lighty that Bilious was going to be just fine.

The stretcher bearers got a very bad fright when Bilious suddenly leaped off the stretcher as they were approaching the ambulance. Bilious' spontaneous recovery was truly an incredible sight to behold everybody said afterwards. Much to the great dismay of all the boys, all the girls, quite rightly, thought and said, that he was the tenth modern day marvel.

Mike Poultney didn't think that it was his fault either when, during the tour, late one afternoon on their way from the Transvaal to Natal, he had decided that a breath of fresh air was quite in order. He had climbed out of a window to perch himself on the roof-rack. It was also so that he could pass cases of beer down to the boys inside the bus. It also enabled him to drink copious amounts of beer and to pee to his heart's content without annoying Archie and the bus driver too much.

It was when the bus was going down a steep hill, with the setting sun directly from behind, that the bus driver noticed, on the road in front of him, the shadow of someone perched on the roof-rack. He braked violently throwing Archie out of his seat and onto the floor, and Mike very nearly off the bus. By the time the bus had been brought under control, Mike was innocently smiling and safely seated inside the bus and everyone was on their very best behaviour.

Lighty didn't think that it was his fault when they had resumed the journey and he had inquired, loudly enough for Archie and the bus driver to hear, about who the fellow was standing in the middle of the road furiously waving his arms about in alarm. The bus driver again braked violently, Archie again fell out of his seat, grudgingly regained his composure, and took another roll-call.

Wollie didn't think it was his fault for showing anyone who cared to take a look at what his bleeding haemorrhoids looked liked. He also said that it wasn't his fault for nearly drowning very late one night in the swimming pool when Lighty had jumped in right on top of him knocking his wind out. Once he had been rescued, been resuscitated, and started to breath again, Chris had remembered his first-aid drill and had promptly tapped a hot bath for him.

'Shock!' it was, Chris said. Wollie had been dumped into the hot bath and had immediately turned a very bright red. He looked very unhappy in a paralysed sort of way. They said at the hospital that night that he had first degree burns all over, but they told Archie at three o'clock that morning that Wollie was going to be OK in a month or so once all his skin had peeled off.

Lighty often wonders a lot about Rugby and about how Wollie inspired a certain man to the greatest of heights. You see, one night, when he was a student, Wolly accidentally fell into a pub in Valhalla for a beer while on his way back to Palm Villa. A very big man came in and sat down next to him. The big man ordered a beer. He looked at Wollie and said "Cheers !". Wollie lifted his glass and said "Cheers" back. They then started to talk about rugby as was the custom amongst strangers in those days to immediately break the social ice.

They bemoaned, at great length, the fact that the very big man had been dropped from the Northern Transvaal team for the two previous matches because he had misbehaved, and had been, not suspended, but just dropped, for the previous two games. They spoke for a long time over a few quiet beers as Rugby players are known to do.

'I am going to score a try, and I am going to convert that try, and I am going to place a penalty and I am going to kick a drop-kick!' promised the very big man in parting that Wednesday night. Wollie promised him that the Palm Villa crew would all be there for the match that Saturday to cheer him along every inch of his way to make the very big man's dream come true.

The Palm Villa crew all had a case of Lion Lager apiece on their shoulders as they walked into the stadium. Wollie's very big beer-drinking friend in the Valhalla pub scored a try, he converted that try, he place-kicked a penalty, and he drop-kicked the ball between the posts and over the crossbar in that memorable Currie Cup game. Frik du Preez is one of the very few heroes to be found in the World Rugby Hall of Fame.

Tex didn't think it was his fault for his insatiable passion for rock 'n roll amongst other things. He didn't think that Archie fully appreciated the finer points of that art-form, especially the part when Tex twirled him around a few times in the bus after Archie had imbibed the odd Scotch too many and had developed an acute case of the wobbles one night in Natal after a reception. Natal had that casual and relaxed sort of air about it. *Natal Fever* they called it.

Tex's fever took on a particular high later that night when, after a pee stop at the President Hotel in Vryheid, the boys had decided to abandon Archie and the bus driver. They decided that it would be more fun going to a rock 'n roll party in progress at the time in the Town Hall instead.

Tex really hit his straps that night. He wasn't just happy dancing with the girls, he had to race them around the room until he drove them into a screamingly hysterical heap in the corner before finally falling down on the floor and laughing himself into a hernia. Such was Tex.

Chris didn't think that it was his fault because he had innocently called for a pee stop. Archie and the bus driver were the first off the bus and the only ones to alight. Chris had promptly closed the doors, got into the driver's seat, and took off.

Archie and the bus driver didn't like running after the bus only for it to take off again for another hundred yards or so. About five times Chris did that with the rest of the mob leering out of the rear and side windows cheering them on.

Chris also didn't think it was his fault for setting a new college record by seeing 21 movies in one week.

CP was offended, and indeed deeply aggrieved, at Archie's total lack of humane consideration.

'CP, meet BP,' was how Nickers had introduced CP to the blow-up BP man at a fuel stop. A love-at-first-sight affection had besieged CP in a weak moment. The BP man was spirited aboard the bus, but Archie had later demanded that BP be abandoned at the side of the road fearing serious repercussion in the event of police intervention.

'It isn't fair,' CP had mournfully claimed for a long time thereafter.

For a long time after the tour Archie couldn't understand why many, many letters from ladies started arriving at his home in response to an advertisement he had placed under the pseudonym *Granite* in the Hitching Post column in the Farmer's Weekly magazine. He also couldn't, for the life of him, understand why his photograph in bed with Delectable Dulcie started appearing on the college bulletin boards and in the college magazine.

Anyway, to get back to the painful original point, the boys started the Wednesday afternoon off at the Springbok Hotel in Rissik Street. The darts game started immediately as did the continuation of the college matches knockout championships, Indian wrestling, bottle walking and general mayhem.

They had all been banned from the Springbok Hotel some two years before, but as there was a new owner, and a new barman, they thought that they were safe enough there. They were so too, until a very proper gentleman walked in for his constitutional evening Scotch on the rocks. He took exception to the unaccustomed racket and antics around him and voiced his strong disapproval.

'Who the hell are you?' Chris asked him casually.

'I am Colonel Viljoen of the South African Police Force,' the gentleman replied calmly.

'And I am Mohammed Ali!' Chris replied, a fraction thoughtlessly and somewhat exaggerated. His best performance was to be the runner-up at the National Amateur Boxing Championships. He then poked his finger in the colonel's Scotch on the rocks.

'Baleka Ngodini!' Tex shouted as Colonel Viljoen flashed his police identification. 'Run down the hole!' They had hardly run fifty yards when the first of many police squad car sirens sounded.

They regrouped at *The Underground*, a basement nightclub at the Ambassador Hotel on Twist Street. It didn't take Lighty long to get bounced after he had decided that to be a go-go guy was a good idea and had joined the go-go girl on stage for a bit of a boogie. He had been thrown out of better places that that before.

The boys merrily wound their way around to the Chelsea Hotel in Hillbrow where they took up position at the bar in the Cocktail Room. Al Willox and The All-Stars were entertaining the patrons to some delicate strains of the music of old.

Al was a Scotsman, and proud of it too, as he always wore his kilt and sporran. He was the only known person who could speak Afrikaans with a Scots accent. Al and The All-Stars were a very popular band, and were well known throughout the whole Witwatersrand and the Transvaal.

Once comfortable settled down with a beer apiece, it was mischief time again. A table next to the stage had been vacated and Duchke was quick to seize an opportunity.

'Come with me,' he said to Lighty grabbing him by the arm. 'The rest of you stay behind and watch' he said to the others.

Duchke and Lighty slipped into position at the vacant table. Duchke then took a notebook and pencil from his briefcase and started making some notes. The more he made notes, the more his critical eye looked upon Al and The All-Stars raising his eyebrows each and every time a false note was played.

Al was becoming increasingly aware of their presence and eventually could contain his curiosity no longer. He called for a break for The All-Stars and immediately approached Duchke and Lighty at their table.

'What are you making notes for?' Al asked Duchke.

'I am Rudi Duchke, the art critic from *Die Burger* in Cape Town. This is my colleague Lighty, who is the art critic from *The Cape Times* Duchke replied.

'What are you doing here?' Al asked, more as an exclamation rather than a question.

'We are on a secret mission to scout around for musical talent to invite to The Cape Town Music Festival next month,' Duchke confided to him.

'I shall see to it that you are very well looked after,' assured Al, and did. The harder Duchke and Lighty drank, the more beers were placed in front of them, and the harder, louder and longer The All-Stars played. Duchke stopped making notes when he realised that he could no longer read what he had written and that his notes kept falling off his note-pad and onto the table.

'I have booked The Banquet Room at The President Hotel for dinner and a party for you and the other Cape Town people on Friday night,' Al came up and told them a bit later, and smiling ever so broadly.

'There are ten of us in all,' Duchke replied.

'Splendid!' said Al. 'I shall invite some of the better musicians in town to provide a greater variety of talent for you to choose from,' he continued.

'We will all be there,' Duchke assured him.

At that stage a dishevelled Wollie made a dramatic, wild-eyed entrance and, on seeing the other boys sitting at the bar, immediately started loudly expostulating to them how he had just been rolled by a bunch of muggers.

'Unfortunately we must go to another venue now to meet some of the others in our contingent,' Duchke apologised to Al. They took their leave followed by the rest of the boys - slowly. Wollie's intact wallet was duly recovered after some interesting negotiations with the muggers.

The party on the Friday night for all ten of the Palm Villa crew was nothing short of excellent, and so too was the very friendly and over-abundant female company. Someone should tell Al about this because Lighty's conscience can't stand it any longer.

When they turned up at the party at Berea Residence at about nine o'clock that night, the whole thing was a rather tame non-event and everybody was sort of sitting around looking at each other not knowing what to do at parties and how to get them started. The best thing to do of course, is for the boys to dance with the girls, and to chat to them.

On their rowdy entrance everybody's eyes lit up. Lively reputations were hard to come by and needed to be earned over quite some period. The mining boys were well-known hardened party veterans by then. The boys swiftly

211

sorted themselves out with the *You take the fat one and I'll take the skinny one,* routine and the party started roaring.

Lighty spotted a rather sweet, angelic and innocent looking wall-flower that he had not seen before and raced her off for a rock 'n roll. She couldn't dance very well, but she was a nice girl to talk to, so Lighty stuck around her for a while. She didn't seem to mind much about that, the sticking around for a while part, which of course, Lighty thought was rather a good thing.

She told Lighty that she was a novice at that sort of thing which he didn't really care about firmly believing that, with every confidence, he would soon put all that to rights. She was in her first year at The Johannesburg College of Education studying to be a music and English teacher she said.

Later that night, at around midnight, Lighty walked her home like gentlemen used to do in those days and ensured that she was safely in her flat in Smit Street, Braamfontein where she lived with her widowed Irish mother. He lightly kissed her good night on the cheek at the front door before walking the very sobering two miles back to Palm Villa thinking pleasantly naughty thoughts about Bern. That was her name, Bernadette O'Something.

Now, for those fellows who have a woman in their lives, fair and well. For those who do not, then find one - but be warned! If the surname is O'Something or O'Other, beware, beware, and tread very carefully.......plenty trouble, plenty trouble. They won't let you just run away because your legs won't be able to run that fast, or far, enough.

God, or whoever, or whatever, is meaningful to you, won't help you either. He will just laugh at you as you dance merry jigs, do cartwheels, and do things that you never thought were humanly possible. You will start to achieve the impossible. It is called living, and that is what you are supposed to be doing.

For some weeks Lighty and Bern had this innocent thing going which, as time went by, naturally started getting less and less innocent. Bern didn't seem to have any particular close friends that she used to hang around with at college, and to do the things that normal women students did. She said that her best friends lived in Robertsham near Crown Mines, south of Johannesburg.

She played the piano very well - Beethoven, Bach, Brahms, Chopin and that churchy sort of stuff which, heathen that Lighty was, didn't mind too much. Bern had told him that a bit of culture would do him no harm at all.

212

Lighty, at the time, was not the sort of guy who used to hang around for too long before moving on, but when a hell-raising young lad strikes the odd lucky patch, he sort of hangs around a little longer than he perhaps ought to, and sometimes for just that fatal fraction of a second too long.

Lighty discovered that harsh reality of life when Bern one day suggested that she had two friends who wanted to go along to the motor car racing at the Kyalami racetrack one Saturday and to have some fun there. Lighty agreed, and thought nothing more of it, until that Saturday morning. That was when the trouble really started.

He told Nickers and Mike on the Friday night that he was going to have two spare girls with him at the races and arranged to coincidentally meet them at Leeukop Bend so that they could check the girls out. Nickers and Mike had both been having a pretty dry run with the girls at that time and it seemed like a very good idea to them.

The Bilious-inspired drought had been so prolonged that Mike had, at a weak and jocular moment, and for quite some time, been contemplating becoming a bi-sexual so that he could double his chances on a Saturday night. Lighty didn't like this trend of affairs at all and vocalised his concern many times. Lighty's mind was fortunately soon put to rest when Mike was being chatted up by a very friendly chappie in the German Beer Hall in Hillbrow one night.

'We are together,' Mike told the nice chappie as he clutched Lighty's hand and held it tenderly. Lighty threw a frightful fit. Mike helped the nice chappie over the bar counter and was cured forever of his misguided malaise.

Mike's big problem was not his enormous nose. His big problem was, as he put it, was that it would have been really fun to have a car that went. His Ford Anglia didn't go because it was a disastrous lemon. It had one of those insoluble quirks that persistently, and at great expense, defied proper diagnosis and rectification.

Nickers' real problem was that his Veedub Beetle did go very well. In fact, it went far too well as it had neither footbrake nor handbrake. Nickers' nerves were starting to give in as time went by because he never had the brakes fixed, and he steadfastly continued to live dangerously firmly believing that it was the only way to fly.

It was firmly and broadly rumoured that the Berea Residence girls wouldn't go within coo-ee of Nickers and his car. None of the Palm Villa crew remotely even considered an invitation to go anywhere with Nickers.

Nickers eventually managed to wipe his Veedub out one Friday night near Witbank where he managed to capsize it at great speed and turned it into a flaming inferno. Chris casually wandered into the casualty department of the hospital rolling the spare wheel in while Nickers was refusing treatment of any kind to the six inch bleeding gash on his head. The wheel was all that could be salvaged from the wreck.

A very, very large nurse was called and managed to gently persuade him to have his head stitched. Lighty later had to remove the stitches from Nickers' head with a nail clipper and tweezers because Nickers hated hospitals.

A few weeks later Chris had taken Nickers to the casualty department of the Johannesburg General Hospital to have the stitches removed. While they were sitting in the waiting room for Nickers to be attended to, a very large, toothless, red-headed, barefooted lady wearing a pink candlewick gown, walked in wearing an axe in her head. Nickers took one look at her and bolted.

Lighty then, after another week, took Nickers back to the same hospital to have his stitches removed. As they got to the gate with the door of the casualty department in sight they met two nurses coming out of the gate. Nick asked them how long it took before stitches had to be removed.

'Seven to ten days,' was their response.

'What happens if they have been in for four weeks?' Nickers asked them. The two nurses grabbed him, arm apiece, and started to drag him through the gate, but to no avail. Lighty joined the fierce scuffle but Nickers rigidly stood his ground. Lighty then took Nickers back to Palm Villa where he removed Nickers' stitches with a nail clipper and a pair of tweezers.

Nickers' aversion to hospitals was really as a direct result of the first false start to his adult life. He had enrolled as a trainee male nurse at the Springs Hospital; not because he was averse to nurses at all. It was quite the contrary, for the female kind were by far in the majority there, and the very real reason that he had become a trainee nurse in the first instance.

His real aversion to hospitals was as a result of a rather prolonged and unexplained absence after which he turned up for work at the hospital one day where it was very rudely and aggressively demanded of him to identify himself.

It wasn't Dr Joss Lurie's fault for being a bit miffed with Lighty for nearly blowing Joss' geology laboratory sky high when Lighty was secretly making gunpowder one day. He was making a stockpile and was going to use

214

the gunpowder to blast Palm Villa off the planet on their very last day in order to destroy any evidence that might have incriminated them all thereafter. Something went a bit wrong. Sorry Joss. *(Guy Fawkes is a distant Welsh ancestor of mine. He very nearly succeeded in blasting the House Of Commons in London off the planet.)*

It also wasn't Flip Pherson's fault for pulling up one Monday morning for lectures dragging a pair of crutches along with him. 'Fell on my arse when my ceramic toilet exploded under my bum while I was reading the *Sunday Times* yesterday morning - cut my bloody backside to ribbons,' he solemnly explained to the boys. The Bushveld's original experiential and pioneering mining man. He could tell you everything that you wanted to know about how to make a twin native-powered Bushveld manual mine hoist really come to life.

It wasn't Lighty's fault for nearly killing Chris when Chris hadn't been keeping a sharp passenger lookout one Friday night while they were on their way home and nearly there when disaster struck. It was raining lightly and the windscreen wipers on the Bomb weren't working. Lighty spied the chevron reflectors on the back of a bus in front of him. He changed down a gear and put his right foot flat to the floor to overtake the bus. Problem was, that it wasn't a bus, but warning chevrons indicating that it was a tee junction. Strait into a three metre deep ditch they went. With the nose of the Bomb in the ditch, and the roof against the far side embankment, and with Chris and Lighty both lying on the windscreen inside the Bomb, Lighty unexpectedly said to Chris:

'I think we had an accident.'

Lighty's high school classmates Gommy Nel, Aitch van der Walt and Ivan van Rensenburg, who, all together, just happened to be passing by. They wrongfully borrowed a nearby tow-truck, hauled the Bomb out, dusted Lighty and Chris both off, and swiftly saw them safely on their way; just as the police were rapidly approaching from a block away to ask some very awkward questions.

It wasn't the Palm Villa boys' fault for going to see the cricket test for nearly a whole week. All ten of them, each with a case of Lion Lager on the shoulder, marched into the Wanderers every morning and spent the day watching the Aussies and Springboks thrashing about for five days. None of them could remember, to this day, who won the game.

215

Anyway, to get back to the painful point, on the Saturday morning Lighty drove to Bern's flat. After a quick cup of coffee with her chatty mum, they set off along the M 1 highway to Robertsham to pick up Bern's two friends. Bern had told Lighty that she had lived there for two years before moving into the apartment at King's Langley with her mum.

Lighty drove into the driveway and parked The Bomb. He saw two young nuns dressed in full habit standing on the verandah who, on seeing them arrive, stood up and walked over to the car. One of them was carrying a picnic basket.

What the hell is going on here? Lighty thought to himself, totally bewildered. Bern introduced the two of them as Sister Thomas and Sister Theresa and the two nuns got into the back seat of The Bomb with their picnic basket.

He had never before seen Bern that chatty before. The three of them, simultaneously and continually, chatted over the top of each other. It was obvious to Lighty that Bern had not seen the two nuns for quite some time, and that it was quite clear that the three of them had been the closest of friends for a long time. The cerebral gymnastics that followed made him reverse The Bomb into the gatepost leaving yet another dent in it - about the thousandth one.

How in God's name am I going to get myself out of this incredible jam? Lighty kept on thinking to himself as he drove along the M 1 Highway North to Kyalami. This wasn't going to do his reputation any good at all. None at all. He was never going to live this one down. Not even with Tex who was a Catholic.

He drove into the racetrack and headed for Yukskei Sweep instead which, he believed, would offer some protection as it was the least favoured viewing position on the track, and totally unlikely that he would be found. He figured cleverly that the fact that he was renown to be a right scatter-brain and might just have forgotten the arranged rendezvous, he would have some time to conjure up something or other to later explain to the boys about his non-arrival at Leeukop. This, unfortunately, was not to be.

After waiting for some two hours the boys had decided that long enough was long enough and that Lighty had, after all, perhaps forgotten the arrangement. They found him. Five parts pissed they were when they turned up too. Not only did Nickers and Mike turn up. There, in front of him, stood the whole Palm Villa crew.

'Look at those nuns over there!' shouted Chris as he pointed to them. Nuns were not known to attend motor race meetings in those days.

'It's Lighty with them!' the rest of them yelled when they saw him.

Tight-lipped introductions were made and the Palm Villa crew took up station with Lighty and the nuns for the rest of the day. The nuns even had a naughty beer apiece offered by the boys and got quite giggly. Not far behind in the reciprocal niceties, Sister Thomas took out of her picnic basket a bottle of secretly spirited bottle of sacramental wine and offered it to CP.

'Hooray Amsterdam Ajax and Jimmy Hendrix,' CP said as he had a casual swig and passed the bottle on to Chris. CP was a Dutch migrant and had formally been a lead guitarist in a travelling rock band and a professional soccer player. He still had dreams of great glory playing stadiums everywhere.

'Long live Bacchus and the Pope!' said Chris, had a swig and passing it on to Tex. Chris was never known to hold a man's religion against him.

'May God forgive me for my sins,' said Portagee Tex genuflecting, crossing himself, and taking a liberty bite out of Sister Thomas' sandwich before taking a slug and passing the bottle on to Nickers. He had just done his Mass for the weekend.

'Anyone who is a friend of the Pope, is a friend of mine,' said Nickers. His encounter with the nuns had shocked him into a moral and Christian consciousness of proportions unknown before.

'There goes Christianity as it was known,' proclaimed Mike and passed the bottle on to Lighty.

'I'll kill you bastards if you ever tell anyone about this,' said Lighty taking a swig and passing it onto Bilious.

'Bleeeech!' Bilious barked his lunch to no-one in particular over the protective Armco barrier and, without taking a snifter, passed it on to Wollie. Bilious could never be taken anywhere a second time without profusely apologising for the first.

'Here's one for the girls,' said Wollie and passed it onto Rudi Dutchke.

'Hooray for the Irish,' said Rudi with an Irish lilt and passed it on to Soutie Foster.

'Chase the English into the sea!' Soutie said with a sip, a burp and then let off an indiscreet loud fart before tossing the empty bottle away.

'Another snort boys?' Bern asked innocently as she lifted the second bottle of sacramental wine out of the picnic basket.

'Liewe Jesus!' said righteous Grey College, Bloemfontein goodie-goodie Basie Pottas when it was his turn, and promptly ran away for the rest of the day. Sadly, Basie was the only Palm Villa inhabitant never ever to have been elected to the Coward Tribunal. He was just too good - or just to good to be caught. No-one could ever find out.

Basie however, and very much to his credit, did manage to get himself and Lighty severely reprimanded by a police sergeant at the Hillbrow Police Station one night. This happened after Basie had crashed a borrowed open Beach Buggy into the back of a one-legged lawyer's Valiant at a red light. It simply still wasn't good enough for him to be voted onto the Coward Tribunal.

They had gone straight from a rugby party, five parts there, to fetch some girls at the Berea Women's Residence to take them to the continuation of the party at Palm Villa. A full case of beer on the back seat of the Beach Buggy had catapulted into the air and went crashing through the Valiant's back window and had then hit the lawyer's wife on the back of the head. The lawyer is still trying to find Basie to sue him for whip-lashing the hell out of his wife.

At the end of the Kyalami races they wound their weary way back to Palm Villa with a determined trio of nuns in tow who needed to know more about how the other half lived. The Vatican Two Council resolution in the 1960's to liberate nuns was the best thing the Roman Catholic Church could ever have done.

'How is the nun today? Are you getting any, none, or are you getting nun? Is she pregnant yet?' were typical of the probing questions and taunts that Lighty had to frequently and frustratingly contend with thereafter, and courageously did. He was eternally condemned to serve out the rest of his time at Palm Villa as Chief Coward for corrupting the morals of a novice nun.

Despite his prolonged, passionate and repeated pleadings to the Pope over many years to be forgiven for his sins, he, to this very day, has consistently refused to recognise his very existence. A very worried Bishop even came to see him deep in the bush late one night, beer in hand, to relay an urgent message to tell him that he could hang himself in hell for eternity as far as He was concerned.

Lighty and Bern continued to see each other openly, and to behave as they normally and naturally had done before believing that what they were doing was right until the end of that year before they parted and went their separate ways.

A year later, when Lighty was a shaftsinking shift supervisor, he was invited to address a seminar in Johannesburg arranged by the South African Institute of Mining and Metallurgy on the rigours, hazards and harsh realities of sinking mine shafts. Early on that freezing winter's morning he was sitting on a bench in Joubert Park recovering from a night of drunken womanising and brawling as shaftsinkers, savage sub-human animals that they are, are wont to do when they find themselves in town.

He saw Bern serenely walking along the path toward him. She looked up and, on recognising him, faltered, and then resolutely continued to walk straight toward him. She had taken her Holy Vows and was wearing a nun's habit.

Lighty stood up and waited for her. When she reached the spot where he stood they both reached out, silently took each other by the hand and sat down continuing to hold hands all the while.

After about half an hour they both stood up and went their separate and disparate ways again without looking back. They had spoken not a word.

* * * * * * * * * * * *

'Ten green bottles hanging on the wall. And if one green bottle should accidentally fall, there'll be nine green bottles, hanging on the wall,' sang CP Wissekerke as a post-funeral Requiem next to Joao Texeira's open grave in Benoni having killed himself in a car crash about a year after graduation.

'Nine green bottles hanging on the wall. And if one green bottle should accidentally fall, there'll be eight green bottles, hanging on the wall,' sang Basie Pottas as a post-funeral Requiem after Wollie's funeral a few years ago. Wollie had senselessly shot his brains out. He somehow forgot that he had eight of the absolute very best of friends in the World that he could talk to instead. Sorry Louise.

The very worried, beer-in hand Bishop is not that very far from the real truth. You see, the Bishop of Cairns communicated with the Pope concerning Lighty's eligibility to becoming a Catholic. This happened after Lighty approached Father Neil Muir of the Cairns North Parish and declared himself a spiritual and Christian derelict. Matters took the course of events they did and the Pope declared Lighty free to become a Catholic despite his being a divorced man - with the proviso that he never goes anywhere near a convent ever again. Father Neil Muir confirmed Lighty as a Roman Catholic at the Freshwater Catholic Church in Cairns over Easter 1995.

Lighty and Father Neil used to watch Super Twelve and Rugby Test matches with the other Catholic Priests in Cairns at their home in North Cairns. Lighty used to turn up there with a case of beer on his shoulder, and he was always warmly welcomed.

Lighty now looks very deeply and intently into his beer. And he does some very serious thinking about the goodness and greatness of the game of Rugby. Lighty is dreaming of being the Captain of the Heaven Rugby First Fifteen because he was secretly informed by the most reliable sources that Rugby was the main game they played There. Lighty has decided that he won't ever teach the Devil and his motley crew of misfits how to play good Rugby.

(Eric Dillon alias Rudi Duchke came to Australia in 1971 straight after graduating. I came to Australia in 1981. I have been looking for Duchke ever since. Last Thursday I called the Salvation Army Family Reunion people in Brisbane and told them that if they could find him for me, I would send them a cheque for $250.00. I found him on my first phone call. We spent an outrageously good weekend in Brisbane where we drank our first beer together in nearly 30 years. I have just returned from a weekend as his guest. (10 July 1999)

220

Chapter Twenty

It was a leisurely start that day as we broke camp followed by a refreshing swim in the river before setting off. I drove all the way from the Wenlock River to Weipa. We were gradually preparing ourselves for the trauma of encountering civilisation again.

As we were approaching the Weipa north turn-off we were astounded to see a 1924 Pontiac pulled up at the side of the road with the driver standing beside it. We stopped and inquired if he was in distress but were assured that he was fine. He was one of a contingent of Veteran and Vintage car clubs on their way to Cape York and was waiting for his son who was driving the backup vehicle. We chatted for a while until his son arrived from Weipa in a Range Rover.

Taking the Weipa north road we could see a pall of smoke rising from the first of the dry season bushfires in the distance ahead of us. As we continued we became aware that we were heading straight into it. It appeared to have started that day. The Pontiac and Range Rover drivers had not reported a fire. We cautiously proceeded west toward it.

'Keep on going!' said Jack. 'Wind all the windows up and don't stop for anything! Go as fast as you can!' I did just that, and we went straight through the blazing inferno raging on both sides of the road and over the top of us. It was very scary, but we made it. Once out of the fire we stopped for a mug of tea and a trembling sandwich.

'We have got to report this fire!' Jack suddenly realised. 'Lets go!'

We reached the junction from the south going to Weipa. We were greeted by a superb flat, wide and well-maintained dirt road. As we reached the outskirts of Weipa there it all was - civilisation, tarmac roads, two-wheel-drive family sedans, traffic lights, roundabouts, a shopping centre, fast food shops, Woolworth's supermarket......????

It was early Sunday afternoon when we arrived. We were just in time for a well-earned steak sandwich and a large pot of tea at the coffee shop before it closed. The ladies in the coffee shop kindly relayed the fire alarm for us.

A notice on the Community Notice Board advertised a *Poetry in the Park* event at sunset so we decided to go. It was being arranged by the Weipa Branch of the Queensland Arts Council. After five weeks of solitude a community cultural event seemed to be an ideal way to make a soft re-entry to society.

We pitched tent at the campsite which, to us, was relatively chaotic but we were reasonably well prepared for that. This was followed by a drive around some recreational lakes which Comalco, the company running the mining town, had expended a lot of time, money and effort to ensure that the social and recreational needs of the community were met.

We stopped off at Centennial Park where we watched numerous fish jumping out of the water. An Aborigine had caught a good-sized barramundi. We had a leisurely stroll along the waterfront chatting to the other Aboriginal anglers until five o'clock, the advertised time for Poetry in the Park. We were hopelessly lost trying to find Rocky Point Park for the event and arrived half an hour late.

In true Weipa style however, we beat the organisers to the spot. We had lost sight of the fact that up there, five o'clock meant in that general time-frame, and perhaps on the same day.

A table was set up and adorned with white, red and rose wines with cheese and biscuits to munch. It cost a dollar for a glass, or a lump sum of two dollars for a bottomless bottle. We opted for the latter and set up our fold-up camp chairs.

Poetry in the Park overlooking the Gulf of Carpentaria, with the sun setting in the west, was ever so civilised. I thoroughly enjoyed reading two poems, one by John Keats, and the other by William Wordsworth. *I Wandered Lonely as a Cloud* was so relevant to me. John Keats, who wrote about how graceful England was, but how one craved for more spectacular scenery.

Jack got hold of three anthologies and looked up the poems that he knew. *Crossing the Bar*. Next. *La Belle Dame Sans Merci* - Oh what can ail thee Knight at Arms, So pale and lonely loitering? The sedge is withered from thy brow and no birds sing....' Next. *Elegy Written in a Country Churchyard*. Next. So it continued, until he finally gave a recital of his own.

222

The Man Across the Road

The Mendelssohn Concerto ever so tranquil,
Came to a halt when ever so frightful,
'Snake! Snake!' he heard one midnight still,
A damsels cry, so clear and shrill.
Great distress, so please come quick!
You've got to beat it with a stick!
It nearly bit me, it is ever so slick.
I nearly hit it with a brick!'

The great big snake lay curled up tight,
In the rafters with all its might.
Wouldn't budge for all the night,
It gave the girls a terrible fright!
The tongue was forked, no fangs could see,
The Man was trembling at the knee.
Didn't know that the scales decree,
The kind of snake it was said to be.

The Fearless Wildlife Ranger came,
With book in arm to find a name.
Couldn't find one to identify same,
Poor innocent snake wasn't to blame.
She looked and looked and read and read,
Through the pages her fingers sped.
'Shoot it now! Shoot it dead!
Shoot it in the bloody head!

The Man Across the Road did look,
At the snake, his head he shook.
Knew not what it was, nor the book,
With great care his aim he took.

Steely eyed they looked at each other,
'In the head, fierce, furious no bother.
'Tis you or I will die now Brother!'
Knew not then that they shared a Mother. (Nature)

The rifle roared and from it shed,
The bullet on its way it sped.
Hit the snake in the bloody head,
Poor blighter hung there and bled and bled.
It writhed in anger and did despair,
Couldn't understand 'Not fair! Not fair!
I mean no harm, no fangs I bear!
I'm a Carpet Snake, I do declare!'

It finally from the rafters fell,
It went to Heaven and not to Hell.
And There it did its story tell,
And There was blessed forever well.
The Man Across the Road was not,
The Intrepid Hero no matter what.
By any means nor great a shot,
For on his conscience it had got!

Australian poetry was by far the most popular, including the obligatory Banjo Paterson's *The Man From Snowy River* – 'There was movement at the station, for the word had got around....', about Clancy of the Overflow. *The Bastard from the Bush*, reputed to have been written by Henry Lawson, but vehemently denied by him, with very good reason, followed.

At the end of the recitals and readings everyone stood around and socialised. I found a guy who had lived on Mornington Island for three years with the Aborigines and had *intensively* studied the dugong during that time. Apparently there were heaps of them, and crocodiles, around Albatross Bay. They were very shy and elusive whale-like mammals found in tropical seas. I so wanted to talk with him about it, but time moved on.

1. *Safe !*
2. *Poetry in the Park*

1. *Starboard Lounge - "Gulf Sky"*

2. *Fly Fisherman*

3. *Juliette, Barry & Fish*

Jack was engrossed in conversation with Jim, the Chief Mining Engineer at the mine. Jim was explaining to Jack, a fellow mining engineer and therefore a kindred spirit, the conflict he felt at being a macho mining man and also having been elected as President of the Weipa Arts Council. Jack laughed, and then went on to explain to him that mining engineers were also human and had a need to appreciate the finer, creative, philosophical pleasures of life in order to balance the harsh and hostile environment all mining people had to deal with. It was certainly a most enjoyable evening and we were the very last to leave.

After Poetry in the Park we retired to the Bowling Club where we had a superb meal of garlic prawns. We decided to return for more the next night, which we did, but we had to walk five kilometres for it.

We were on the wharf very early on the Monday morning, reported to the office of Gulf Freight Services, and checked ourselves and the Toyota in. They wanted the Toyota alongside by eleven o'clock that morning so that she could be loaded on board the 'Gulf Sky'. We were to be wheel-less for the day, which was very inconvenient but far less painful than the one thousand, two hundred kilometre drive to Normanton.

We then took the Toyota to the local garage to have her checked out. No water had found its way into the vital components and she was mechanically sound. What a relief it was to know that after the savage beating she had taken.

With limited time at our disposal we rushed around to the shopping centre to do some shopping then delivered the Toyota to the wharf. We felt a sense of loss as we temporarily parted. She had been our constant, faithful and reliable companion for five weeks, and had not once let us down. The fuel cap and flat tyre were purely due to our negligence.

We met John, the Master of *Gulf Sky* at the office when we delivered the vehicle. He had been raised in Shere, Surrey the same small village where most of my family had come from. He kindly dropped us off at John Evans' Landing where we spent the rest of the day fishing off the wharf. I caught two of the blighters but three very, very large ones got away. Jack got five big hits and lost his rig every time. Poor Jack. Everybody and everything but the fish liked him it seemed!

The day passed quickly. We had a nice cold beer at the local watering hole and then set off on the five kilometre walk for dinner at the Bowling Club.

We were sensible enough to call for a taxi to take us to board the 'Gulf Sky' before twenty two hundred hours. We said a fond 'Hello' to the Toyota where she was lashed down on the deck immediately forward of the bridge.

Sharon, the ship's cook, took us below, gave us a quick guided tour and then saw us comfortably installed in our cabin. We had to walk through Graham and Eve's cabin to get to ours, which was a bit unfortunate for them, but we did have a curtain separating our quarters from theirs. It was all very pleasant.

Sharon had placed some flowers on our pillows - a lovely touch. We went topside and got acquainted with the rest of the ship's passengers while the crew cast off and we headed out to sea. Once we had altered course to the south we fell into our bunks, lulled to sleep by the steady, comforting throb of the diesel engines and other shipboard noises and bumps in the night.

The slowing down of the engines at zero four hundred hours, followed by the anchor being run out, woke us. We ran onto the deck only to find that we had arrived at the mouth of the Archer River and we had to wait for first light to enable us to steam upstream to the Aurukun Aboriginal Community to deliver 30,000 litres of diesel fuel and building material. It was still dark so we went back to sleep again.

At sunrise we weighed anchor and chugged up the Archer River to Aurukun. We kept a beady-eyed lookout out for birds and crocodiles. When we arrived I started fishing with the handline while the crew pumped out fuel, and off-loaded housing material and other supplies. I had a bet on with John the Master who said that I wouldn't catch a thing.

Aurukun was a *wet* Aboriginal settlement that meant that there was a wet canteen to dispense beer. Some of the locals had also found a way around being dependent on the canteen hours and the outrageously expensive *sly grog* outlets, and had mail-order brewing kits and supplies delivered in addition to beer and stronger liquor.

There was a general reluctance to fill this dubious need, but the purveyors and conveyors were obliged to do so by law. Others got their brewing kits and liquor by going to Weipa by boat and getting it there, especially the *sly grog* operators. The irony of it all was very saddening.

It had crossed our minds that a visit to the Aurukun township would be interesting but we had been told that we had to cast off and be under way before the tide started ebbing leaving us stranded on the beach for twelve hours.

We did get to see the mission - unplanned, unexpectedly and at great speed when a catfish I had surprisingly caught, stabbed me in the inside of my right foot near the navicular when I was kicking it off the ship while wearing thongs.

I bled profusely and was in absolute agony. Jack had not been feeling well and had previously gone to lie down in his bunk so Eve patched me up while Graham went below to wake Jack up. John the Master, told me to go straight to the clinic which I was glad I did.

Catfish barbs sometimes break off in the flesh and a very nasty infection, left unattended, can ultimately result in an amputation. John said that if we were not back in time for the cast-off, he would put out and anchor midstream to wait for us. He arranged for a motor boat to ferry us across if that happened.

Bill drove Jack and I, plus a load of Aborigine women, their children and their dogs, into *town* and on to the clinic. The ladies had taken their children the previous night and had gone to camp out by the river. The previous day a new brew was ready for sampling. They were supposed to be much safer camping out on the beach.

One Aborigine lady told us their sad story. They had camped too close to the water and were pestered by a crocodile all night. It kept charging into the camp and terrorising the lot of them. On one of its marauding excursions it had taken one of their dogs from within the camp, right under their very noses. It could very well have been one of the children. The poor souls hadn't slept a wink all night.

Bill appeared to be rather nonplused about it all.

'It happens all the time. It's a way of life around here,' he said.

Ted, the nurse at the clinic, immediately gave me top priority treatment and I held Jack's hand as I was informed of how painful it was going to be. A local anaesthetic, a twenty five millimetre incision to drain out all the dirt and a good look-around sufficed. Thankfully Ted did not think there was a barb inside.

The most painful part was the tetanus and penicillin jabs. Thereafter I had very little pain. I did get a lot of sympathy and attention though. Ted gave me a set of crutches and I was under orders to keep the foot up which was much easier said than done.

We were rushed back to the barge just as they were casting off. I hobbled back on board without a minute to spare. I was immediately nicknamed *Catfish* and suffered the name for the rest of the voyage. Apparently kicking the darn thing wasn't a very intelligent thing to do.

227

We were supposed to spend two nights on board, but fate had it that it turned out to be three. What happened was that we ran aground on a submerged sandbar coming out of the Archer River on an ebbing tide. We were stuck fast. Sandbars in that area shifted continually and their locations were totally unpredictable.

'Your catfish kick might have something to do with us running aground,' Jack said to me to make me feel guilty.

There was no bump or detectable impact at all. The ship just slowly crept up onto the sandbar and imperceptibly stopped. John dropped both the anchors to prevent us from drifting any further onto the sand bar. He then signalled full ahead to blast a channel astern of us to create sufficient draught for our later disengaging on the rising tide five hours later. Clouds of sand and silt fluffed up as the screws thundered away at creating the channel.

We were scheduled to be alongside in Karumba harbour in the late afternoon. The entrance to Karumba could only be made in daylight, so we would have to anchor offshore for the extra night.

Naturally enough, John the Master, Frank the First Mate and the crew, Phil, Sharon and the ships Engineer, were none too pleased about it as they had their families and loved ones to go home to after a week at sea. The rest of us passengers Eve, Graham, Larry and Ray empathised but silently were delighted at our good fortune.

The instant I dropped my line in the water a catfish took it, again and again and again. Ray kindly did the honours for me every time. He was a professional fisherman, had been at sea for four months, and was on his way to meet his new wife in Karumba. I was the first to catch a large blue-fin salmon and Jack caught one not long after.

He was thrilled - he had caught his first real edible fish. He fought the thing furiously for twenty minutes on very light tackle before getting it on board. What really puffed him up was that it was bigger than mine. I took a photograph of him and his salmon. It was a pity that his fly was open otherwise I could have sent it to his mum!

Amazingly, I caught more fish from the horizontal position - flat on my back with my sore foot in the air. Every time I hooked one, I would haul it in and Ray below would pull it out of the water, take it off the hook, bait up for me, and then cast my line in again. How much easier could fishing be?

It came to an end when the tide had risen and we had to up lines as we slipped off the sandbar and continued south. We later caught a tuna on the trolling line which was let out astern. Sharon served it up as a delicious mornay one lunchtime.

What a great time we had on board *Gulf Sky*. Sunny, clear skies, spectacular brick-red sunsets, calm seas, great fishing, dolphins, whale lookouts, delightful ship's company, afternoon snoozes on deck, sundowners in the *Starboard Lounge*, excellent cuisine. It sure beat the pants off thundering back down the dry and dusty track and west on to Normanton.

The ship had a very friendly, fun, but professional atmosphere. It was kept spotlessly clean and well organised - all with the exception of our cabin which fortunately no-one saw. One night we played Canasta with Graham and Eve. That time we didn't fight. It was Larry's birthday one day, so Sharon baked him a cake. John showed us around the bridge with all its advanced navigation aids and we also paid a visit to the engine room.

We spent the third night anchored off Karumba as rescheduled. At first light we weighed anchor and steamed in. Ray's wife was there and the two of them waved their arms off at each other. Sharon's boyfriend was also there and they did likewise.

The Toyota was slung, hoisted off the deck, and then deposited on the dock. Only then were we permitted to disembark. We drove the Toyota behind one of the sheds where we hosed the salt from her to help prevent her from rusting later.

We visited the clinic first for the nurse to dress my catfish wound. It was doing well and there was no infection. We bought ice, fuel, some supplies and cooked prawns for a scrumptious lunch, and took the tarmac road south to Normanton.

A short distance from Karumba, Jack suddenly braked for no apparent reason, leapt out of the vehicle, and vomited rather violently. When he had recovered he asked me to drive to Normanton to find a doctor. On our arrival in Normanton we were directed to the clinic where Chris, the doctor examined his sore throat.

'You have tonsillitis,' she diagnosed. He had been staggering around like that for over a week. She prescribed, and supplied him with, antibiotics similar to those we had been carrying around in our first aid box. She told Jack that she originally had come from Sydney. She and her husband had bought a catamaran with the intention of circumnavigating Australia. Three years and two babies later they had got as far as Normanton where she had set up a practice.

We had past the *Purple Pub* on our way to see Chris. It was an absolute classic Outback pub. It was very *Aboriginal* and few whites, if any, dared go in for a drink.

We set off West in the heat, and the dust, and the sand, and the flies with me driving for the four hundred and sixty kilometres of dirt road and bulldust to Lawn Hill National Park.

Chapter Twenty One

I thoroughly enjoyed the sparse, dry, extensive landscape. It was almost like I imagined parts of Africa to be. Wildlife was the biggest red kangaroo I had ever seen, a real boomer, and heaps of wandering Brahman cattle roaming all over the place. They were a serious traffic hazard and very good reason to have a bullbar fitted to the front of the Toyota.

'If you crash into a large animal, you throw away the bullbar but you get to keep the truck. Don't swerve out for them. Just hit them and then stop. We don't want to overturn the vehicle and wipe ourselves out,' was Jacks sensible logic. We encountered very little traffic on the way and did not hit any animals. I, inadvertently, did manage to give the odd emu and a good few kangaroos very bad frights.

At Riversleigh we saw, or rather tried to see, some fossilised remains. It was an archaeological site where significant finds of prehistoric animal life were known to occur. It was either our untrained eyes, or the midday heat, or something else, which prevented us from seeing anything of significance.

Later that afternoon, and still some 100 kilometres from Lawn Hill, we stopped at the Gregory Downs Hotel where the publican very reluctantly served us with a cup of tea. He wasn't quite used to serving tea to anybody it seemed, and our request was a unique experience for him. There was not another hill in sight until we reached Lawn Hill, and when we did see some, we caught them at a pure magic sunset.

Our arrival at Lawn Hill Ranger Station and camping ground was a fraction after dark and far too late to collect firewood. We had not the faintest idea where to camp so we just flopped down on the first vacant spot we found.

We scrambled up a very forgettable dinner, decided that putting the tent up was just too hard, and we spent the first of many nights under the stars which was a lovely sight but, boy oh! boy, was I freezing cold. Sleeping next to a warm campfire would have been absolutely ideal.

Jack kept waking up from the unexpected cold so he dragged out a groundsheet, folded it over, spread it out on the ground, and we slipped in between the folded-over groundsheet. It kept the chilly wind out and we slept much better. I slept exceptionally well all snuggled up in my sleeping bag.

Perhaps it was the weariness after the very long and tiresome drive. It was also gently assisted by a few large, hearty, and perhaps reckless, draughts of a Hunter Valley Cabernet Sauvignon to pre-warm the cockles.

That morning I awoke bright, early and alert for a birdwatch, and to climb up the Garra for a magnificent view of the sun rising over the surrounding gorge country, river and tropical vegetation. Dry, red and spectacular it all was. I saw a white-browed robin en route to the Garra; a most uncommon encounter and I was thrilled about it. An elderly gentleman told me later that morning that he has been photographing birds for 50 years and had never seen one.

I returned to camp to find Jack just surfacing after 12 hours of solid sleep. We then discovered that we had flopped down in the dusty group camping area that night. After a mug of tea we reported to the Ranger who assigned us a grassy site and we set up camp there. Bookings normally had to be made two months in advance as it was a very popular park and also accessible by family sedan. We felt a little guilty about not having booked a site beforehand but the Ranger was kind enough to be forgiving.

Lawn Hill National Park was a comparatively small park being some 12,200 hectares of lush, tropical vegetation on the banks of Lawn Hill Creek and Gorge in the middle of parched, open plains, stunted trees and scrub, and secretive arid-zone fauna.

For the first time we were surrounded by a multitude of people, far too many we thought on the first night, but it was after a very long drive to get there, and we were very tired. It was a little difficult to adjust to the 50-odd people already there, and it did feel, to us anyway, a bit claustrophobic. It was a very small National Park after all.

We decided to have a completely restful day without too much activity to recover from the long 600 kilometre drive from Karumba. It did us both the world of good to relax and enjoy the odd short walk.

There were heaps of birds, especially in the campsite itself with sprinklers on the lawn and it being situated next to the very picturesque river. The beauty of Lawn Hill National Park more than adequately compensated for the crowd. The tall canyons, rivers, waterfalls and clear, warm water were precisely our style. The daytime temperatures were perfect, but it got really cold at night.

The following day, feeling very energetic and satisfied that we could cope with the exercise content, we decided to canoe up-river. This unfortunately occurred in the afternoon, as we had actually decided to do so in the morning, but things didn't quite go according to plan. We waited for two hours for a canoe, and by the end of it, I was going crazy and promptly had another tantrum attack. In the end, it was well worth the wait and the tantrum.

'When you have decided that you have made enough noise, kicked up enough dust, and had your wobbly, you can sit down and wait like everyone else has to,' Jack said calmly. I could have throttled the endless patience out of him!

We finally secured a canoe and paddled up to a couple of superb waterfalls. There were grand, red canyons and tropical vegetation on both sides. We then raised the canoe via a portage up to another tranquil river section. I had a swim in the rapids at the very top in surprisingly warm water.

After that exercise we stuffed down some smoked oysters before rushing up the gorge to take in the last of the day's light. The eternal bloody flies were everywhere!

We had well and truly seen the lot at Lawn Hill and the next day we were off to the desert. We were both back to full fitness again despite a revival of my fascitis and thorax pain after the canoeing. I said nothing about it, so Jack didn't know about it. It was the cold nights that brought it on. I thought it best not to say anything to Jack. If I had told him, then he probably would have called in the Royal Flying Doctor and had me flown back to Cairns Base Hospital.

We very reluctantly left Lawn Hill. It was to be a twelve hour, 800 kilometre haul for the day to the Northern Territory, which included Camooweal, Barkly Homestead and Three Ways Junction. That was all there was, and very little of each of them.

Jack started the driving doing a four hour, 250 kilometre stint until we reached the sealed road at Camooweal on the Queensland-Northern Territory border. There were many kangaroos, and wedge-tailed eagles scavenging off the carcasses of dead animals.

We refuelled the vehicle and then ourselves with mega-hamburgers at Camooweal, which we thought, were better than the Archer River ones. It was fun and quite enjoyable having something to eat at the three roadhouses.

'The desert shouldn't be too far away now?' I asked Jack. I had been looking forward to the desert for a long time. It was surprisingly cool, dry, red and sweet, flat nothing.

'Around here, whenever you ask people at a cattle station where the desert is, they will tell you that you do not have far to go and that it is dead ahead of you. Eventually, you will find someone who will tell you that you have just come through it,' Jack replied. Funny place Australia.

The scenery got drier and drier, flatter and flatter, and for miles, and miles, and endless miles. We generally cruised at around a sedate 150 kph until dusk when Jack made me slow down.

'There are kangaroos, cattle and buffalo all over the road at this time of day,' he warned. He kept on going on about my driving until he was comfortable at around an excruciatingly slow 80 kph. I had to drive like that for over an hour before I was allowed to creep up to 100 kph.

The Australian sky put on a great fireworks display for us 60 kilometres north of Three Ways Junction in the Northern Territory on the Stuart Highway. As I was driving north a meteorite with an enormous fiery tail entered the atmosphere from the west in front of us illuminating the night sky to almost daytime brightness.

We spoke to a truckie about it on the radio a short while later. He was quite blase about it as he had seen many of them in his travels. He told us to be on the alert for UFO's as well which, he said, were seen quite often in those parts - deadly serious he was about it too and we believed him.

We were a million miles from anywhere when Jack decided that we would stop for the night. We spent it under the stars in a roadside gravel quarry that protected us from the cold wind. I never thought that I would ever sleep in a quarry.

After our customary huge mug of tea the next morning we were on our way north again. We stopped for an enormous breakfast at Elliott before our next six hours on the road that was all sealed for a change.

The Daly Waters pub encouraged us in being one of the oldest in the Northern Territory. Jack was quite disappointed, as it catered not for the locals as in days of old, but for bus loads of tourists. It was full of interesting relics and many pioneering stories. The staff were friendly and had hysterically funny signs hung on the walls.

'We don't serve women, bring your own.'

'A dingo's breakfast - a pee and a quick look around.'

'Stake sandwich,' and a few more much too racist ones.......

The famous overland explorer John McDowell Stuart left his mark 'S' carved on a tree nearby. Next to it was a 44 gallon drum full to the brim with dead beer cans and buzzing with flies.

We visited the graves of the *We Of The Never-Never* people. It was a peaceful place, full of atmosphere, and gave us an idea of the hardships those pioneers encountered. I shall have to read the book one day.

Mataranka Hot Springs was set amongst beautiful tropical bush in the middle of the desert. The water was very clear and refreshing but there were heaps of people again. I took myself off downstream to another hot pool where I swam with some turtles. I had it all to myself and didn't tell anyone about it.

We met Katie and Alan via the radio as we overtook them. We somehow ended up meeting up with them en route several times after that. They were both ex-Pommies with an eight-week old baby and they were looking for somewhere in Australia to live. Like us, they had a penchant for gravel pits and river beds.

As the day progressed we got wearier and were both nearly falling asleep. A short nap south of Katherine revitalised us. Katherine was not very welcoming with its rat-race, tourists and people. It was hot, we were irritable and wanted nothing more that to get the hell out of the place. Suddenly after six and a half weeks of solitude we were back in civilisation again. Yuk! I realised how lucky I was to be with Jack and not catching buses all over Australia.

We drove out to Edith Falls, some 60 kilometres northeast of Katherine, to have a look at the camping facilities there. There were far too many people and generating sets - no thank you. We went for a swim in the pool below the falls. Freshwater crocodiles swam around us. We headed back to a place on the Edith River bed that Jack knew about. Peace and quiet at last.

We were very glad to have a rest day at the dry Edith River. The sky was full of birds and their sweet sounds were deafening. It was friar bird country, varied lorikeets and lots of them.

Late that afternoon we took to the bush and headed along a track toward Mount Todd where Jack had started a gold mining operation some years before. He wanted to have a look at what had happened after he had handed over the management of the mine once he had got it operational. It made Jack think a lot, as he was a lot less talkative there. He got into a lot of trouble there because he had forgotten to consult with the Northern Lands Council concerning possible Aborigine sacred sites occurring in the area. However, he eventually got away with it.

The views from the mine and the ridges were marvellous, the edge of Katherine Gorge National Park and sparsely covered hills in the east to the magnificent sunset in the west. We took it in from Jack's favourite spot where he and his troops used to sit and watch the sunsets over a bundle of beers after a hard, and very thirsty, day's work.

Jack was bestowed the nick-name of Bushpig while he was there and he felt greatly honoured by it. It appeared that, despite his outward refinement and sophistication, he was totally capable of being as wild as, if not wilder than, the very best of the Bushies. He told that to me with a broad grin and with fond memories written all over his face. Then he laughed a lot and infuriatingly told me nothing about why he was laughing. Boys will be boys when they are on the loose.

'Peter, Geoff, Damien, John, Barry, China, Lincoln and the rest of the mob will know why,' he said as if that explained it all and he continued to laugh. There was a good story there that badly needed some very serious telling. I understood it to have been something to do with Rage in a Cage at Lim's on a Sunday afternoon. Instead, that night around the campfire, he went into miner mode and told me about what happened to Lighty after he left college.

Chapter Twenty Two

Lighty had decided to take up shaft sinking after completing his course as part of his chosen career as a mining engineer. Lighty had chosen to sink mine shafts in South Africa as it was the most strenuous, demanding, glamorous and elite occupation in the mining industry in addition to being extremely lucrative financially. It ranked second only to mercenary soldiering as the most hazardous, savage and unforgiving profession anywhere.

He had explained to The Baron von Maltitz that he had decided to get some experience that would build a stronger character because he was a bit short on that even though he was pretty long on brains. He also wanted to acquire an equally strong practical mining background and wanted to make a bundle of money before going on to easier, conventional mine management which meant progressing through the ranks until he could reach his then perceived career dream and peak - Mine Captain by the time he was forty. On reflection how frightfully naive Lighty was then.

The Baron, who had some very good connections and was not short of intelligence, practical experience or strong character, arranged two choices for Lighty. He could sink shafts in South Africa for a year or, of equal value, was to work on an exploration project in the Yukon Territory in Canada on the Alaskan border.

'Lighty, you and the Palm Villa crew have taken this college by the tail and you have shaken it very badly,' the Baron told Lighty when Lighty went to bid him a final farewell.

'I want you to leave here with the firm understanding that it will never ever happen again,' the Baron continued. 'That applies to you in particular. You have the incredible ability to get up to the most sinfully innocent mischief and miraculously get away with it. You might be graduating as a mining engineer, but my personal reference, should I ever have to write one, would include your majoring in beer, women, beer, rugby, beer, non-conformity, beer and general mayhem on a massive scale.

'Your subtle defiance and contempt of authority is already legendary and well known throughout the mining industry. I would not have arranged something similar for any other student. It was your incredible academic results that brought to my attention your exceptional ability. Don't ever abuse it, for it will become your worst enemy at a time when you are going to need it most,' the Baron warned in conclusion.

Lighty managed to remember that warning for a while, for about two months perhaps. Lighty chose to sink mine shafts in South Africa.

'For Christ son! What the hell do you think you are doing?' his father had said to him. It was the first, and last, time that Lighty had ever heard his father swear. It was also the first and last time that his father got angry with him. He was very, very, very angry indeed.

The Baron sent him to see Norman Beresford-Smythe, the Managing Director of Shaftsinking Incorporated Limited. Norman's prediction was that Lighty would never make it but, because he was gutsy enough to attempt it, and his reasons for wanting to do it were sound, he would give him a go.

'The only thing you have got going for you is your youth and wide-eyed innocence. Your academic record, past mining experience, beer drinking ability and athletic prowess count for nothing. You remember that for the rest of your life!' Norman told him. 'Marauding Mike Murphy will be your field manager and Shorty Bester will be your mastersinker. They might be able to put some marrow into your bones for you. I have already told your father that I accept no responsibility whatsoever for your decision.'

Lighty had to undertake not to make a decision on continuing or quitting until he had been on the job for at least six weeks at which time Norman would talk to him again and a learned assessment could be made. Norman sent him to see Mike Murphy first, and then to see Shorty Bester.

'I will see to it that you either get worked out of the system very soon to prevent you from getting killed,' was Marauding Mike's greeting. 'You have no business being here. Get out of my sight before I take an intense disliking to you,' he added. He oozed the blatant and bitter resentment of the School of Hard Knocks graduate toward the silver-spoon fed, college educated, runty twerp.

'Goddamnit Lighty! You'll get yourself bloody well killed in the first week!' You simply can't do it!' Shorty told him when he went to see him. 'Why don't you be sensible and become a surveyor, or geologise, or do something appropriately poncy? Those Basutu drillers will probably eat you up in the first two days. You even smell like you have just crawled out of a bloody multi-racial brothel in a brewery!' Shorty continued shaking his head in dismay, all five foot two inches of him, his eyes four inches below Lighty's.

The low pitched, controlled growl of Shorty's voice, delivered in a flat, thinly veiled, threatening monotone, the piercing slits of black for eyes, ever-shifting, ever-searching, and eternally void of humour, the totally controlled, over-abundant aggression and his slightly forward-leaning, hands-on-hips stance, told Lighty that this was one man you don't dare defy.

Nobody argued with the man who set the world record for sinking concrete-lined shafts. Nobody. Shorty's native name was *Nyonga*, bile. He gave everyone who was bad and errant the most terrifying heartburn.

Shorty was endowed with additional attributes vital to all successful mastersinkers and mine captains. He was of sound judgment, decisive, just and upright, forthright and fair to a fault, and had the rare ability of listening and reacting to sound reasoning. He commanded respect rather than demanded it.

With those characteristics a team could be led to, and indeed be driven beyond, the very gates of hell - the conscious general directional objective of shaftsinkers, and of all men mining. They never ever really get there. They all end up in The Other Place Above.

In stark contrast stood the diminutive, one-eyed, bespectacled, soft-palmed, soft-spoken, smart-arsed, inexperienced, book-learned Englishman - the most despised, unworthy and disrespected of all men. Shorty wasn't at all happy with what he saw. He told Lighty, somewhat sadly, that Lighty was to learn the hard way as that was exactly as Lighty had explained his needs to Norman Beresford-Smythe.

'A word of advice to all newcomers,' Shorty added. 'Diplomacy is lost on me - I view it as legitimised deception. Discipline and grievances are not my job. The group dynamics under which we operate determine the outcome of those aspects, and how well you do, and your integration into the team, or how fast you get worked out of the system. The mining school might have taught you all you need to know about engineering, but they taught you nothing about people.'

'It is my opinion that it is a tragedy for the educational institutions to totally overlook the most important things you will ever need to know - organisation behaviour and people management. You may make mistakes, any amount that you care to, or dare to, but make them early and don't ever repeat them. Any major transgression on your part, you can depend on my full, unqualified support no matter what, even if it costs me my job. Make the same mistake again and you are on your own. I will even help the Philistines

239

when they crucify you. You remember that always,' he concluded. Lighty did, and he also remembered not to argue. Perhaps he just forgot to.

Shorty assigned him to the drilling crew on his first shift. Dressed in oilskins far too big for him, and wearing a double hard hat, Lighty descended in the kibble down the shaft with the black Basutu drillers. Lighty had been told by Shorty to do exactly as he was told to do by his Jackhammer Number 1, a Basutu from Lesotho by the name of Nglubi, The Pig. There were two men to a drill and Nglubi had a Jackhammer Number 2, Ngundwan, The Rat. Lighty was there as a novice to learn the ropes from them. He was Jackhammer Number 3.

Nglubi told him to stand at the drill-hole collar and to look up at Ngundwan who was sitting on top of the Seco 25 jackhammer so that Lighty could see what Ngundwan was doing. They placed the six foot drill steel with a carbon tungsten bit on the collar of the hole, lifted the jackhammer and attached it to the drill shank.

Ngundwan effortlessly lifted himself onto the handles of the jackhammer, perched there like a monkey. Nglubi held the whole assembly in place with his six foot four, two hundred and twenty pound frame and again told Lighty to look up at Ngundwan to see what he was doing.

As Lighty looked up Ngundwan threw the compressed air and water levers. The jackhammer violently barked into action spraying him from head to foot with a thick mist of oil and water which spewed out of the forward pointing exhaust ports rendering his spectacles totally useless. Blind in the one eye and seeing next to nothing out of the other. The taste of thin lubricating oil was dreadful as Lighty copped a mouthful of it with his mouth agape as he looked up. Lighty was not very happy.

Day in and day out, drenched to the bone, oil bespattered; arms, legs and back muscles wrenched to far beyond human endurance lifting the jackhammer and drill steels. Half blind without his spectacles, ears shattered by the incessant roar, the auditory senses dysfunctional for some four hours after the last drill ceased.

The only way to communicate was by the shaftsinker's hand signals that Lighty had to learn from hard experience. When he misinterpreted the signals, or got something wrong, a whack on the back of the head with the flat of a shovel was delivered swiftly and decisively. Twin hard hats had their purpose then because the outer one always fell off. Lighty learnt very fast.

Lily white hands turned to a mushy, red, bleeding pulp as the raw, cold steel tore the tender skin and flesh away on the first shift. A large sterile dressing from the first aid box, held in place by a triangular bandage and leather gloves over it, all helped in preventing further disintegration, but the stinging pain was a constant.

At the end of the first shift Shorty told him to report to work with the mucking crew first up in the morning. Lighty was to be there when the freshly blasted rock was lashed out and hoisted to the surface.

He was in the blasting cabin when the sinker on the previous crew detonated the blast his crew had charged. They descended down the shaft immediately thereafter through the thick plug of smoke and sickly-sweet smelling nitrous fumes, the latter turning into nitric acid in his eyes, his respiratory tracts and his lungs.

The eyes constantly watering, and the rawness in the nose producing a constant drip of blinding tears and snot, left to just drip unnoticed being mixed with sweat, oil and water. The shallow hack, hack, hack all day to clear the lungs of the fluid build-up. Sleeping at night in a semi-inverted position to allow the lungs to keep clear by providing a natural gravity drainage system so that Lighty could breath, stop coughing and get some sleep.

The cactus grab operator commenced his function. He opened the jaws of the grab, dropped it down onto the pile of broken rock, took a bite, closed the jaws, raised it over the ten tonne kibble, and dropped the load into it - again, and again, and again. Full kibbles went up, and empty kibbles came down, the double-drum hoist never ceasing until all the blasted rock was on the surface.

Nglubi and Ngundwan came down the shaft in the last empty kibble. It was their turn in the cycle again. Three eight-hour cycles a day, six days a week.

A popular trick for the crew working on the Galloway stage directly above the shaft bottom was to urinate directly over where the initiate stood at the bottom of the shaft. The hilarity of it all was that the victim was totally unaware of what was happening at the time.

Shorty had told Lighty to assist the explosives crew to charge the drilled holes with gelignite after the drilling cycle. There was no time to waste on the silly Mines and Works Act and Regulations which stipulated that explosives could only be charged once the drilling cycle had been completed. Halfway through the drilling cycle the explosives crew were on the shaft bottom charging up the drilled holes with explosives and giving the drill crew heaps of hurry-up.

Lighty arrived at the shaft head one day to find the place in total chaos. A drill team had drilled into a misfired sidewall hole still loaded with gelignite. The charge had gone off killing the Number 2 driller who was perched on the jackhammer. The drill steel had broken, and he had impaled himself on it - in his stomach and out of the back of his neck. By the time the Inspector of Mines arrived on the scene no evidence of any explosives was to be found.

While helping the explosives crew to charge up the holes with gelignite, Lighty was kneeling down dropping gelignite down the hole and had unwittingly wiped the sweat from his forehead with the palm of his hand. Before the shift was over the literally blinding gelignite headache drove him to the very brink of insanity. That night was the worst night Lighty had ever experienced in his life.

The maddening, incessant pain aggravated by increased high blood pressure whenever he vomited provided a sleepless night. The next morning, barely able to stand up straight let alone keep his eyes open, Shorty told him to stay on the Galloway stage and to watch the concreters drop the ring of shuttering and pour the next six feet of concrete lining.

Dropping a monkey wrench from the Galloway stage to the shaft bottom while bolting the concrete shuttering into position for the next pour had its decisive moments. The choice was to take the next kibble up and to disappear off the face of the earth, or to clamber down the chain ladder to retrieve it.

Lighty chose the latter, and took his medicine. The blows rained down all over his body - delivered by a somewhat intolerant and irate drill crew with the flat backs of shovels to any part of his body. One blow per man - sixteen blunt blows. No incisions. Then climbing back up the chain ladder to the safety of the Galloway stage to spend the rest of the shift crying in a corner. For the first four weeks Lighty cried a lot.

One Monday morning Ngundwan didn't turn up for work. He had been stabbed to death the previous day while drinking in an illegal shebeen having lost an argument over a s'febe, a prostitute. Nglubi signalled to Lighty to mount the jackhammer. He grabbed Lighty by the scruff of the neck and gave him a swift, unexpected lift.

Lighty scrambled up and, mounting the machine, rode it like a baboon. Lighty hit the water lever followed by the compressed air lever and the machine barked into vibrating life beneath him. Vision totally blurred by the vibration, the sense of control and power was exhilarating. Riding the jackhammer!

'If only my mum could see me now!' Lighty thought as he laughed hysterically for the first time. The rest of the drilling crew all took a moment to look at him. The flashing of white teeth and a flick of the hand or finger told him that he had become one of the fraternity. His yells and hoops of delight went unheard - even to himself.

John, his lifelong Zulu friend, joined the crew as a driller a week later and took over Lighty's job as Nglubi's Number 2. John had recently completed a Bachelor of Arts degree with the University of South Africa. It took him eight long, hard years to achieve this by a correspondence course. He was working hard to save up enough money to go back to university to complete a law degree. Practicing law was one of the very few professions exempted from the Apartheid Job Reservation laws.

Lighty was promoted to the shaft bottom sinker supervising the drilling, explosive charging, the blasting and the mucking-out of blasted rock. When his six weeks probation expired Lighty was given two weeks notice to report to Norman Beresford-Smythe as arranged.

'You're doing just damn, fine, splendid Shorty tells me. Next month report to Allan Greenwood. He needs a good supervisor on his Galloway stage,' Norman told Lighty.

Life became a bit easier then, and more tolerable. Allan was a huge, grizzly-bear like man with cauliflower ears and the face of a prize-fighter with a justifiable reputation to accompany it all. He took trouble from no-one but dealt it out in massive proportions when he considered it prudent and judicial to do so.

Doing compressed air, freshwater and waste water, concrete and ventilation piping extensions, and dropping concrete shuttering for the next concrete pour to form the shaft side-wall, was easy by comparison. Lighty absolutely revelled in it. He consulted and collaborated with Fanie Botha, a former rugby playing friend and company colleagues of his who had completed a double major in chemistry and civil engineering.

They came up with an additive mix, which caused the concrete to set half an hour earlier than before. This gave Lighty the opportunity to put competitive pressure on the shaft bottom crew that he did with great relish.

Six months later Lighty was promoted to shaft shift supervisor on Carl 'Mehlwan' van der Merwe's shaft. Lighty was running the operation for the whole shift. Carl's mehlo, his eyes, saw everything because he had spies everywhere, and he used to beat the black workers who wouldn't co-operate in his twenty four hour a day espionage. He used to fart, scratch his balls, hack, snork snot and spit greenballs indiscriminately and cared not in whose presence he did it. Mehlwan and Marauding Mike were as thick as thieves, and both of them used to womanise with the wives of Lighty's men while they worked on the night shift.

Another eight months later Lighty was an Acting Mastersinker - he had his very own shaft. The Acting Mastersinker part was The Law's way of saying that he did not have the required statutory practical experience of three years to sit for the Mine Captain's Certificate Of Competency. He was some twelve years younger than his youngest peer Shorty.

He wasn't acting for anyone. He had temporarily been appointed as such while Mehluan went on annual leave. Mehluan had a massive heart attack on the first day of his holiday driving in his car, and had died while on his merry way to Plettenberg Bay. One man dead - another man's bread.

'Jou tier is dood' Speenvark (Suckling Pig) had said to Lighty in lighthearted mock jest the following morning in front of all the men in the changehouse. Your tiger is dead. Speenvark was one of Mehlwan's known spies and was the electrician on Lighty's shift. He got his name from sucking up to Mehlwan. He had a temporary lapse of memory forgetting that Mehlwan was really dead and that he no longer had protection.

'Don't you ever forget who rode that tiger until he died!' Lighty spontaneously replied in a gruff, flat monotone without looking at anyone in particular, his blood pressure rising ten points. The strange, new, hostile tone in his own voice momentarily startled Lighty. Flashes of insight and hindsight crossed Lighty's mind as he remembered a number of mysterious stoppages at critical moments in the operation, and the premeditated fury from Mehlwan he had to endure and resist after such an incident. His blood pressure rose another ten points.

No-one spoke to Lighty for a long time after that preferring instead to put as much distance between themselves and him then, and to walk very fast. Speenvark's days in the shaftsinking business had suddenly become numbered to three. Lighty had nothing whatsoever to do with his demise, knew not who did, cared not who did, and did not bother to find out what became of him.

Lighty knew that the job that lay ahead of him was not only formidable but virtually impossible unless he made the right moves and took positive action fast to control the monstrous job that he had been promoted to. It called for every ounce of his limited capabilities, and very limited they were.

Late that afternoon he summoned his three shift supervisors Whitey van Aswegen, Stoffel Beukes and Dick Thornton to his field office.

'You men taught me virtually everything I know about shaft sinking. The time has come for you now to prove how good a job you did in teaching me the trade,' Lighty said to them matter-of-factly. It was difficult to talk harshly and to give orders to his former colleagues and superiors, all of them much older than he was.

'Ja, Meneer!' Stoffel said. Yes Sir!

'Meneer se moer,' Lighty said flatly looking the three of them straight in the eye in turn. Formality flew out the window and the four of them risked a smile apiece.

'Now, I intend being the best, fairest, safest and most honest mastersinker in the business. I assume that we would all agree to that,' Lighty said continuing to look them in the eyes. No 'Ja, Meneer!' was necessary.

'I want to know from you what it is that you expect from me in order for the three of you to do your jobs properly and safely,' Lighty continued. 'I want the three of you to get together and determine exactly what it is that you want me to do for you. When you have done that, write it down and bring your requirements to me,' he concluded.

Serious discussions followed for the next few days, and there was much debate amongst the entire crew about their new boss who wanted to be told what to do, and how to do his job, when everybody knew that he already knew. He was, in fact, supposed to know everything.

Shorty, Allan and Lighty got very drunk and disorderly late one afternoon sometime later instead of going to Mehlwan's funeral to celebrate the occasion. They weren't quite sure if the occasion they were celebrating was Lighty's lightening-fast promotion to mastersinker or Mehlwan's death, but, in all likelihood, both events.

'The miserable, inconsiderate, poxy, son-of-a-bitch could have at least contracted a more prolonged and painful disorder as a way of dying,' was how Allan summed up his own personal feelings toward Mehlwan as they walked into the pub, not as if they owned it, for they cared not a single, solitary, goddamn who bloody-well did.

They cleaned the twenty-odd souls in the pub out in two minutes flat just for the hell of it, and primarily because the frivolous and puerile merry-making of mere mortal men was irritating to them for they liked to drink alone. Two cops walked in, each took one look at the three of them, and then told the rather vocal and sadly disillusioned bruised and hurting egos outside that it seemed to be a very good idea for them to go and drink elsewhere.

Lighty was working, walking, talking, fighting, drinking and being with living legends in the mining industry.

The next day the three shift supervisors walked in and presented Lighty with their list of expectations. The list had been very well prepared and had already been typed out and four copies made. Lighty read the list, signed all four copies, and gave each shift supervisor a signed copy.

'If you gentlemen would kindly reciprocate and sign my copy, we will have a firm agreement,' Lighty said to them. The three of them eagerly signed Lighty's copy. They had never in their lives been addressed as gentlemen before.

'If ever a time comes that I don't deliver as we have now contracted,' Lighty said, 'you are at liberty to immediately bring to my attention the error of my ways. Are we agreed?' Lighty asked them.

'Ja, Meneer!' came the three concurring, unified responses.

'Meneer se moer,' Lighty reminded them for the umpteenth time. It was totally in vain as the habit had set in and refused to be eradicated thereafter. It was one of the burdens that Lighty had to carry - that of not being addressed by his Christian name. The lonely chill of the system-imposed regimen bore heavily upon him.

It took less than a fortnight for the other five of Mehluan's spies to be flushed out and dispensed. One of them whispered a sweet nothing into Lighty's ear one day so Lighty made a note of it. The next day he summoned Spy and prospective Victim to the cement storage shed where he confirmed the accusation with Spy; then closed the door to the shed firmly behind him. Spies became fair game, the men no longer felt that they were being ruled by fear, and the operation started running with the precision of a Swiss chronometer. Shorty had taught him well.

Once the purge had been completed Lighty again summoned his three shift supervisors to his office.

'Menere, now it is your turn to tell me what it is I can expect of the three of you and your respective crews. We will follow the same procedure as before except that this time, consult with your men and take your time,' he told them. Their eyes lit up. It was around this time that he acquired the Bantu name of Thanda Bantu, the man who likes black people.

It was some time later, after a very satisfying six weeks of spectacular shaftsinking seriously threatening Shorty's world record, Lighty decided that a party was in order. It had taken him twenty short months to go from Palm Villa Chief Coward to the World's No. 2 Mastersinker. He was acutely aware of the fact that he had not a single black hair on his chest yet.

He duly arranged a 'braaivleis' (barbecue) late on a Saturday afternoon after the last shift had knocked off. Whitey van Aswegen was appointed to lead the fore-party that did the necessary procurement of booze and meat and to set the fires going.

Whitey coped well for a man who had the misfortune of having a broad, flat nose, large nostrils, very tightly curled hair, came from the Cape Coloured District Six in Cape Town with an accent to match and was clearly Eur-African. His slanty eyes indicated a faintly noticeable ancestral connection with a Malayan slave, or perhaps a Hottentot, but he was classified to be of European descent.

He had *tried for white* in the Transvaal, and had succeeded. He was a brilliant shift supervisor, played the guitar, banjo and concertina very well and did just about everything else to perfection including roasting an ox over the spit.

The sun had no sooner dipped its lights over the horizon in the west, following the example set by some of the crew, when the long arm of the law took a hand in matters. Four plain-clothes policemen materialised from nowhere and started to demand 'Name, address and also where you live!' from everyone present including Shorty and Allan.

One of the policemen, whom Lighty recognised from a previous and unpleasant non-police encounter, headed straight for the explosives magazine and started to inspect it. The bastard had needlessly bashed Lighty senseless some eight years before after he kicked, then killed, Lighty's pet mongrel stray puppy dog by wringing its neck.

One of them who appeared to be in charge of the raid started reading out reams of rubbish from all sorts of sub-sections of God only knows which Acts of Parliament. Mixed-race, drunken parties in the veldt among the black-wattle trees were severely frowned upon. No amount of explanation from Lighty was heeded in the slightest.

Lighty had no sooner decided that, if they were ignored, they might go away when the man Lighty knew inspecting the explosives magazine returned and read out a charge of breaching The Explosives Act to Lighty. One of the locks on a gelignite carrying box had not been closed properly. The fact that it contained no explosives at all meant nothing to him.

'You must disperse immediately or face further charges under the Riotous Assemblies Act,' the policeman said to them all. His goons stood waiting at the gate to the site ready to make driving under the influence of alcohol arrests. There could have been many, including Lighty. In fact, all of them were leglessly drunk by then.

Lighty ordered the black men to return to their compound nearby, and to carry and help the disabled with them. He ordered the white men to his office where he started making phone calls, the first of which was to his boarding school Afrikaner room-mate Ghandi.

Ghandi said that he would take care of matters and that he would also rectify the puppy problem. Perhaps goon was the only white man to jump from a window. Lighty then called one of the local farmers who was a beneficiary of some of the engineering services on site. He soon arrived in a lorry, loaded them all into it, and delivered them all home safely.

Nothing more was ever heard of the incident thereafter. This seemed to displease Marauding Mike more than a fraction. He was more than conspicuous by his absence at the party. Lighty started wondering whom it was that informed on him.

The adrenalin constantly surging uncontrolled through the system, mental faculties at a constant peak, the muscles as taught as stressed springsteel and reflexes as sharp as an enraged and entrapped Black Mamba. This resulted in a never-ending loud buzz in the auditory senses totally drowning out the thunderous cacophony of eight unsilenced jackhammers roaring in frantic military unison in a confined eight metre diameter hole deep down in the earth - incessantly going closer to the very gates of hell than perhaps was really necessary. The ever-present crawling of the skin a constant reminder of the last ice-cold chill of fear when the last man was killed not very long before. *Ngonya* - jaws of the lion.

Two years and one week later, which included five fatal accidents, the last of which was Lighty's black brother and life-long best friend John who was crushed in a fall from the shaft sidewall, about ten tonnes of it, was enough.

John's battered dead body was dug out, unceremoniously slung onto the pile of broken rock in the kibble, hoisted to the surface, and then dumped on the concrete slab at the shaft head to await the meat wagon. The operation resumed as if nothing had happened - the round being drilled had to get blasted by the end of the shift. A fatality was purely of nuisance value.

Lighty followed on the next kibble up and, taking John's left arm with him, tossed it onto his forever still and motionless chest. He proceeded to the changehouse where he was confronted by the field manager Marauding Mike while stark, bollick naked, smoking a blood-stained cigarette, and about to have a shower. As the mastersinker, Lighty had every right to be there at the end of the shift, or anywhere else nearby that he considered appropriate.

Lighty was still recovering from the death of his father Nyanyan five months previously. His younger brother Ivor had been buried two months before, and he had attended the funeral of Joao Texeira from Palm Villa the previous week. Joao and Lighty had been to an all-night hockey party, and Joao had been killed in a high speed car chase on his way to work from the party - but not by the police. It was well known at the time that Joao had a paternity claim on him.

Lighty was also still smarting after he had been jilted by his fiancee who had eloped to Cape Town with her very best girl friend. It was a very badly timed confrontation.

'What the hell do you think you are doing just walking off the job? If that round isn't taken all hell will break loose over your bloody head!' Marauding Mike roared, angrily thumping his fat finger into Lighty's chest.

Marauding Mike got the chest part wrong. He spent the next six weeks recovering in the Cottesloe hospital after he had slipped and fallen down a long flight of steps next to the changehouse. That was what had been written on the accident report. It was later rumoured, somewhat loosely, that he was going to summon Lighty before a court of law as soon as he was able to walk and talk properly again. Lighty never saw the inside of a court of law in that regard.

Marauding Mike never walked properly again, and when he spoke after that, he spoke a lot less, and with greatly diminished conviction. The steel end of a pick handle could do a lot of damage.

Lighty got dressed without showering, a legal offence, and drove into town in The Bomb. He still had it because he couldn't give it away let alone sell it. He bought a brand new Alfa Romeo 2000 Spider sports car and then went to arrange for John's body to be taken to Manzi Mhlopi for burial.

He then proceeded to the pub to have a few quiet beers. The pub rapidly emptied itself the moment he entered leaving a number of half-full glasses and smouldering cigarettes on the bar counter, and Lighty completely alone with the barman. Word had got around - the complete savage animal.

He took off for Manzi Mhlopi late that night arriving there at sunrise. Ndlovo and Katie had heard on the grapevine that John had been killed. Lighty's unexpected and untimely arrival at sunrise merely confirmed their worst beliefs.

The funeral was attended by the police, as a white man who lived with black people, and who went to black funerals, was a marked man. Added to that was the facts that he was known to have been initiated into the Zulu tribe, was treated by the indunas as an equal, and that he was a co-owner and trustee of Manzi Mhlopi. His future was predictably made very difficult. The name Thanda Bantu did not make his life any easier.

The day after the funeral Lighty left Manzi Mhlopi, for he could not cope with the deep grief of Ndlovo, Katie and Nondwe, and he needed to grieve on his own. He returned to the Transvaal to defend himself on a mandatory culpable homicide charge for John's death at a Mines Inspectorate Inquest. He then set off for Jeffrey's Bay riding pipelines, and then to nearby Cape St. Francis. He spent the next four and a half months surfing there unsuccessfully trying to becoming a human being again.

Shaftsinking was to bring out in Lighty the true spirit of the mining fraternity where one obliviously thinks nothing of selflessly giving of one's self, and sometimes one's very life, in order to save another in peril, or in the hour of their most need. It also delivered the mental toughness, strength and tenacity which, together with an abnormally high intellect, enabled him to outdistance, outgun and outlast anyone who got in his way, or anything else that had to be resolved. It was an all too rare phenomenon called having hard balls.

These personal intangible assets and attributes he intended to acquire were something Lighty had, as a student, found to be somewhat lacking in the leaders of the mining industry he had encountered which happened to be taking a turn for the worse at the time.

Shaftsinkers are well known to prefer fighting to fornicating anytime. The stress release and sense of comfort was swifter, more lastingly satisfying, and far more pleasant a recreational activity. The physically visible wounds were far less painful than the women-inflicted invisible kind. They were men of very few words, and they bore many wounds, of many kinds.

They expounded the belief that women were a double-breasted pastime in order to hide the deep inner conflict they felt of their own inherent femininity, all the while weeping with their heads between the soft, tender breasts of the women upon which their very masculinity fed. The former they did loudly, unwittingly, and to their own detriment, but they had to do it. They were outwardly apparently untouchable sub-human animals and simply did not fit into regularly ordered society. They were a breed apart.

Shaft sinking was also to bring to his attention, and to bring out in him, the inherent animal savagery, ruthlessness, hatred, resourcefulness, resilience and grim determination of the human spirit which comes to the fore when one is constantly and visibly stalked by the prospect of a violent death as one goes about defying Mother Nature deep in her very being, for she commands and takes her toll at will.

Behind the coarse, brash, tough and unforgiving facades were some of the finest, kindest, most dignified and most proud human beings that Lighty had ever encountered. They were truly the salt of this earth. Lighty was one, fiercely proud so, and he probably still is one at heart. The sudden, unexpected sound of a jackhammer roaring to life on a city construction site elicits a surge of adrenalin, followed by an acute sharpening of the senses, an exuberant elation, a razor-sharp awareness, and a subtle reminder that he once truly lived.

It was a cloak that Lighty used later in his life with great effect, but now that he doesn't need it, or even want it anymore, he has found it virtually impossible to discard - painfully so.'

My godfather Jon, who had been in publishing for thirty years, as well as Adrian, my father's longstanding friend, both read the first manuscript of this story after Jack had posted it to me. They both said that it was impossible for anyone to write such a story unless they had personally experienced the whole series of events themselves. I know all this actually happened. I just know it.

'I rest my case,' was all that Jack wrote and told me.

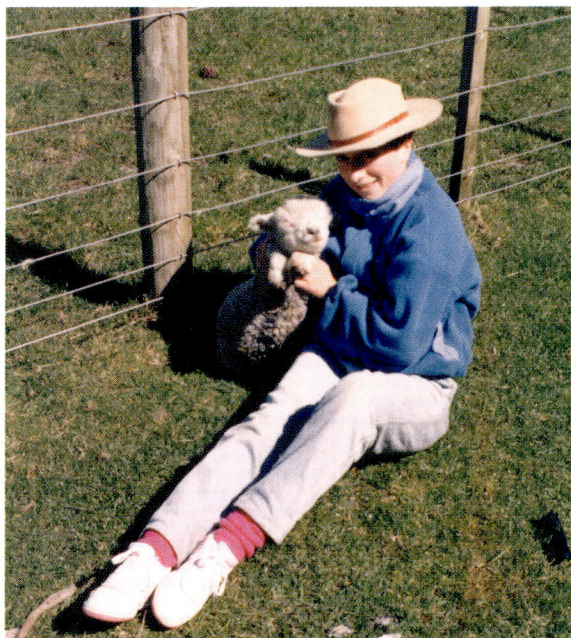

1. *Takaka,*
   Golden Bay,
   New Zealand

2. *The Lambs*

WANTED

Chapter Twenty Three

Jack one morning mentioned to me that Kakadu National Park was not far away, and that he knew of a trackless shortcut through the bush to get there. I didn't tell him that my back was hurting and that four hours in the rough was something I couldn't handle. Jack wasn't to know. Besides that, we were very tired after the long drive from Lawn Hill National Park and we both needed the rest.

We left our Edith River bed camp reluctantly and headed for Western Australia - the Kimberley. We were in the mood to drive, and the drive was again spectacular, especially the red gorges of Gregory National Park. The boab trees were in full splendour at sunset and full of corellas. We drove into the beautiful orange-mauve sunset behind the ridges in front of us. The enchantment was totally unique and far more than just magical. I didn't miss the flat country in the least.

'Slow down! Slow down! For God's sake, slow down! Get the bloody hell off the road!' Jack screamed at me from the passenger seat as a road-train loaded with cattle came hurtling toward us. Suddenly, as we came off a concrete causeway at high speed, a large, head-sized boulder was thrown up from the wheels of the passing road-train.

I remember seeing it bouncing up from the ground at great velocity, and then smashing into the windscreen right in front of my face. I was suddenly covered in broken glass chips. It was so, so, oh! so close! A fraction more speed and it would have knocked my block clean off at the neck! Life is terribly short.

I could see nothing through the windscreen as we tore off into the scrub. We got out of the vehicle and I started to cry from shock. Jack kept me calm at the time by reassuring me that it was an accident and not my fault. There was a large hole in the windscreen almost as big as my head. That boulder came so close to breaking through the windscreen and decapitating me that it was no wonder that I was in such a shocking state.

Jack made me get back in the driver's seat and then made me drive for a few more kilometres before he took over the driving. My fifth life gone. It was obvious that my number was not yet up. In that sorry state we headed for Kununurra in the Kimberley.

We stopped at Timber Creek Roadhouse to refuel and to check if there was anywhere we could have the windscreen replaced. Kununurra was the only place to go to we were told. Straight ahead.

When we arrived at Kununurra at 10.30 pm that night it looked absolutely awful! We were exhausted and just wanted to find a bed and a hot shower. There was only one room left in the whole town as there was a rodeo taking place for that week. We just booked in and crashed despite all its deficiencies. There were no blankets, no bed linen, the loos and showers were miles away, and all that for $55.00 for the night. We were dead-dog tired after an eventful day which could very well have been my last.

Civilisation in Kununurra, The Kimberley, Western Australia was another shock to the system. Haircuts, beard trims, (Jack's, not mine!), washing our laundry, real coffee in a coffee shop - the whole works. It was quite a thriving metropolis and very relaxing and enjoyable. Luckily the windscreen took no time at all to be fixed the next morning. In those parts of the country windscreens were a common replacement part and the repair works chaps knew and did their jobs well.

We asked around from people we spoke to, to advise us of a good camping spot in the vicinity where we could while away a few days. Some fellows gave us a very rough mud-map and sent us on our merry way. Unfortunately, it turned out to be a bum steer as we found ourselves in a cul de sac in a rubbish tip in mid-afternoon. The guides obviously didn't like tourists very much or they had an appalling sense of direction.

Eventually, we intuitively followed a track and arrived at an irrigation farm homestead where Patti and Nigel were extremely friendly. They told us where to find a very special camping spot close to their homestead. They offered us a bunch of bananas which they grew on the farm, and which I politely refused saying that we had already bought some. Jack later told me that I had committed a faux pas as bush hospitality must never be refused. Bananas went very well with Jack's biryani as it so happened.

We set up camp on the banks of the Ord River on a sandy patch under some palms that ensured that we had shade throughout the day. I went for an absolutely magic stroll along the river after we had established our new temporary home. I then walked up the hill for a view of the surrounding gorge country, the red sunset and the large boab trees.

I returned to camp to find that Jack had set up a campfire, which would have done Guy Fawkes proud. We set it alight and sat there in front of the roaring fire watching flocks of magpie geese and cockatoos silhouetted in the sunset. We were honoured by a visit from some wild horses called brumbies and a mob of wallabies who skipped away noisily after a long, curious peep at us. It was so peaceful and so very Australian.

There were saltwater crocodiles flopped out on the banks of the river and floating close to the reeds not very far from camp. It made us more wary of getting too close to the river's edge, especially while fishing. Another family camped up-river from us saw a very large one very close to their camp.

We had morning coffee overlooking the river with its pelicans, egrets, cormorants, ibis, spoonbills, magpie geese and avocets. The place was brimming with activity and it was a pleasure to be a part of it. The day was hot and we spent the greater part of it under the tarpaulin trying to stay cool, but oh, I so wanted a quick dip in the water. Jack's incredulous glare at my suggestion made me rethink that notion.

'Happy birthday Mum!' I wrote in my notebook. 'Well, I'm stuck here in the midday heat in the Toyota. She has decided to give us some trouble - the solenoid on the starter motor has gone and we can't go anywhere! We were looking forward to a day at Lake Argyle, the rodeo and then (a) cuppa tea with Patti and Nigel at the homestead by the campsite. Jack's gone to get help. There is nothing we can do. S... I'm getting hot. At least we just made it into Kununurra.'

Jack walked to the Toyota garage in the 45 degree centigrade heat and returned with the proprietor who sat in the Toyota and made it start the first time he tried. I was relieved and Jack was highly embarrassed. The owner warned us not to flood the self-starter motor - a fraction too late I thought.

We continued our planned day starting with a visit to Lake Argyle, which was superb. Azure blue water surrounded by steep red hills with pelicans dotted on the waters surface. Lake Argyle had 12 times the capacity of Sydney Harbour but it was so large that we saw only a fraction of it.

Apparently they didn't know what to do with all the water which we had seen being put to good use irrigating farms in the Ord River area where we were camped. We had lunch at the bottom of the dam with a massive volume of water spurting out of three spill pipes. I was getting good at spotting crocodiles and we saw a number of fresh-water ones in the reeds.

We wandered back towards Kununurra. We first dropped into the rodeo that was in progress. It was a picture in a classic Australian bush setting. There were wild brumbies and bulls, all bucking and kicking, with riders falling all over the place. Dust, heat, sand, flies and two rider casualties. There was some very skilful riding by the men who caught the horses afterwards. There were spectators of all shapes, sizes and colours, all having a great time. I had realised another of my impossible dreams.

We dropped in on Patti and Nigel at the homestead for our cup of tea. Jack and Nigel fearlessly went out to give the corellas in the banana plantation a fright to chase them away while Patti and I discussed matters of great import. There was a small domesticated orphaned calf, a poddy, which was romping and frolicking with the dogs on the lawn and, much to our amusement, was getting highly confused every time it moo-ed in reply to the dog's excited barking.

I phoned my mum from the homestead to say 'Happy Birthday' and we had a good, long chat. They were off to St. Mawes in Cornwall the next morning for the annual family holiday. Mum told me, much to my great delight, that she, my father and elder brother Simon, were planning on going to New Zealand to visit me on my return there.

That night we spot-lit seven pairs of salt water crocodile eyes watching our camp. Crocodile spotting was to become part of our lifestyle there. On the opposite bank we saw six of them one morning, one of which was a three metre specimen lying in full view on the bank. Every night our spotlight picked out many pairs of eyes watching us in the camp.

The Monday morning was an early 6:00 am start to the day so that we could pack up camp, and for Jack to get the Toyota into Kununurra to be serviced before setting out on the Gibb River Road. He left me behind at the camp finishing my breakfast before I walked up to the homestead, my companions a cereal bowl and a mug of coffee.

Patti and I had arranged to have an early morning ride from her parent's Ord River bank farm a few kilometres away before they took me into town to meet up with Jack. Nigel brought the children along for the ride and to help catch the horses. Nigel was thrown off the horse I was to ride which did my self-confidence no amount of good at all. Nigel reassured me, and I mounted my steed, my New Zealand bolting incident some months before very fresh in my mind.

I enjoyed the ride and the scenery of irrigation canals, fields of corn, the brolgas and red, hazy canyons behind us. It took a lot of courage to get the horse to leap over an irrigation canal. I was quite ready for the horse to baulk at the last instant and for me to be thrown into the canal.

On our arrival at the farm I scored a refreshing cold shower before Nigel took me into town. I met Jack at Duke's Loo, a coffee shop in Kununurra for lunch. He, for some inexplicable reason, and a pleasant change it was, was more cheerful than I was.

'Blame it on the heat!' I said to myself.

We spent a relaxing three hours at the local swimming pool while waiting for the Toyota to be serviced. It was more like a resort with many international travellers at the poolside. I eavesdropped on some of the conversations as Jack started to write, and very hard at that. He kept looking at me a lot.

Our drive to the Gibb River Road at sunset was very pretty. The Gibb River Road was established as a cattle droving track many years before but had been replaced by cattle road-trains and tourist caravans.

We met Rusty. She was one of the most unforgettably beautiful people I have ever met. Rusty was the caretaker of a patch of hot, dry and very red dust called a camping ground at the entrance to Emma Gorge.

She lived a simple, uncomplicated life in a caravan there in the Kimberley with her two lovely little girls aged two and three. The girls, when we saw them on our arrival, were very dusty and weary from playing in the dry, red earth. A clean, healthy dirty they were as children who grow up in the bush with nature are wont to be.

'I'm just a dusty little scrubber,' Rusty told us around the campfire that memorable full-moon lit night in early August. Five foot nothing she was, with flaming red and very wild hair. Dressed in a bright red cotton frock enabled her to blend in perfectly with her environment.

She collected the five dollar camping fee from travelling campers such as we who made use of the dusty patch to rest their weary bones after a day of travelling in the dry, sweltering 45 degree heat of the Kimberley.

'There is no dignity in the dole' she told us. 'The camping fees I collect here, I hand over to the landlord, who, in turn, supplies me with about fifty dollars worth of groceries every week and some clothing for the girls. We are happy and make do on that. I spend the wet season with an Aborigine tribe further to the north of here, and I then caretake the camping ground in the dry.'

She had lived in a town once where the father of her two children came from, but she didn't marry him.

She couldn't spend much time with us as one of her children kept squawking, and she had to make a few dashes to investigate the problem. After a few drinks and the odd yarn, she went home to bed.

We settled down in our sleeping bags and stared up at the stars and the full moon. We had long before abandoned sleeping in the tent, preferring instead to stare at the stars, meteorites and the moon at night from our sleeping bags. A smouldering mosquito coil downwind from us took good care of that problem.

'What the hell has happened to the moon?' I asked Jack as we were settling down to sleep for the night.

'If I am not mistaken, we are about to witness a total eclipse of the moon tonight,' Jack assessed. 'We seem to have unwittingly positioned ourselves in one of the best vantage points in the world to witness this very rare event.'

And so it was. The eclipse began at about nine o'clock that night and continued until the total eclipse was complete at around midnight. When it slowly started to peep out from the other side again, we went to sleep with the comforting knowledge that the world was not coming to an end.

On the Tuesday morning we walked up Emma Gorge at 7: 00 am and had a cool dip in a pool on the way down in the early morning light. We got talking to John and Joka for quite a while. They were a Dutch couple who we had met at camp on our return. We then packed up camp in the screaming heat of day and set off for El Questro Cattle Station further along the Gibb River Road.

The dry heat and going troppo every day was not doing me any good. The heat kept hitting me on the head like a heavy sledge hammer, cooking and scrambling my brain to an incoherent pulp. I avoided too much discomfort by doing very little, in fact, being horizontal from midday and leaving Jack to do all the work. It did start to cool down after 4:00 pm and I could go for my birdwatches then.

We arrived at El Questro to find the best spots had all been taken and we were frustrated by the inconvenience. We went back to the homestead where Margaret heard out our story of dismay and our needs. She then drew a map of how to get to John Rat Gorge telling us that it was the very best there was, and that there was no-one within miles of the place. Margaret also promised not to let anyone else come anywhere near us. We had a chat with her and she told us that El Questro was an all-woman cattle station.

We set up camp at John Rat Gorge, another paradise despite the infuriating flies. Our 'boudoir' was surrounded by pandanus palms and established gum trees which provided excellent shade next to clear water and in a beautiful gorge. The sunset was unbelievable as the hills shone red, later shading to purple, and then black as did everything else at that time of day. We slept under the stars as usual.

It was a Garden of Eden as I saw azure kingfishers, the nankeen heron and the striped honeyeater, all of them for the first time. I watched it from my perch up a gummy while we were having our breakfast coffee.

When it started to get a bit hotter we drove to a place where Margaret had told us that we could find a hot spring in which to have a swim. After a short walk we found a family of six wallowing in a shallow pool. Not wanting to invade their privacy we asked them if there were any more pools above them. They told us that a short walk up the hill there was one absolutely ideal for us.

Surrounded by gleaming pandanus palms and 45 degrees of heat we wallowed for three hours in a small, shady pool that we had all to ourselves. Our roaring laughter was deafening as the echoes resounded from the surrounding cliffs. It was so good to hear Jack laugh as he did. At last!

The following day we were again lolling around in our pool when a retired Army officer and his wife turned up and asked us if they could join us. When we told them that they were most welcome to, they took all their clothes off and jumped right in! Funny place the Kimberley?

Chapter Twenty Four

Between 11:00 am and 4:00 pm, we simply didn't do much so as to conserve our energy, and we said nothing at all in case we were misunderstood and offended the other. We had decided that we would do our travelling during the heat of the day and make full use of the air conditioning in the Toyota at that time. The intense heat was very noticeable at smoko stops when we got out for a leg-stretch and a pee.

The scenery beyond El Questro station remained outstanding, but as we progressed west along the Gibb River road, it flattened out and became very arid. However, as we approached Mount Barnett Station, the cliffs rose up in front of us again.

An Aborigine community lived across the road from the Mount Barnett shop and we saw most of them there. Seemingly, they were quite a happy crowd with a lot of laughter, but the older generation looked a bit dirty, neglected and haggard. The children were dressed up very brightly and ate ice creams virtually non-stop.

The shop was brand new and had been in operation for only four weeks. It was re-supplied by road-train every fortnight and, as the venture was still new, there was not much available at the time. The owners were still finding out what was most in demand in the community.

We liked the Aborigine and white relationship there as it seemed to be a mutually balanced one. We didn't like the way we were herded through a special electronic gate to the camping ground though. It was dirty and full of bloody tourists. However, we luckily, again of course, managed to find a quiet spot away from the crowds.

The walk up to Manning Gorge late that afternoon turned out to be much better than anticipated with a steep scramble over loose rocks and spinifex for commanding views back over the water and to the distant hills beyond. We had a refreshing swim in a pool there as we watched the flocks of corellas and cockatoos going to roost at sunset.

We had a fun evening with a good hearty campfire going. I even had Jack ask me to dance so we had a bit of a rock 'n roll on a dusty patch until the dust cloud we had kicked up became totally ridiculous. The dunny, quite fortunately, was not too far away from camp and spared us the spadework in the hard ground.

I awoke at sunrise and, with binoculars in hand, watched the activities of the fauna around us. I was very dirty, and I had endless trouble when trying to phone Qantas from the shop to confirm my flight from Melbourne to New Zealand. A hot shower at the shop afterwards was much appreciated.

We had heard how pleasant Bell Gorge was, and after an hour's drive on a nasty patch of wash-outs, sand, bulldust and potholes, we arrived there. So had everyone else, and in a way, we felt disappointed at the campsite, as the best had gone. However, after we had slowed down and revitalised we headed to the gorge that was well worth the visit. There was a shallow but large waterhole from which a four-tiered waterfall fell. It was no doubt a magnificent picture in the wet.

Sunset was creeping up fast, and I walked into it, and up and over the rocks further along the gorge. I found another nice waterfall and waterhole but, unless I fell a hundred metres, I couldn't get there for a swim.

Stupidly I got too hot and started going troppo again but a refreshing swim soon cured that. There was no one else around and it was starting to get late. On the way home, the flies licked the moisture off us by the gallon. The Western Australian fly was not our friend. We decided that we were justifiably allowed a little whinge about the heat, the flies and the people. Could it be said with an element of truth that they combined to prematurely drive us south?

The drive to the western-most point we planned to go, where we turned southeast at the junction toward Windjana National Park, had been ravaged by fire. We had some good views back over the ranges.

Soon after we had turned southeast, we started to relax together a little more and felt the better for it. Perhaps it was because we had achieved the western-most point we had planned for, or perhaps it was that we were heading south to cooler climes.

The campsite at Windjana National Park wasn't exactly what could be classified as shady so the first thing we did was put a tarpaulin up in the heat. When Jack suggested that we go for a walk at 2:00 pm in the scorching heat I thought that he had gone totally mad. He hadn't been with me on my many walks and birdwatches, and I thought that he couldn't possibly outwalk me. He did! He was forever more than 100 metres ahead of me and kept on stopping to wait for me to catch up with him!

'Where I come from, we used to run for hours on end in this kind of heat' he said. Walking in the shaded gorge itself was, in fact, the coolest place to be.

Windjana, Tunnel Creek and Geiki National Parks were all part of the Devonian Reef which was made up of coral reefs once submerged beneath the sea. It was supposed to be one of the best preserved fossilised reefs in the world and had been carbon dated to be some 350 million years old. That was well before I was thought of.

We walked for about 5 kilometres between the towering rock formations on the dry, sandy river bed. The freshwater Johnson crocodiles were by no means shy except when a stupid tourist started throwing empty beer cans and rocks at them so that his friend could take a video of him. We remonstrated loudly at the two of them. About 100 crocodiles lay basking on the rocks with their mouths agape and with birds picking their teeth.

Jack took a photograph of me as I appeared to be just about to kick a crocodile in the bum. Wow! No-one will ever know it wasn't vicious would they! There was no need for a telephoto lens to click away at crocs there.

That night we had a roaring fire and met our neighbours. They were Steve from the USA and Michael, a 'whingeing Pom' architect from Bristol who we talked to until late that night. At least I did, as Jack had gone to sleep early. I was not surprised after the long walk in the gorge.

We all got very excited about a hungry boobook owl that had perched above our camp and had flown very close to us. Steve had been to Kunming and Dali in China and was a keen birdman so we had a lot to talk about. He was, as I had been, in China when the Tianamin Square massacre took place. I thoroughly enjoyed the different company for a change. The stars surrounded us totally as we sat around the camp fire. It was as if no-one else was there.

The next morning we packed up slowly, made the most of a cold shower, and headed to Tunnel Creek, part of the coral limestone Devonian Reef. Again we stayed cool in the 750 metre long tunnel and, equipped with torches, walked the whole way through to the opposite end. There were moments of total, scary, darkness when Jack told me to turn my torch off. A good few stalactites and stalagmites had formed over the ages.

An Aborigine named Pigeon was supposed to have hidden in there about a century before. He made white settlement in the area very difficult and uncomfortable and was eventually, after four years, found and shot stone dead.

Our next stop was Fitzroy Crossing, a small community. When we arrived there and were refueling, Jack and I had a major misunderstanding about a hamburger. All I did was order one for him while he was refuelling, and he blasted me out of my boots for my kind and considerate efforts.

'Listen Tweethead! I am a hamburger gourmet, and I know big stuff about how hamburgers are supposed to be made,' he said to me.

So what if I was a tweethead? He hurt my feelings.

We were in a hurry, just the once, to catch a tourist boat which patrolled the Geiki Gorge nearby. The rush to get there in time for the boat didn't do us any good. We also patiently had to wait in a queue alongside 100 other tourists. It was the first touristy venture we had undertaken but we eventually did enjoy being piloted up and down the river.

I got a great photo of a jabiru stork, and the crocs were so numerous I happily clicked away. I was glad to eventually get out of the sun and it was a restful and peaceful hour and a half. The Ranger, who really knew his birds, gave us an excellent running commentary until I rudely interrupted him:

'Penguin!' I shouted, when it turned out to be a nankeen night heron. Everybody laughed at me. After the boat trip I went in pursuit of the purple crowned wren, but none of them were at home then.

Camping was becoming less inviting and so we decided to opt for a hotel with a decadent hot shower and all the mod-cons. This was all fine and splendid, until we had a power cut for an hour and the air conditioner stopped working. We went to sit outside on the verandah to catch a bit of the evening breeze to keep cool. None of the lights were working either, so I couldn't finish the letter I was writing to brother Simon.

Later that evening we dined with two 55 year old Aussies touring the country on motor cycles. A couple of jolly good characters and they were adventurous, devil-may-care, knockabout types. I had a delicious fish dish washed down with a good bottle of red wine while Jack had a huge medium-rare steak. We spent the rest of the evening chatting away to these two happy chaps.

On Tuesday morning Jack got very dirty as he did some checking on the vehicle and then gave it a good wash while I washed some laundry and did the shopping. We were quite relaxed as Hall's Creek, our next destination, was not far away and it was all on sealed road.

There was nothing much to Hall's Creek really. We noticed many Aborigines and their dogs and all were seated on the ground everywhere.

There were beautiful old faces and I wished I could have photographed some of them. Jack had told me that they were likely to disapprove as it was an invasion of their privacy which needed to be respected.

We spent a lot of time at the roadhouse with its chatty owner and drank gallons of tea. I just loved the ten-gallon Stetson hats that some of the Aborigines were wearing. Some of them looked like they had just walked off a western movie scene as they swaggered down the road.

Aboriginal art at the roadhouse was abundant with didgeridoos, boomerangs and engraved boab pods. I bought one of the latter for $10.00 - a nice present for someone.

Then we were off through the Tanami Desert, 1,040 kilometres to Alice Springs with next to nothing in between. We arrived at Wolfe Creek Meteorite Crater at sunset. Part of it glowed orange and the other part black. It was 850 metres in diameter and 50 metres deep. There was no wildlife or birds to be seen anywhere. It must have been a mighty big bang a million years ago when it came to earth and rattled the old globe around!

We stayed the night camped out at Carranyn Cattle Station nearby the crater after we had met Heather at the homestead. In the cool of the desert we were, at last, alone. Yippee!

It was there where I knew I had finally made the crucial breakthrough. Jack had barely woken up that morning when he momentarily thought that he had lived his last day. He was peacefully lying in his sleeping bag next to the Toyota while I was taking an early morning stroll around the campsite. A sudden, violent gust of wind had risen from the southeast, and our pots and pans went flying off with the wind. I took off after them at great speed and, after a mighty struggle, finally brought them all under control.

Quite upset that Jack had not done a single thing to assist me, choosing instead to just lie there and watch me, I charged around the Toyota, arms outstretched, a frightening look on my face.

'Lets get the (quite unpronounceable adjective) hell out of here! Right now!' I screeched at him. On and on I went, jumping up and down all the time I was. He just shrieked back at me with outrageous laughter for a very long time until he lay there like a completely paralysed pulp.

We had set up camp next to the cattle yards where the scrubbers were held after a muster. A gust of wind had blown straight across the cattle yards, and I was covered from head to toe in a thin film of silvery, powdery cattle dung. The real laughing Jack had finally emerged, but I most certainly had not.

We got the hell out of the dangerous, dignity damaging deluge of dung and quickly raced down to the homestead where Heather made some comforting hot coffee for us in our big mugs. We had a nice chat with her - after she had a rip-snorter chuckle at me.

The station was 800,000 acres of free-range grazing with a large muster to take place that following weekend with aeroplanes and helicopters. The old horse riding cowboy days were fast disappearing. She welcomed the cool change in the weather for the muster, but I really wished that the wind did not come up quite so suddenly. Further down south it was freezing cold we knew. We topped up with fuel, had a cool shower to get me clean again, and we were off into the Tanami Desert.

It took me another two days in the Tanami to regain my composure. Jack did not in the least bit make the job any easier for me. For the next two days he would burst out in fits of uproarious laughter for absolutely no reason at all.

As we were driving along toward Rabbit Flat we came upon a rather unusual situation. A little chappie had parked his four wheel drive ute along the side of the road and appeared to be changing a tyre. We stopped and Jack went to see if he could assist.

'Get the hell away from that vehicle!' Jack screamed at the chappie and raced toward him. The chappie had parked on the verge of the road and was using a high-lift jack on the soft edge off the road. The jack was leaning at a dangerously awkward angle, and the chappie had just undone the wheel nuts and had taken the wheel off.

'You stay well away from here,' Jack said to me when I got closer to see what was happening.

The two of them had barely got themselves clear of the vehicle when it fell off the jack and very nearly down the embankment. The two of them were still standing there when the two-way radio came to life. The language and verbal abuse that came from it, and which was directed at the chappie, cannot, under any circumstances, be repeated. Jack took a look at the mining company logo painted on the door. He went to the Toyota and brought back a notebook.

'Write down your name and that of the man that was on the radio a moment ago,' Jack told the chappie.

'I can't write,' the chappie replied.

'How old are you?' Jack asked the chappie.

'Sixteen,' the chappie replied.

'Bull! You are not yet sixteen, and you don't have a licence to drive this vehicle in any case,' Jack told him.

'I know. I'm only fifteen, but my boss made me do it,' he replied and paused. 'And he makes me do other things that I don't like,' he quickly added then burst into tears. Once he had explained what it was he didn't like, the radio started screaming the foulest abuse at the boy again.

'Is that your boss on the radio?' Jack asked.

'Yep' the boy replied.

'Does he talk to everyone like this?' Jack asked the boy.

'No. Just me,' the boy replied.

Jack answered the radio and spoke with the boss. The boss didn't like what Jack said to him.

'He will never do you any harm ever again,' Jack calmly told the boy while trembling with homicidal rage in every fibre of his body. He hated bullies. 'You are safe now. The despicable mongrel won't be there when you get back to camp, and he never will come back again. I will tell the right people to look after you and what to do about him. You are no longer alone my boy.'

Jack wrote down the boy's name as well as that of the boss. Jack wrote a letter to the manager informing him of events, and that he was going to contact the managing director of the company as soon as we reached a telephone.

'Give this to the manager as soon as you get to camp!' Jack barked at the boy as he gave him the letter. 'If you don't, I will be after your blood!' he growled.

The truck was dragged back onto solid ground, the wheel was changed, and we waved the crying but smiling boy on his way. I had just witnessed what epitomised to me to be the dinkum, down-trodden little Aussie battler getting the lend of a helping hand.

Rabbit Flat really was the arsehole of the earth. On the way there we spent a lot of verbal energy discussing how we should approach the proprietor to ask for petrol which he didn't serve on Tuesdays, Wednesdays and Thursdays. That day happened to be a Wednesday. We found that we could not even meet him because he had cordoned the whole place off with drums, tape and barricades. We were forewarned well beforehand that he did not tolerate visitors on his days off and was known to shoot at people with a rifle when they turned up to ask for fuel and beer.

Luckily, as it was cool, if not cold, outside, and no air conditioning was necessary, we could conserve our fuel and gain an additional 200 kilometres on a full tank. We decided that we would reach Yuendumu without much difficulty where, we were told, fuel was available. Beautiful purple, pink and white flowers along the desert road indicated recent rains. We also saw huge flocks of green budgerigars.

The most unusual phenomenon we encountered however, was a lone Western Australian chap named Bruce. Sandgropers they are colloquially named. He was harnessed to a two-wheeled cart and was pulling it along the dirt road northward with all his gear on board. We stopped to inquire if he needed any assistance.

He told us that he had been serving a prison sentence for fraud in the Fremantle Jail near Perth. He didn't like it there, and he had another two years to serve before he qualified to be considered for parole. He diligently applied his intellect and ingenuity and had made plans to escape. He set about acquiring a number of private companies to sponsor his escape project. The sponsors had agreed to his escape and to provide equipment and the wherewithal, together with a backup vehicle driven by another ex-prisoner friend of his, to achieve his objective.

He presented his escape plans to the parole board. He had been granted early parole from prison provided he completed his objective of pulling the cart for the ten thousand kilometres from Perth across the Nullarbor Plain to Port Augusta, up to Alice Springs, into the Tanami Desert, and was heading for the Gibb River Road before taking the Western Australia coastal road back to Perth and finally to his freedom. He had left Perth with the objective of raising $40,000.00 for the Royal Flying Doctor Service.

Good on him! Without asking for it, he got a cool drink, a dozen beers, and a very healthy donation towards the Royal Flying Doctor Service. Howyergoin' Bruce?

I found I could read and sleep in the Toyota which made the long distances, when I wasn't driving, quite bearable. We camped alongside the Tanami road stopping after eight hours on the road from Wolfe Creek meteorite crater. By 4:00 pm we were quite ready to stop. It was a good drive - a lot of green spinifex, orange sand, and even the occasional 'hills' being waste dumps from gold mining operations and taking on the appearance of miniature Ayer's Rocks all over the place.

With a stroke of luck I found a portable, fold-up camping table on my evening walk which we promptly named Tanami. We built a roaring fire to keep the desert evening chill at bay but it was difficult as we had to sit to windward to avoid the smoke and only one side got warmed at a time. The residual light from the sunset was just enough to get a few notes jotted down as the gas light had given up the ghost and the 12 Volt fluorescent light didn't want to work anymore.

We kept warmer that night by using the tarpaulin as a windshield and snuggling up tight. The stars were brilliant and shooting everywhere but we were much too tired for the show. We were huddled around a superb campfire and it was a cold shock moving away from it.

We decided the following morning to stay there for another night. Sitting at our newly-found table in the desert with a very cold breeze, accompanied by a warm sun and clear blue skies, was a treat. A group of Aborigines in a station wagon got a flat tyre nearby and we were keeping an eye open just in case it was their table and they might have decided to come to claim it!

The desert was such a wonderful place with an enchantment of its own. One either loves deserts, or one hates them intensely. We were in an area of saltbush and spinifex (ow!) which rushed and howled with the strong wind. Every time a road-train came by, I would remember. A combined effort with the biryani that night resulted in an extremely hot feed with heaps of tears and runny noses.

That was our very last campfire together. Jack started to laugh again while he was sitting in his camp-chair pensively staring into the fire. I mockingly lunged at him with the barbecue fork, tripped over a log of wood, and fell on top of him. His camp-chair, which had been giving serious indications of final notice for quite some time, finally collapsed. So did we, together with it, into a screaming, laughing, helpless, dusty heap.

That night, in the stillness and quiet of the desert, after a silence of about an hour, I asked him to tell me about his late daughter Kate. He had, until that far, said nothing more about Kate or the bootie.

I was just about to discover new depths to the man. He silently went off and rummaged around in the Toyota and came back with some crumpled papers. He told me that it was the very first poem that he had ever written and that I was the very first person ever to see it.

'I didn't mean to write a poem. I sat down one morning to write Kate's short life story and accidentally ended up with a poem late that afternoon. I didn't really write it. Kate told me what to write,' he explained.

He told me to read it for myself because he had never been able to read it back to himself from the day he first wrote it. I sat with my arms folded and left him standing there with the papers in his proffered hand.

'Read!' I said, steadfastly staring into the campfire. It was something I felt that he had to do for himself. I reached out with my right hand and picked up the hand axe lying next to the campfire and put it down on my lap. He eventually, with great difficulty, and at great length, recited to me the story of Little Kate.

The First of May, it was a rainy day,
When I first saw, the light so grey.
Frantic action did abound, around,
Great alarm, everywhere resound.
'She's going to die! So please hurry!'
Never seen such a flap and a flurry.

I was badly startled, with a jerk,
Oh! Dear God, my lungs won't work!
Fought tooth and nail, for my dear life,
Why does it have to be, such strife ?
For I was born, with much deform,
Why couldn't I, just be the norm ?

Ten toes I had and fingers twelve,
No child like that, come off the shelf.
Tiny lungs, but a king size heart,
No mouth, no nose, a hell of a start!
Bet you can't match that, try as you may,
Even born, on that fateful Day! (May Day)

270

My chest did ache, my lungs did rent,
Enclosed I was, in an oxygen tent.
True Blue I was, as I fought to respire,
My nerves on edge, taught as a wire.
Racing heartbeat, Why ? Oh why ?
I've got to live, to see the sky!

My Dad he said, 'Now listen Kate,
Before you go, through the Pearly Gate.
We'll give our best, to beat this evil,
We'll fight as if, it were the devil!'
In mighty battle, did we engage,
My Dad determined, I would come of age!

The kindly Reverend, did finally come,
With great haste, from his distant home.
He took one look and did despair,
For he couldn't, touch my hair.
I was baptised, on neither head nor tum,
I was baptised, on the bum!

All night we fought, 'til early morn,
Looked out to see, the break of dawn.
A pretty sight, the sun arose,
And I was breathing, how, no one knows!
I did improve, as days did speed,
They even let me, have a feed!

'They took me home, one sunny morn,
Fifteen days, after I was born.
My Dad he took me, to the park,
And there we had, so many a lark.
I knew great warmth and we gave chase,
A sunbeam shone, upon on my face!

271

Then we did lie, upon the bed,
That afternoon and as he read.
With me beside him, under his arm,
Like a football, I was his charm.
And we became, ever so fond,
Of each other, as we did bond!

So ecstatic, did we sleep,
Great tears of joy, did my Dad weep.
Had never known, in all his life,
No sharper arrow, no keener knife.
And I did sleep, knowing well,
That he was going, through sheer hell!

Four days later, on the stroke of noon,
My time had come, it would be soon.
My lungs did stop, I knew not why,
'Too long!' cried Dad. 'She's going to die!'
My lungs did start and stop and start,
But soon there was, to be no heart.

I battled on, for a length of time, (9 hours)
In the distance, did a faint bell chime.
'My dearest Kate, your time has come,
I'm glad you were baptised, on the bum!
Give my regards, to our Sweet Lord,
I'll see you soon as, the fare'll afford.'

And then my skin, started turning blue,
Great colours appeared, with many a hue.
My Dad he soothed me, ' You must let go!

Go to the Lord, but don't be slow!'

He held me in his arms, I'm told,

Till my little body, it did turn cold'

I was left to lay down the hand axe at its place next to the campfire, and to swamp up whatever was left of him off the Tanami Desert and put it in his sleeping bag.

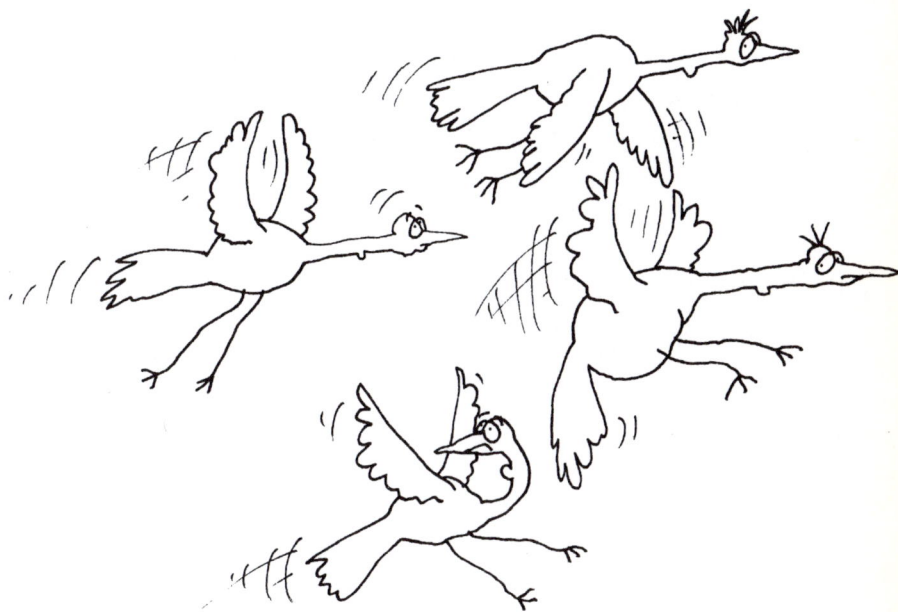

Chapter Twenty Five

I awoke after an excellent sleep and had a long walk with the binoculars following bird sounds. I saw a large flock of crimson chats and two zebra finches - both firsts. We were in no rush at all to get to the metropolis of Alice Springs.

On it was to Yuendumu, an Aboriginal settlement 300 kilometres northwest of Alice Springs. The welcoming signs looked promising - especially the petrol signs, but, we could not find anyone to serve us when we arrived there. It was 2.30 pm and the attendant had gone to lunch - for the rest of the afternoon!

Yuendumu was our first experience of what appeared to be a real Aboriginal settlement - rubbish, and filth, and corrugated iron, plastic and cardboard humpies everywhere. I felt uncomfortable there and the few photos I took were not easy to take.

Jack explained to me that the Aborigines who came in from the desert preferred to live in their traditional humpies and to follow a traditional lifestyle in preference to western norms. Even then, he didn't sound very convincing to me. He was of the opinion that it was immoral to force a foreign culture onto an indigenous people. I couldn't understand it. I was very glad to leave - even without enough petrol.

'We will make it to the Stuart Highway,' Jack said to me. 'If we don't make it into the Alice tonight, tomorrow morning we will put you on the side of the road with a jerry can in your hand, and we will see how good you are at pulling up road trains.'

As we drove further southeast there was more evidence of recent rains as we saw white, mauve, pink and yellow flowers on the side of the road. The desert was quite green as we approached Alice Springs on the flood plains. We drove along a flood plain with cattle grazing on fluorescent grass. The floods of the previous two years would have looked spectacular.

Once on the sealed Stuart Highway we realised civilisation was looming with the radio tuned into Radio Alice. We limped into Alice Springs on a wing and a prayer at 8:00 pm that night. The two jerry cans of fuel were empty and the fuel tank was bone, bone, dry. The Toyota started to splutter and cough at the lack of fuel, the engine died, and we coasted the last 200 metres to the fuel station.

Arriving in the Alice was a complete shock to the system - all the traffic and the people were totally bewildering to us. We took the first motel available and relished the hot water shower and clean sheets. We had a tremendous meal at the Memorial Club that night.

The following morning we found a self-contained apartment close to the town centre. We had colour TV, a kitchenette and all the luxuries, but I can tell you, I missed the bush so much. We were reminded of this when we played an Aussie bird tape that Jack had bought for me, 'A Symphony of Australian Birds' it was titled. I burst into tears and immediately blamed Jack for making me cry.

Jack made a telephone call to a friend of his in Sydney who was the managing director of a mining company and satisfied himself that the illiterate and innocent child alone in the desert was in safe hands, had very good job security, and was being looked after very well. His boss had done a rapid runner.

We paid a quick visit to the School of the Air. Jack was upset by seeing all the children and the surrounds, so he took off to the car park where he had a little cry on his own. On to Anzac Hill for a view of the sunset that evening. I had seen three firsts that day - grey shrike thrush and two honey-eaters. My bird score by then was an absolutely incredible 185 species!

That Friday was a little difficult for us both. We were both a bit short-tempered and less tolerant of each other. We didn't know if it was being back in civilisation again, or what it was that was causing our intolerance and discontent. Jack and I wanted to do different things at different times, and to take off in different directions. We argued in the car-park about what it was we wanted to do, but not for too long. We didn't know what it was we were fighting about.

We huffed off on our separate ways and had an early shop. We later collected ten packs of photographs which we laughed at hysterically in a coffee shop. Jack was exhausted and so decided to go back to the apartment to have a rest as I continued to do the food shopping. It was a problem having so much choice and stimulation after so long in the bush. We bought so little - what does one really need?

Jack and I spent most of the afternoon chatting intensely about our disagreement in the car park.

'I think I know what our problem is. We are both showing symptoms of pre-separation anxiety,' he said eventually. It seemed to me to be a perfectly logical engineering observation as could best be found, so we agreed to recognise it for what it was, and to be on the alert for further impulses to express our agitation.

We visited the Royal Flying Doctor Service in Stuart Street. They operated in a 1,000 kilometre radius using Navaho and Kingair aircraft. We also visited the grave of the Reverend John Flynn who founded the service.

That evening we went to Chateau Hornsby for a sunset overlooking the vineyards and a delicious wine-tasting followed by a self-cooked barbecue steak. Ted Egan's entertainment afterwards was hilarious and, at times, quite sad. Ted is part of the Aussie Outback culture. He is a living legend in fact, and he shared his experiences in jokes, stories and songs. Jack asked him to sing Willie *The Whingeing Pom* for me, but Ted couldn't oblige.

The next day we got away from Alice Springs and went west to Simpson's Gap, Stanley Chasm and as far as Glen Helen Gorge. We saw a frilly lizard along the way, lots of tourists and many buses. We just didn't care about them any longer and it was good exercise and a change of scenery. The evening light on the hills looked marvellous.

'Mmm... that smells good!' I said to Jack that evening on our return. He was cooking up a superb lamb stew that we washed down with a Chateau Hornsby wine.

That night after dinner we decided to visit the casino to try our luck. I got bounced before I even got to the front door because I was wearing my Reebok runners instead of acceptable footwear. We went back to the Toyota where I changed into a pair of Jack's old holey desert boots which he had decided to discard and then walked right in. Jack lost $ 100.00 on the roulette wheel in two minutes flat without scoring a single win. He didn't think that casinos were overly user friendly.

'Happy birthday Mum!' Jack said into the telephone to Johannesburg early the following morning. Didn't he cop an earful! He hadn't told anybody where he was going to, and nobody had heard from him for more than four months! Mums will be mums and they will make themselves heard despite all the 'buts'.

We set off for Coober Pedy to the south. A short distance past The Gap Jack pointed out to me a collection of buildings named Old Timer's.

'It is a place to go to for Aborigines who come out of the desert for the first time. Some of them come in hot.' he told me.

'What do you mean by 'hot'? Are you talking about the heat, or are they wanted by the police?' I asked him.

'They sometimes inadvertently wander into the Marralinga area where nuclear bombs were tested by the British in the 1950's. They are radio-active as a consequence,' he explained.

Jack also pointed out to me Pine Gap, the ultra-secret communications centre near Alice Springs. He didn't know what happened there and didn't want to know.

We stopped for a leg stretch at the right hand turnoff to Ayer's Rock and the Olgas. Jack had been there before. He confessed to me that he had climbed as far as 'Chicken Rock' and swore me to eternal secrecy about that.

'We still have time to go in. We can also then take the Gun Barrel Highway through the desert clear across to the west coast and come back via Perth and the Nullarbor. You are driving from here on so pick whichever destination takes your fancy. I couldn't bloody well care less,' said Jack.

Realising outrageous dreams far beyond my wildest imagination, or realising harsh realities, is what it meant to me. I now deeply regret my reluctant decision at the time. Realising dreams is what living is all about.

Later that afternoon we stopped for another leg stretch at the left hand turn to Oodnadatta.

'That is another way we can go. We are already at the Back of Bourke. Oodnadatta Track to Marree, Birdsville Track to Birdsville, Strzleki Track to Cameron's Corner, Bourke and on to Sydney. Take your pick,' Jack said to me.

I would have dearly loved to have gone to Birdsville. A great uncle of mine had left Birdsville to cross the Simpson Desert many years ago and had perished in the attempt to be the first to do so as had many others before and after him.

Perhaps next time Sydney, Bourke, Birdsville, Oodnadatta, Ayer's Rock, the Gibson Desert and who the hell cares where to thereafter.

Coober Pedy, an opal mining town, was 630 kilometres from the Alice. It was also exactly the maximum distance the Toyota could go on a full tank of fuel. We put it to the test. It was desert, desert and more empty desert.

A few minutes after sunset, as we were going down the very last hill with the lights of Coober Pedy in sight some three kilometres away, the engine again coughed, spluttered and died. Jerrycan time again.

Wearily we found a motel where we slept that night. The motel had been tunnelled out of a hillside and we slept in a very posh tunnel that night. Jack felt quite at home. Most of the population of Coober Pedy lived in houses under the ground. That was because the screamingly hot summers and bitterly cold winters were totally unbearable.

We encountered the Redex Variety Club Bash the next morning. It was a motor rally for vehicles over twenty five years old and was held to raise funds for handicapped and under-privileged children. Rule Number One was to cheat. If the crews didn't cheat, they were penalised. The cars went hooning up and down the main street all morning making a hell of a noise and the whole town joined in the fun.

One of the vehicles, a massive mid-1950's Chevrolet Yank Tank, was a real screamer. It was painted bright red with Qantas Flying Kangaroo logos on it. It had two enormous jet engines mounted on the boot. Inside the jet engines were massive loudspeakers connected to a tape recorder inside the car. They took off from the starting line with jet engines at full thrust and disappeared down the road with the jet engines helping them along until they, and the sound, disappeared into the desert. We took off in the opposite direction headed for Port Augusta. It was again all desert.

We stopped for lunch at a roadhouse near to the Marralinga area. The pub was crowded with hippy-like protesters who had come in from a 'Ban the Bomb' rally on the security fence surrounding Marralinga. Jack was in conversation with the barman when I joined him.

'Racing them through the sheep dip three times followed by a good steam clean would do them no harm before they are let loose,' I overheard the barman say to Jack. Then they changed the subject. Men!

That evening in Port Augusta in South Australia was our last together after being on the road for more than ten weeks. We had an uneasy Chinese meal that night and the excellent champagne tasted distinctly bitter.

'These belong to you now,' Jack said to me as he hung the Nikon binoculars around my neck early the following morning. He then drove me down to the bus station for me to catch my bus to Adelaide.

We parted dry-eyed as we had previously agreed to do, and I boarded the bus. Jack watched it go up the hill and then turn left and out of sight. He then slowly walked back to the Toyota to drive to Sydney to rebuild his life.

All resolve about putting up a brave front disintegrated as the stiff upper lip, lion-hearted, keep the upper hand, British bulldog bunkum I had been taught all my life went flying out the window forever. The little old lady sitting next to me, a roving sheep-shearer's wife who knew a lot about these things, dried my tears away and comforted me all the way to Adelaide. Jack called me on the phone that night from Wagga Wagga in New South Wales.

'I just sat in the Toyota, looked at the seat beside me, and exclaimed, 'It's empty!' I cried alone for a long time before setting off,' he said.

I had taken my last walk on the wild side. I had lived and realised many, many dreams and my life had changed forever. I knew then that I had lived life to the full!

Epilogue

This is Jack talking to you now, so don't get confused about the identity of the author. I write in the third person as I have been unable to do so in the first, so keep your wits about you.

Some weeks after they parted Jack joined Juliette in New Zealand for a month. They furiously tramped the snow-capped mountains of the South Island until Juliette had developed thighs and calves of steel. She occasionally walked with a slight limp and with a noticeable stiffness in her hips. She said nothing, so Jack could do nothing but see and feel.

While the summer approached and it got warmer, Juliette got better and the symptoms abated. She later met a very special and quite unique new friend while wind-surfing in New Zealand - Doris the Dolphin. She and Doris were to frolic for hours on end every day in Golden Bay.

Juliette had been living in Takaka for six months when, at the advent of autumn, she was eventually struck down by the most savage attack of Ankylosing Spondylitis and Reactive Arthritis she had ever had and was totally incapacitated. Virtually every joint in her body became inflamed with arthritis as time progressed. It was also the beginning of the slow process where the vertebrae start to fuse into one solid, inflexible bone which, if left untreated, results in deformity.

Jack was living in Sydney at the time and made arrangement to fly to New Zealand to bring her back to Sydney to look after her. A more sensible approach to the problem eventuated when Juliette's father called Jack on the phone where they made other arrangements. Her twin brother Pete flew from London to New Zealand to take her back to England. There, her family took better care of her than Jack could possibly have done in Sydney.

She spent the next six months in either bed, or was carried down to the kitchen to spend the day on a reclining chair and talking to her mum. Thereafter, for a further ten months, she was wheelchair bound and had to be pushed wherever she went. She was inspired to write:

Reflections on a Dolphin.

You approach the wharf,
Full of anticipation, pulse rate high.
Eyes skim the water for any sign.
'Dolphin, dear, where are you?'
But why do you swim with us?
Two lonely hearts perhaps
Awaiting ecstatic union.
She senses your presence.
The fin approaches fast on your horizon,
You dive down to meet her, nose on.
She calculatingly avoids collision
And both entwine in chase
Oh, how she swims so close,
Above and below, around and around
Enticing gentle caress alongside her silky body
She sets the game rules
And trust is never misplaced.
Then the offering game.
A piece of seaweed is nudged gently towards you.
You take it, hopefully the correct response,
And the bond deepens.
Then she zooms away and takes half of you with her
You are alone and lonely,
But not for long, as suddenly she is back,
Reared high above you
More exited than ever.
Both dolphin and human are in unison again.
Your weariness soon returns however,
And reluctantly you drag yourself away.
Back to the wharf she speeds
For a well earned dinner on kingfish and herring.

And soon it is all a dream.

At the time that he commenced writing this book, Jack was engaged in the fiercest battles of his entire life. The tragedies that had befallen him were only the comparatively mild beginning of an outrageous onslaught. On his return to Sydney he was assailed by further multiple, major life events, both natural and man-made, the likes of which you wouldn't ever want to experience, or even hear about.

These, which added to the former, combined to leave him reeling and drunkenly staggering against the ropes like a lobotomised baboon. Compounded, the whole left him with profound psychomotor retardation virtually unable to respond to the demands society placed on him.

He was directed by six doctors never again to play wild man to the mining industry in the jungles of Borneo, or anywhere else on the planet for that matter. He was also declared totally and permanently disabled, completely unable to work again in any job for which he was qualified by education, training or experience.

He had given far too much of himself, was totally and completely burnt out and had nothing left to give anymore. His so-called very superior intelligence, together with his relentless, dogged determination, neither of which had ever failed him before, were to become his very worst enemies. The harder he tried to get better, the sicker he became.

He couldn't read, he couldn't count, he couldn't do sums, and he couldn't understand what people, the radio and the television were saying to him. All he heard was noise from them.

The Mosman police found him on two occasions immobilized and frozen on the spot in the middle of two busy streets. They loaded him up in the police car and took him home both times. He was brain dead.

Jack believes that he had lost his sanity, and that his will to live had been totally extinguished. The raging inferno that once drove that devil-may-care, fearless, race-around, scatter-brained, in-control, fix-anything, turbo-charged, pocket-rocket dynamo flickered with the faint dimness of a lonely Toc H lamp in a screamingly devastating Category 5 tropical cyclone.

Jack continually dug deep for those vital resources he so desperately needed, and he continued endlessly to came up with nothing, for there was nothing left anymore. The chilling horror of that realisation of nothingness, and the associated utter powerlessness, is indelibly imprinted on his mind forever.

Friendless, as Bill the Flying Dutchman, his only real mate in Sydney at the time, had frantically, but thankfully temporarily, also run away from home to the jungles of Venezuela. Without a family in Australia to provide him with moral support, he was in very, very deep trouble. He had absolutely nothing left going for him then. Nothing!

Jack had a complete and total mental breakdown, something he was never supposed to have. It was later identified as the result of massive stress overload, chronic fatigue syndrome and mental bi-polar depressive disorder, all together. 'Battered But Intact', a detailed chronology of events over the past seven years is well in progress. It is unlikely to be published for quite some time, if ever.

When the human hyenas and vultures of this planet descend on a vulnerable victim, they do so with an unconscionable savagery and ruthlessness that leaves one fleshless.

He remembered what Katie, his Swazi wet nurse and nanny, had told him many years before when he just was a little boy. He also recalled the Baron von Maltitz' sage advice. He no longer had the slightest ability to even think as Edna Plumstead had taught him to do so well. Everything that Edna had taught him about thinking was totally gone.

'Physically he is fit but mentally he is walking a tightrope from which added stress could cause him to fall' his GP, Gillian Davison had written in a report. She had the most incredible insight and intuition. Thank you Gillian.

Jack had a great deal to think about, totally lacked the ability to do so, and had very little time in which to do it in. It was during this period that Jack started writing this book.

Four months after Juliette returned to England, Jack recalls that, late one night, while driving along Military Road back to his flat in Mosman Bay, Sydney, he was beating the steering wheel relentlessly and screaming to himself over and over again:

'Why? Why? Why?' Again there were no answers. None whatsoever.

He didn't go home, but drove to the North Head of Sydney Harbour instead, not another soul within miles, parked the Toyota, walked along the path to the viewing platform, climbed over the safety rail, placed his feet halfway over the edge and stared down at the rocks and the seething turmoil of the angry sea which he loved so dearly, sixty metres vertically below him.

He looked up and around him, slowly casting his gaze over the Sydney city and suburban skyline. It was a crystal clear, cold winter's night, his acutely sharp one-eyed focus boring into the late-night hustle and bustle of city life around him, but so far away, and for thousand of miles in every other direction. And to the infinity of the heavens above him while rocking gently back and forth on the balls of his heels into the stiff southeasterly breeze.

'You are bigger and better than the bastards who couldn't care less whether you lived or died! You know who you really are!' someone silently said.

'It's about bloody-well time that You turned up and got back on-side for a change!' Jack shouted back. Someone then just laughed at him. Jack then slowly put his best foot backward. It was the very first time in his life that he had ever taken a backward step for anything. It was also the smartest move that he had ever made.

He mindlessly walked right past the Toyota, perhaps he walked over it, or right through it, he can't remember, and then the ten kilometres home. He walked through the doorway and sat down at his desk with his word processor in front of him - the dead screen staring mutely into his vacant nothingness. On the desk in front of him lay Juliette's painful letter that he had received that very day. Alongside it was Bryce Courtenay's letter that he had received, also on that same day, urging him to start writing.

'Tell the glory of overcoming defeat and diminish your enemies with humour,' Bryce had written. Jack slowly reached out with his right hand, kick-started the word processor, and started his life anew.

He knew that there was absolutely nothing that anybody, including himself, could do for him. He decided that the next best thing he could do was to be of some assistance to Juliette.

He had just finished reading a simple book titled, 'He' by Robert Johnson. Amanda Monteith, a psychologist from Sydney had given it to him as bibliotherapy and she had made him read it. It dealt with the inherent femininity that lies within every man, and it is that very femininity which is the very heart and soul of the source of man's creativity. Jack decided to do some outrageously wild experimenting. It probably offers the best explanation as to why he wrote as 'I, Juliette'. It very nearly killed him. Sanity is self-imprisonment. The next time someone asks you, "How are you?" you must declare yourself to be *Sanity Free.*

Jack picked up a photocopy of a scruffy notebook Juliette had kept of the trip, started deciphering the cryptic hieroglyphics, arranged a chronology of events filling in the text from memory and the things Juliette told him, accurately reading and anticipating Juliette's thoughts and feelings at the time, and then getting her to confirm the accuracy thereof, and then he finally created an intelligible record of her most extraordinary adventure.

Jack did his absolute very best, and he gave everything that he had totally depleting his limited resources many, many times in the process. Juliette would give him sufficient time to recover, and would then kick him in the guts to get him going again.

Being a man writing as a woman has been the most difficult task Jack has ever undertaken, and is definitely not looking forward to doing anything similar ever again. It was an extremely painful task for him indeed. He has walked some of the most dangerous and hazardous of paths imaginable in his life, but none as tortuous and near-fatal as the writing and final completion of this book.

If you perhaps one day contemplate doing something similar, be warned! Your footwork will have to be as slippery as your mind will have to be nimble. If you need a good friend, then you must be prepared to be a good friend. You will have to stick to that friend like bubble gum sticks to an army blanket. It is all part of living a meaningful life, and that, I believe, is what we are all supposed to be doing.

Jack disclaims entirely all responsibility and liability for the mental and physical damage which will definitely occur should someone else attempt to do anything of a similar nature. Juliette can throw neutron bombs with pin point accuracy.

Almost every week for six months Jack would post the latest manuscript to Juliette. She would then proof-read the text, do some editing, remind Jack of events that he had missed, filled in with some of her own comments and, of course, kept Jack very honest. It made her laugh a lot at herself, it gave her something to hang onto, and something to look forward to when the postman arrived. It was the very best that Jack had to offer at the time. It also enabled Jack to laugh and to belatedly enjoy the trip through Juliette's eyes.

It was never intended that a book be written, but a life-long, two-person reminder to them both that they had actually done something worthwhile together in their lives. It has been a team effort, for Juliette made a significant contribution by being the subject and doing the things that she did, but she has, quite rightly, despite Jack's protestations that other people wouldn't believe that he wrote the book, insisted that there be one author. So mote it be. He has to live with that.

Once the first primitive draft was completed, and another two months had elapsed proof reading the manuscript, Juliette started getting mobile again - wheelchair-wise. She prefers that the living nightmare be kept totally and completely private. Her wishes are respected.

Juliette started getting involved in the activities of The National Ankylosing Spondylitis Society of Great Britain (NASS). She established a branch in the Chichester and Bognor Regis area. She started, and coordinated, a weekly Ankylosing Spondylitis exercise group in Bognor Regis co-opting fellow physiotherapists to conduct those activities that she couldn't.

She kept a register of all the Anky Spond victims in the area and conned, cajoled and bullied them all relentlessly into doing what she knew was good for them. She recruited and coordinated a voluntary transport fleet including ambulances to ferry them to and fro so that they could offer no excuse whatsoever for not attending the therapy sessions.

She went on a two-week sailing trip in the Canary Islands on board the *HMS Lord Nelson*, a brigantine built for disabled people including those in wheelchairs. Hoisted to the very top of the mast one night she was, under full sail, to rectify a technical hitch. She had progressed to Watch Leader by the end of the voyage. Shortly thereafter Juliette started to walk a few steps a day again without any assistance.

One day, when Jack was looking at the dolphins at play in the breakers, he was inspired to write a poem to Juliette to let her know that she wasn't alone in her plight:

The Paths of Life.

As we wander through the paths of life
Leaving some dreams behind us.
Some realised, some unfulfilled
And others just forgotten, alas.
We toil and struggle as we go along
To see what we can do.
We strive, we achieve, all so painfully slow
We wonder, how about you?

We know we've many great things achieved
And paths so many we've travelled.
Our guts did wrench as we did heave
Our shoulders pained and withered.
Many people did we meet along the road
Many crooks and thieves and cowards.
Many liars, cheats and bastards too
As we move forever forwards.

We also see such wondrous things
As can be done by the deeds of others
Who love and care for us as we grow
Like Mums and Dads and Brothers.
'Tis them, the very special people
The kindest of them all
Who are always close and help us
Especially when we take a fall.

They help us through our suffering
As we sometimes lay very still.
They keep us warm and are always close
When it seems that we'll always be ill.
How little do we realise
When we are well and free again
The medical fraternity are always there
To ease the ache, the pain.

The appreciation of ones self
The most vital factor of all, they say
Once found, in one's aloneness
Ensures we live profoundly, every single day.
But we cannot always live alone
In mindless isolation.
Doing the things we've always done,
When we come to choose the next destination.

Jack finally managed to slay all the proverbial Philistines that he needed to, and to lay down his broadsword and battleaxe - hopefully forever. He had, in his uniquely forthright and honest way, finally out-mongrelled the lot of them.

Jack then managed to disentangle himself from his other peripheral difficulties and went to camp out alone with Big Ted and his new friend Spiffy Martin at Ruby Gorge some 200 kilometres east of the Alice where he spent a long time licking his wounds.

(Big Ted and little Gavin Rawlins of Toowoomba are looking after each other now. Big Ted has very fierce radar. Spiffy Martin was kidnapped from my hotel room in London. Scotland Yard and Interpol are still looking for him)

It took Jack a month of Sundays to come to the realisation that his big battles were finally over and that he was free to move on again. He drove back to the Alice to find out what was going to happen to him next.

On his arrival there he found that all the flights to South Africa were fully booked because every fellow Australian Rugby maniac was going to Cape Town to see the World Champion Wallabies versus Springboks Test match. It was the Springboks' first game for the New South Africa.

Juliette then told Jack to go to England instead. He finally left the Alice for England in the northern mid-summer to see what he could do for Juliette to, you know, gently help her along a little bit.

On his arrival at Chichester he was, quite unexpectedly, confronted by some thirty or fifty wonderful people, he could barely read or count then, who had all come to welcome him to England, and to have a good look at this strange colonial chappie that they had heard so much about and who wrote funny stories as a woman. Juliette's family looked after him exceedingly well then, and for that he is at a loss, for he can find no words to express his appreciation of their gratuitous hospitality.

Juliette had, by then, progressed to managing some twenty to thirty steps a day without the aid of crutches. She started working voluntarily in the NASS office in London occasionally. Candy, the Labrador was still there. Candy and Jack went on endless walks in the English countryside every day for hours on end.

Jack met up with his sisters Margaret and Verity in London and didn't they have a good time! It was like re-living uninhibited childhood days the way they had fun.

Jack went to visit his cousins in North Wales for a fortnight and drank copious amounts of Guiness at the Black Boy pub in Caernarvon - far too many and far too often. The dozen or so Welshmen he was with initially spoke English in deference to him until Jack insisted that they revert to their native Welsh tongue, and then answered them in his colonial English. For that gesture he was accepted as solid Welsh blood in song, poetry and heart. His cousin loaded him onto the footplate of the little steam engine which went from Llamberris to the top of Snowdon Mountain and back again. It was exactly like old times with good old Bill.

Jack and Juliette went to Scotland for two weeks touring the magnificent north-western coastal area. They had a terrible row when Jack insisted that a wheelchair, or at least a set of crutches, be taken with.

Jack lost that fight very badly. He got a lot of exercise piggy-backing Juliette all over Scotland for his troubles instead. It was a jolly good thing that he had strong legs and a strong back. He admits to having veiled thoughts about slamming Juliette's fingers in the boot of the car and making her run sometimes. They looked very hard for the Loch Ness Monster but unfortunately, it didn't oblige as it was in hibernation, or so it was rumoured.

They spent two days with Anne, Juliette's nanny who lived near Inverness, and didn't the two of them half go on about good times past! The mischief that Juliette used to get up to as a child would fill another two volumes the size of this book!

Juliette then started to get involved in raising funds for the Chichester and Bognor Regis branch of NASS and was very successful at that. At one such fund-raising event that she organised Jack played croquet for the first time. He was comprehensively thrashed by the highly adept but very wicked Mayor of Chichester who had himself Anky Sponded. Jack made a mental note to check if wickedness was a chronic post-Anky Spond disorder because he didn't like recovering from the duck pond all the time.

Juliette then started working every Thursday morning as a metrologist at the Swindon Hospital. She had a two hour drive to get there and another two hours back to Chichester. Jack went with her every time.

Weekends were spent racing *Joy*, the family yacht. Juliette was the skipper with Jack and twin brother Pete crewing for her. Juliette was the Under 30's Club Champion that year. They had an outrageously good time at Cowes Week. When she was leading a race one day, and everyone was looking at her, she ran *Joy* aground.

They spent many hours in The Piggery working on the manuscript with Candy lying asleep at their feet. During a family discussion over dinner one evening Jack was reluctantly convinced by Juliette's father that the book was publishable, and that the story should be published.

They went to see plays, to the Proms, to the movies - a lot of piggy-backing of course. Jack realised one of the very last of his boyhood dreams - the Farnborough Air Show when Pete especially took him there for the day. Juliette started singing again, beautifully, accompanied by Jack's very bad guitar playing.

Toward the end of the summer they went on a three week trip to the southwest of Ireland. Jack unashamedly fell in love with Ireland, Irish music and the Irish. Juliette's two little nephews one afternoon collusively led Jack up the garden path and, taking him by the hand, led him to the woods and showed him where the leprechauns lived!

They perchance had the occasion to visit a convent in County Cork; Jack very reluctantly so. As he was chatting away to Mother Superior and the Sisters exchanging pleasantries and satisfying their curiosity about his background, one of the nuns blanched, choked on her mouthful of tea, started trembling violently, and tipped her cup of tea over herself.

She hastily retreated to effect repairs and, standing in the doorway, she deeply and intensely stared at Jack for a long time. All conversation gradually ceased to a deafening silence as everyone in the room stared back at her.

'You will return here soon to continue your writing,' she softly said to Jack. Mother Superior and the other Sisters eagerly, noisily and unanimously agreed with her. They all seemed to like Jack a lot despite his being a non-Catholic.

As they were being walked to their hired car by the nuns for them to be seen off, the distraught nun walked next to him and held his hand for far longer than nuns normally hold hands with a man, if they ever do. She was weeping freely and quite unashamedly. So too was Jack, very deeply inside, and his mind raced off to kill leprechauns.

While in Ireland, and when she was playing with the dolphins again, Juliette managed to walk for some five kilometres one day. She was totally unaware of this fact until Jack brought it to her attention. On their supposed second last day in Ireland they turned up at a village to discover to their amazement that the Irish National Folk Festival started that night. They promptly delayed their departure for another week to attend the festival. A few days after that Juliette started to run again, and to play with the children.

Jack's job was finally done, it was autumn and starting to get cold so he took off for the warm bosom of his Mother Africa with almost indecent haste. The Call of Africa was totally overwhelming by then for he hadn't seen his mum and the rest of his African family for almost seven years.

When Juliette saw Jack off at Heathrow Airport in October 1992 he perchance was asked by a Zulu behind him in the South African Airways queue if he could play the guitar that he was checking in.

'Very fiercely but very badly,' he replied. Joseph Shabalala invited him to jam with them one day in Soweto - Ladysmith Black Mambazo. "The Journey of Dreams" never ends. Go Joseph!

On his arrival in Johannesburg he found that his mum had bought a racy little sports car and was cheerfully terrorising everything that got in her way including his step-father Mike who had gone partially blind while Jack's mum was recovering from a mastectomy due to breast cancer, receiving chemotherapy, and recovering from a total mental breakdown which was long overdue. Jack's Welsh grandmother had died aged 99 when his mum was in hospital.

Three medical practitioners, after having done everything humanly and medically possible, had pronounced his mother an irretrievable case, had ceased medical treatment, and had left her to die. That was when Jack's two sisters Margaret and Verity took total control of the situation, fought non-stop for more than a week successfully bringing her back from the brink, and then told the doctors to start looking very busy. They are a rare breed indeed.

Jack spent a lot of time with his mum and his family, and with the black people on the farm. He, Djaji, Willem, Maria, Tsets the Kehla African Zionist Christian Church Umfundis, Big Skabenga and little Tsotsi planted orange trees and looked after the cattle, sheep and chickens while they looked after each other, as all South Africans should be doing, and they all know perfectly well how to do it!

He went to visit his old boarding school and tracked down The Chief. He found The Chief and spoke to him just in time in hospital because The Chief died of cancer two days later. He went to visit Wilks after the funeral, but he had to do so in the same cemetery. He also went to visit Nyanyan, Joao Texeira, Ndlovo, Katie and John Gumede, Bonnie Koeleman and his wife and many significant others in similar manner - far too many.

He tracked down, stalked and surprised Shorty Bester, Whitey van Aswegen and Allan Greenwood late one afternoon, lawless as ever before, on the banks of the Sabie River drinking beer and smoking trout together - the poached kind.

He miraculously survived two attacks from black mambas, the most deadly neuro-toxic snake that Africa has to offer. The first was a 70 centimetre diddy tiddler which charged him while he was on his hands and knees driving tent pegs into the ground in the Bushveld. He back-handed and slapped it into senseless semi-unconsciousness with his left hand before his brother Derick caught the poor thing and put it back in the bush again where it belonged.

The second black mamba was quite another matter. The fang wounds on his left calf were 16 mm apart. It was a real biggie of over three metres in length which, somewhat inconsiderately, objected to being trod on. Having survived that ordeal he figuratively raced ahead in leaps and bounds toward snakeless Ireland where he thought he might play with those errant leprechaun fellows over there and realign a few of their priorities, or perhaps get realigned himself. His had softened his attitude toward leprechauns by then.

After Africa he went on to the peace, quiet, solitude and timelessness of his beloved Australian Outback. He continues to write. Poetry falls out of him occasionally - he uses it to express his deepest emotions. He eventually posted Kate's bootie to her because she told him that her foot sometimes got cold. She also complained that she was missing a feather.

'It's Lighty!', a continuation of the collection of chronological funny and some not-so-funny short stories is coming along very nicely and is nearing completion. **"The Problem With Palm Villa"** might be the Magnus Opus after that.

Later Juliette also took off for a four week holiday in New Zealand by herself. Shortly after her return to England she started work as a Research Assistant at The Royal National Hospital for Rheumatic Diseases in Bath doing research into arthritis related illnesses and specialising in Ankylosing Spondylitis in addition to her Swindon job.

Juliette then left Bath to start work as the Senior Physiotherapist at the Southampton General Hospital managing the Rheumatology and Orthopaedic Departments. She also started doing a Masters degree in rheumatology specialising in Ankylosing Spondalitis. Being close to home and the sea again she is again racing *Joy* with the most wild abandon.

It didn't take her long to establish an Anky Spond self-help group in the Southampton area, mustered the lot of them, acquired a transport fleet as before, and then, in her own way, got them to do the things that she knew was very right for them.

She started coxing the University of Southampton rowing team raising their achievements to previously unthinkable heights by demolishing all opposition they encountered. Having asserted herself with the impact of a neutron bomb, the shell-shocked crew profusely thank her for her efforts after each race. She continues to take charge of, and to supercharge, the social lives of everyone around her.

Juliette was, at last, soaring with the eagles.

"Finger On The Trigger!" was the headline to the last publication Jack saw about her contribution to rheumatology. He started to run very scared.

He still has in his possession a book titled 'Why Am I Afraid To Tell You Who I Am?' by John Powell. The answer of course is 'You may not like who I am, and that is all I have.' Jane and Ben, two very good friends of Juliette's who really cared about her, gave it to her as a present and had signed their names in it. It was in her backpack when she first met Jack in Cairns, and she inadvertently left it behind in the Toyota when they parted in Port Augusta, South Australia. Jack will return it to her in due course, but he doesn't believe that Juliette needs to be afraid anymore.

The rotten, bomb-dodging, sanity-free, incorrigible Palm Villa Chief Coward was last seen slithering over the horizon into the Deepest Australian Outback, a thundering cloud of red dust trailing behind the Toyota, alone, teddies, guitar, laptop and printer in tow to see if he could finish this book - his path and destiny quite unknown.

* * * * * * *

Jack has been granted the Registered Trade Mark "Crocodile Juliette" under the seal of the Commonwealth of Australia. It is registered for books, films and ladies wear. Jack has now suddenly become incredibly busy. His ultimate objective is to internationalise all three. He knows that he can do it. The Zulu translation is in progress.